Dear Anne,

A special gift for you.
Just an appreciation of all
your dedication for work
done at Sask. Wheat Pool.

Love
Dad & Mom.

December 2004

Building Our
FUTURE

A PEOPLE'S ARCHITECTURAL HISTORY OF SASKATCHEWAN

Building Our FUTURE

A PEOPLE'S ARCHITECTURAL HISTORY OF SASKATCHEWAN

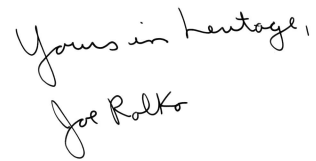

JOE RALKO

Red Deer PRESS

A Saskatchewan Centennial project of the Saskatchewan Architectural Heritage Society

PUBLISHED BY
Red Deer Press
813 MacKimmie Library Tower
2500 University Drive N.W.
Calgary Alberta Canada T2N 1N4
www.reddeerpress.com

CREDITS
Cover and text design by Erin Woodward
Edited for the Press by Lee Shenkman
Cover images courtesy the Saskatchewan Archives Board, Saskatchewan Heritage Foundation &
Saskatchewan Property Management Corporation
Printed and bound in Canada by Friesens for Red Deer Press

ACKNOWLEDGMENTS
Financial support provided by the Canada Council, the Government of Canada through the Book Publishing Industry Development Program (BPIDP), the Alberta Foundation for the Arts, a beneficiary of the Lottery Fund of the Government of Alberta, and the University of Calgary.

NATIONAL LIBRARY OF CANADA CATALOGUING IN PUBLICATION
Ralko, Joe
Building our future : a people's architectural history
of Saskatchewan / Joe Ralko.
"A Saskatchewan centennial project of the Saskatchewan
Architectural Heritage Society."
Includes index.
ISBN 0-88995-308-2
1. Architecture--Saskatchewan--History.
I. Saskatchewan Architectural Heritage Society II. Title.
NA746.S3R34 2004   720'.97124   C2004-906686-2

FOREWORD

There is a Greek proverb that says "a civilization flourishes when people plant trees under whose shade they will never sit." What a beautiful sentiment! What a profound message about foresight and stewardship! It leads one to question how thoughtful and committed we have been, in our beloved Saskatchewan, to understanding and preserving the gifts of our ancestors.

The courageous newcomers, who arrived over a century ago, discovered a land foreign to them in every way . . . a blank canvas devoid of roads, buildings, materials for construction, and even food supplies . . . a place inhabited for 10,000 years by the ultimate survivors—aboriginal peoples. Their willingness to live in peaceful co-existence facilitated the growth of settlements that required ingenuity and unparalleled determination. Hope itself did not build the churches and the post offices and the town halls. Faith in the future did. And the result was a flourish of buildings modeled on the architecture that the settlers had left behind but with a decidedly prairie flavour.

Built heritage is a commentary on a society. It speaks to how the people of a particular time in history saw themselves, their obligations to their neighbours, as well as their confidence in making their dreams for a better life come true. The preservation of built heritage also makes a statement. It says that citizens recognize the contributions of those who came before them; it says that there is immeasurable value in "remembering" and that, by doing so, people will have greater insight into how the past, the present, and the future are connected. Preservation gives each generation one more way of comprehending and defining itself.

Saskatchewan, like Canada, is young. Perhaps this explains why so many of our precious buildings are being discarded. In the past 30 years, our nation has lost more than 20% of its heritage buildings—that is nearly one-quarter in one generation. It is unlikely that our province's record is any better. This is why *Building Our Future—A People's Architectural History of Saskatchewan* is so important. It documents places that hold a special place in the hearts of our people—not just those of obvious stature like the Legislative Building or Government House, but treasures nonetheless. Each story captures memories and protects them for all time.

In April of 2001, His Royal Highness The Prince of Wales spoke in Regina. A lifelong advocate for built heritage, he said, "We have so much to discover nowadays that has been lost or thrown away deliberately during the 20th century—that century which was characterized, in my opinion, in so many fields of brutalism and soullessness."

I believe His Royal Highness has put before us a great challenge for the next 100 years. Let us begin by celebrating our past, fostering pride in what we have become, and demonstrating to our children, by example, that we cherish what they rightfully should inherit.

Dr. Lynda Haverstock
Lieutenant Governor
Province of Saskatchewan

CONTENTS

INTRODUCTION

Building Our Future: A People's Architectural History of Saskatchewan is a snapshot of how our people have lived, worked, played and worshipped during our first 100 years within the Confederation of Canada. It's a view of how Saskatchewan has grown and evolved as a province through anecdotes, stories and testimonials from those associated with the 100 buildings or built structures featured in this project.

This is a history book with a twist. Buildings and built structures featured in the book were "nominated" by persons from all walks of life across the province.

A process to generate nominations began with a media relations campaign in the fall of 2003 that included interviews on the John Gormley Live show heard on the News Talk Radio stations in Saskatchewan and CBC Radio's Afternoon Edition. The 83 members of the Saskatchewan Weekly Newspaper Association (SWNA) pitched in by encouraging their readers to nominate buildings as well. In addition, articles were published in the periodicals for members of the Saskatchewan Architectural Heritage Society (SAHS), the Saskatchewan Urban Municipalities Association (SUMA) and the Saskatchewan Association of Rural Municipalities (SARM).

Electronic communication tools and techniques raised the profile of the nomination process with the 12,000 groups who receive funding from SaskSport. All Directors of Communications for Saskatchewan agencies, departments and Crown corporations were invited to seek nominations of their co-workers.

There were 745 properties with a heritage designation in Saskatchewan when work on this project began. As a result, a three-member panel had the tough job of culling the hundreds of nominations to our book-size goal of 100 buildings and built structures to celebrate 100 years.

They selected 98 buildings, one bridge and one water tower from 45 communities represented in *Building Our Future*.

Geographic location and size of the community vary from Big Beaver, a stone's throw from the Montana border in southern Saskatchewan with a population of less than most hockey teams, to Saskatoon, the province's largest city, to Stanley Mission in the north.

The editorial plan for this book also changed once the nominations were reviewed because it became clear that adaptive reuse, as a concept, was being embraced across Saskatchewan. So a chapter featuring adaptive reuse techniques became one of the largest in the book even though it wasn't part of the original editorial outline. A proposed chapter on sport and recreation had to be dropped from the book as a result.

Choices were often very difficult to make, but guiding the process was a mandate to provide balance among the many types of structures nominated and the geographic regions across the province. We may have erred in some of our decisions, but our benchmark was consistent throughout the entire editorial selection, research and writing process.

I offer my special thanks to everyone who submitted a nomination and to the hundreds of people who helped provide background information, research material or personal testimonials that make this book unique.

Thanks, also, to the Board of Directors of the Saskatchewan Architectural Heritage Society for having the faith to believe in the project promoted by Al Rosseker, their dedicated, tenacious and tireless Provincial Director.

SAHS is a provincial organization funded by the Saskatchewan Lotteries administered through SaskCulture. Major funding for the project was provided by SAHS through its partnerships with the Province of Saskatchewan Communiy Initiatives Fund, the Saskatchewan Heritage Foundation (SHF), Saskatchewan Gaming Corporation and Harvard Developments Inc.

Let me extend a special debt of gratitude to Bernie Cruikshank of Saskatoon and Bill Henderson of Regina whose personal knowledge of each city and where to obtain more detailed information on various buildings was priceless. As well, heritage expert Frank Korvemaker came through supplying a wealth of images from the SHF database. Without them, this book would not have been possible.

Although this is not an academic or scholarly publication, it can and should be used by individuals and groups of all ages in this province—and by those who once called Saskatchewan home—to see where we've been.

My goal is complete—to research and write a history book with a twist in honour of Saskatchewan's Centennial year.

Hopefully, there will be nuggets of information that you can mine from within the pages and photographs of this book which make you say: "I didn't know that! or "Wow!"

Joe Ralko,
Author

ADAPTIVE REUSE

"The unique architectural features complement the adaptive reuse from a land titles office building to a gallery, gift shop and café."

–Artist Yvette Moore of Moose Jaw

Buildings reflect the pride and passion of the people who erected the structures, planned their original use and those people who invested their hard-earned cash to complete each project.

Over time, the buildings' use sometimes exceeds even the wildest hopes and dreams of the original occupants and owners. Use of those buildings often evolves according to the needs of those who live, work or play in them.

From an architectural point of view, it's called adaptive reuse. Taking a building constructed for one clearly defined purpose and adapting it for another new and innovative use may be a philosophy based on the hardy spirit of finding a use or value in virtually everything we have in Saskatchewan.

Think of adaptive reuse as recycling on a grand scale, except the tangible products being recycled are buildings and not newspapers, plastics or glass. The building receives a new lease on life instead of being torn down, bulldozed or abandoned.

People from literally all regions of Saskatchewan have embraced the concept of adaptive reuse in their communities. Where some see an abandoned or unuseable building, others are stepping forward with a vision of the future that utilizes the exterior almost exactly the way it was constructed but undergoes often extensive interior renovations.

The first building designated a Provincial Heritage Property by the Government of Saskatchewan in 1977 is a textbook example of adaptive reuse. Constructed as part of a wave of land titles buildings in the major centres of the province, the facility was renovated by the provincial government—that was the owner—for multiple use as the Saskatchewan Sports Hall of Fame and Museum along with office space for member organizations of SaskSport.

In other communities land titles building have being successfully transformed for different, yet effective, purposes.

In Moose Jaw, artist Yvette Moore has established a retail shop to display and sell her work, while in Saskatoon, the Brayford Shapiro law firm has been conducting business in the city's oldest (former) provincial government building since 1994.

Other unique examples of how creative Saskatchewan people have been in adapting buildings for new use include converting a former bank into a private residence and changing one of the province's first grocery warehouses into a multi-use facility including a brew pub, condominiums and offices.

Saskatchewan people have become innovators in adapting structures built for one purpose into another. Examples of the adaptive reuse of buildings can be found throughout the province from tiny villages and small towns to the province's largest cities. In fact, the ways buildings have been adapted to new uses are as diverse as the needs of people across the province.

One could possibly imagine Dale Dancsok's trepidation at being approached to handle some heritage restoration work on a project in

Whitewood, Saskatchewan. A former Whitewood church's interior was being changed to become an archives building, while the exterior was being restored to its original appearance. This church, constructed in 1892, was taken over the Masons from 1920 to 1987.

Dancsok was chosen as general contractor for the project. The work on the building, which was taken over by the McKay Historical Society in 1997, involved removal of an unsightly addition, re-incorporation of an original circular window, and closure of various openings to return the structure to its original design.

Dancsok took on the church/archives building project, including doing the restoration woodwork himself. His fine work was recognized by the Saskatchewan Architectural Heritage Society in June 2003, when he became one of the recipients of the Lieutenant-Governor of Saskatchewan's Heritage Architecture Excellence Awards.

Dale Dancsok is legally blind. An impediment, perhaps, but overcome by that Saskatchewan spirit of ingenuity and adaptive reuse.

HENDERS DRUG STORE
Arcola

Leigh Robinson, an Arcola school teacher with a passion for heritage restoration projects, has renovated and adapted the local drugstore, a building made famous in the 1977 movie *Who Has Seen the Wind*, for a new use.

Featured as McConnell's drugstore on movie posters, video cassette covers, and the book by author W. O. Mitchell, the structure was built in 1903 and is one of the oldest buildings in the community, situated 198 kilometres southeast of Regina.

James Donaldson, who graduated from the College of Pharmacy in Winnipeg, built what he called a Medicine Hall in Arcola, a boomtown on the Moose Mountain Plains at the turn of the century. He sold the building in 1918, and the property changed hands several times until Dick Henders acquired the drugstore in 1926. Henders operated the business until 1956.

Over time, the building was bought and sold again. In 1998, Robinson cut a deal with the town

to waive taxes until his aggressive renovation work was completed.

"The structure's unique front façade, its remarkable construction, and its kinship to Main Street Arcola's other landmark buildings convinced me the building should be restored and adapted to the community's need for good commercial and residential space," Robinson explained. "It was important to restore the exterior to its original appearance while adaptively reusing the interior space to create a period look with new infrastructure."

His timing was perfect, because Arcola has discovered that heritage draws tourism.

The Town of Arcola gave Robinson a tax holiday until completion, provided heavy equipment for the removal of debris, and got the old water and sewer lines working again. People in the community donated Arcola brick, old doors, millwork, and radiators. Local craftsmen were happy to recreate lost exterior mouldings and repair stained glass. A local oil

The store's exterior renovation received a Saskatchewan Architectural Heritage Society Vintage Building Award in 2000. PHOTO COURTESY LEIGH ROBINSON

company donated a crane to remove the old boiler sections from the basement.

"Friends and family donated time preparing the tin ceilings, mixing mortar, scraping paint, salvaging millwork and removing crumbled plaster," Robinson said. "It has stood the test of time and neglect."

The building is constructed of tan-coloured Arcola brick. Thick walls and cast-iron columns framing the street entrance support a brick bay on the second floor. Five layers of brick form the basement walls, three layers form the main floor walls, and two layers complete the top floor.

Floor joists were set on the brick ledges at each level. The second floor is 20 inches thick, a composite of 2 by 12s and 2 by 6s sandwiching a 2-inch layer of mortar, probably for fireproofing.

"This unique and durable building has served generations of the community as everything from late-night emergency dispensary to daytime ice cream parlour and gift emporium," Robinson noted. "Overall, the building's design and construction are rare for this part of the prairies. The building style appears to derive from European origins adapted to early eastern and American frontier structures. Brick basements are rarely seen in this area, and brick veneer over frame was the standard approach to using brick."

Some persons still have fond memories of the Henders Drug Store.

"That drugstore was really something," recalled local resident Ida Brownridge. "The stuff in it was so interesting—it was a fascinating place."

Contractor Danny Hawman made a curious discovery when he was helping Leigh Robinson with some renovation work.

"I found their safe deposit box when we were doing renovations in the main floor apartment," Hawman explained. "I could see that there was a cutout in the floor, so I took out a couple boards and found a shoebox-sized metal box under a trap door. That was where they stored their receipts for the day and their valuables."

He suggested the owners of the day would cover the trap door up with a carpet or throw rug so no one knew where the money was kept.

"There was nothing in it when we found it, but it was a neat kind of hideaway for the day,"

Hawman said. "It was painted black, so if you were in the basement you couldn't see it."

Robinson believes the building's massive structural brick construction and clear span fir joists prevented collapse.

Because of neglect and previous drainage problems, much of the back wall had to be rebuilt along with all four corners and upper window arches. The building's plumbing, heating, and electrical systems were replaced. An efficient new steam boiler was installed. There now are three complete baths.

"The reconfigured main floor makes the building very functional and flexible to use while keeping its historical integrity," Robinson said.

An antique shop, massage therapy clinic and bathroom occupy the store front area, about two thirds of the main floor space. The other third includes an apartment and an entrance hall. The hall provides access to all parts of the building from the parking lot at the back. Upstairs is a large apartment with restored antique bath fixtures.

Robinson also installed some modern conveniences, including a central vacuum system and cable television.

It's a far cry from the building's original purpose. And it's even further from the drugstore in the movie that told the story of a prairie boy's initiation into the mysteries of life, death, God, and the spirit that moves through everything: the wind.

Starring Gordon Pinsent and Helen Shaver, *Who Has Seen The Wind* was filmed in and around Arcola. The film was the Grand Prix winner in the Paris Film Festival and was the best grossing Canadian feature film of 1977.

Robinson and his friends have retained the original exterior façade and have brought the building back to the former grandeur of the boom era of southeastern Saskatchewan.

The Henders Drug Store, located at 107 Main Street in Arcola, was designated a Municipal Heritage Site in 1998.

OLD POST OFFICE
Humboldt

Visitors and city folk in Humboldt have been able to tell time for more than 90 years by listening to an 800-pound bell chiming every hour on the hour in the tower of the former red brick post office.

Mayor Dennis Korte, said that when Humboldt was chosen as the site for a new public building in 1911 residents regarded the decision as a celebration of the town's growing prestige as a centre of development in the west. Red brick, an expensive material in comparison to the clay brick often used in the west, reflected the opulence of the age, he said.

The structure still towers over the downtown core today.

"Our historic post office building stands as a symbol of the optimism of our community—both past and present," said Korte, who is also a local businessman. "It was an impressive structure when built in 1912 and has served our community well during its usage as a post office."

He said the community saw the value of its architectural heritage when it was purchased in the mid-1970s.

"Today, we treasure it as one of the community's greatest assets, with its adaptive re-use as the home of our community museum."

The building now is home for the Humboldt & District Museum and Gallery.

A historic site, the original style of the exterior has retained with the words "Post Office" clearly etched in the Tyndal stone over the main doors. "We still have a good number of people each year, who come in to mail their letters or buy stamps," laughs museum curator Jennifer Hoesgen. "Unfortunately, they are about 29 years too late. The post office moved out of the building in 1975."

The Brown Construction Company was awarded a contract on August 16, 1911, to construct a federal government building measuring 79 feet by 36 feet. A bandstand originally occupied the site selected.

Saskatoon architect Bob Rajani led the exterior renovation project to maintain the appearance and character of Humboldt's Post Office Building.
PHOTO COURTESY SASKATCHEWAN HERITAGE FOUNDATION

The Post Office Building was two storeys tall with a wooden mansard attic and parapet gables. A four-storey clock tower anchors the principal corner of the structure. The final estimate for the construction was $42, 275.

A contract was awarded in December 1952 to Shoquist Construction Ltd. for the construction of an addition to the building. The new addition was one storey with a basement on the north end of the structure. The final estimate cost was $101,370.

The building is constructed of red brick with Tyndal stone coping and foundation.

This national historic site, located in the heart of downtown Humboldt, has served the community in various capacities.

The primary use of the building was as a post office, but the second floor served many purposes. A customs office was located in the building from 1912 to 1932. The local detachment of the Royal Canadian Mounted Police (RCMP) was located in the post office from 1933 to 1964. And the War Time Price and Trade Board had offices in the building from 1940 to 1946. Throughout the years, a caretaker apparently lived in a third-floor suite.

The building became vacant in 1975 when the Post Office built a new building. A variety of community groups used the building sporadically until the town purchased it in 1977 for $60,000.

In 1982, the Humboldt & District Museum and Gallery opened.

"The tower clock is a unique feature of the building," Korte said. The clockworks were made by John Smith and Sons of Derby, England.

"Unlike similar clockworks in the country, which have been converted to an electrical wind system, the Humboldt clock remains authentically mechanical, wound every three days, which keeps the 800-pound bell striking every hour."

The Old Post Office is located at 602 Main Street, at the corner of Sixth Avenue in downtown Humboldt. It was named a National Historic Site in 1977 and was declared a Municipal Heritage Property on October 9, 1984.

ASSUMPTION CHURCH
Marysburg

The Assumption Church at Marysburg, about 10 kilometres north of Humboldt, is being adapted to become a unique concert hall.

The red brick church is a natural acoustic masterpiece undisturbed by air conditioning, carpeting, or traffic. Amazing musical performances by choral groups as well as brass and string ensembles are the result of the church being constructed in a neo-Renaissance style with Romanesque arches and an un-ribbed barrel vault over the transept, all conducive to rich sound.

Adapting the church for use as a concert hall is an evolutionary process that began in 1998, when a group of area residents banded together. The church had been slated to be closed because there were only 25 families still in the parish.

The rebirth into a concert facility began when Alphonse Gerwing, a musician from neighbouring Lake Lenore, and Gregory Schulte, a Saskatoon musician, organized the Marysburg Regional Chorus of 42 male and female voices.

The chorus holds annual concerts as fundraisers. Since these proved to be very popular, the decision was made to organize a concert series, The Marysburg Summer Festival of the Arts, described by Gerwing as "Saskatchewan's Salzburg of the prairies."

"This festival took root quickly, ensuring the building's continued use after ceasing to be used as a church," Gerwing said. "The festival gives young musicians the opportunity to perform in public and brings joy to audiences."

From 1998 to the end of 2003, new furnaces were installed, the foundation and brick exterior was repaired, insulation pumped between roof and ceiling, and both nave and side wings given new roofs.

Funding came from the summer concert series and local initiatives.

"It's a beautiful church," said cellist Sarah Pomedli, after her 2003 concert in Assumption Church. "It has great sound for strings. It sounded as though the music went winging through the

The Marysburg Regional Chorus of 42 male and female voices hold annual concerts in the former Assumption Church.
Photo courtesy Al Gerwing

A choir of angels, the 12 Apostles and an image of King David adorn the ceiling and walls of Assumption Church.
PHOTO COURTESY AL GERWING

western Canada, as an example of the Baroque of Bavarian altars.

Four large stained glass windows bring light into the transept. This glass is marked by a fiery component that gives the windows a rich glow in sunlight. The same glass characterizes the windows of the nave and clerestory.

Assumption Church's columns have Corinthian capitals. The church is built of a rust-coloured brick from Redcliffe, Alberta, while the interior brick is from Bruno, Saskatchewan.

Father John Hable, who was pastor of the church in the 1950s, purchased several paintings from Count Berthold Von Imhoff of St. Walburg, Saskatchewan.

The Nine Choirs of Angels are in the apse, the 12 Apostles are in the clerestory, and images of King David and St. Cecilia in the choir loft.

Louis Schober, an Austrian immigrant, donated a wood-carved statue of St. Konrad of Parzham, as well as two wood crucifixes to Assumption Church in the 1930s. Unfortunately, the parish has no record of the artist, except that he was from Italy.

The Assumption Church, named a Municipal Heritage Site in 1983, is about 10 kilometres north of Humboldt on Highway 20 and 3 kilometres miles east on Marysburg Grid Road 756.

church." Pomedli performed in Marysburg a few weeks after playing in Carnegie Hall in New York.

"What a tremendous pleasure it was to play in this marvellous old church! And the audience was wonderful," bass player Wilmer Fawcett wrote from Vancouver after his internationally famous Viveza ensemble played in the Assumption Church in 2002. "With the warmth and enjoyment of the listeners and the terrific ambience of the building, we thought the concert was quite special. We feel a real attachment to Marysburg."

Recordings of Viveza can be frequently heard on CBC Radio's FM network.

People attending the concerts are enthusiastic in their praise as well. "The full rich sound came from all corners of the building, from ceiling, from the choir loft," an audience member wrote following a 2002 performance by Lisa Hornung and Dianne Gryba. "Here was stereo without technology."

A tornado completely demolished the first pioneer frame church at Marysburg in 1919. Only the bell and a statue modelled on Titian's painting of *Our Lady's Assumption* survived intact. The bell still rings and Our Lady's statue graces the high altar of the church.

The Bonas Brothers of Muenster were contracted to build the Assumption Church. No architectural records remain today.

A magnificent Baroque high altar built by Frank Berker and Jacob Schmitz in Milwaukee, Wisconsin, was erected in the church in September 1921. It is unique in Saskatchewan, and perhaps in

LUTHER ACADEMY
Melville

Luther Academy in Melville, built as private boarding school for boys in 1914, now is a museum that holds one of the largest collections of German literature in the province.

"This building has had three lives," explains Marg Redenbach, who has been the volunteer manager of the Melville Heritage Museum since 1988.

"It served the community as a boarding school from 1914 until 1926, then it became one of the first nursing homes in the province, and since 1983 it has been a museum."

The two-and-half-storey, buff brick building was constructed only a few years after Melville, a railway hub serving eastern Saskatchewan, had been incorporated as a city.

"This building is very significant in the history of Melville because it was the original Luther Academy in the province," said Bruno Kossmann, Melville City Manager from 1998 to 2002. "Melville is very proud to say that we were chosen first over Regina as the site for the school."

Both Melville and Regina were being considered as a location by the Lutherans for their private boarding school, he said. "The deciding factor was the offer by the City of Melville to build a wooden board walk from the downtown area almost one mile to the proposed site of the Lutheran Academy," Kossmann said.

Redenbach said Melville was projected to grow to become a city of 50,000 people, but the lack of an adequate supply of water hurt the community.

"Ironcially, we now have one of the best water quality and supply systems in the country but back then we couldn't match the needs of the optimism of both Luther Academy and many businesses," she said.

In 1926, officials opted to close Luther Academy in Melville and open Luther College in Regina, a school that still operates to today.

"We have found some interesting records from the early days of Luther Academy," Redenbach said. "We know that the first three teachers who

Luther Academy was originally established in Melville because the city offered to build a one-kilometre board walk to the school.
PHOTO COURTESY SASKATCHEWAN HERITAGE FOUNDATION

The chapel contains artifacts and furnishings from several area churches of varying denominations.

Two of the former classrooms are dedicated to military memorabilia from the Boer War, the First World War, the Second World War, and the Korean War. Material on display includes medals, uniforms, weapons, photographs, and a scale-model of the HMCS Melville, a minesweeper used in the Second World War.

The Railroad Room traces the history of the Grand Truck Pacific and Canadian National Railways. Another room depicts the nursing home era of the building.

More than 100 original black and white photographs on display provide visitors a glimpse of life in Melville during its first quarter century of growth.

The Melville Museum is open 10:00 A.M. to 4:00 P.M. Tuesday to Sunday from May 15 to October 15. The museum is closed for lunch. There no admission charge but donations are welcome. There is limited wheelchair access.

The Melville Heritage Museum, located at 100 Heritage Drive, was designated a Municipal Heritage Site on June 29, 1981.

came to Melville to work at Luther Academy were educated in Chicago and that the language of choice was German."

There were three classrooms on the main floor and nine study rooms on the second floor. The building had steam heat and drew water from nearby wells.

"There were two dorms for 16 boys each on the top floor," Redenbach said. "Girls were allowed to enrol in the school in the early 1920s providing they could stay at homes approved by Luther Academy in Melville."

She said students came from the three prairie provinces, though some records discovered by researchers show two students who attended came from Latvia.

"You have to remember that when Luther Academy began the three teachers must have felt like missionaries coming to a frontier town in western Canada," Redenbach said. "The school opened just six years after Melville was established, yet they taught subjects such as Greek, Latin and English."

The building was converted for use as a nursing home from 1926 until 1975, when it was closed. It was not used for several years.

A museum reflecting Melville's past, German-language roots, as well as involvement by local residents in military campaigns around the world, opened in 1983.

"Many of the German-language books date to the 1800s but we have one that is called a Bible, but really is a collection of sermons in German that is clearly dated 1721," Redenbach said.

LAND TITLES BUILDING
Moose Jaw

Canadian prairie artist Yvette Moore has successfully transformed the picturesque Moose Jaw Land Titles Building into her own business.

"If I had to start from scratch, I couldn't have designed or built it better," said Moore, about the building through which land was registered in the Moose Jaw district for 88 years.

"The unique architectural features complement the adaptive reuse from a land titles office building to a gallery, gift shop, and café. The construction of the building, with its concrete, Tyndal stone, brick, plaster, and steel, has created the ideal noncombustible location to house and showcase irreplaceable art and antiques. It's a win-win combination of historical architecture and prairie art that has attracted people from around the world."

The single-storey building, with very high ceilings, was designed by Regina architects Storey and Van Egmond, and constructed in 1910. Because of a high volume of land transactions, the building was enlarged in 1922. The provincial government's land registration office operated in the building until 1998, when it closed and then was sold to Moore, who had already established a high profile in western Canada as a successful artist.

Restoration work and the change to its existing use as an art gallery began in 1999. Moore got lots of help from her friends and family.

"The project consisted of plaster repair using over 2,500 pounds of plaster, removing the paint from the copper using 30 gallons of stripper, removing the original flooring, and refinishing as much of the original furnishing to be used as part of the décor," she recalled.

"The colour scheme used was taken from the original plaster on the ceilings, which dated back to 1922 but had been hidden for the last 50 years with suspended ceilings."

Chandeliers in the main gallery are not originals but are reproduction copper fixtures that blend perfectly with the décor.

The building received a Saskatchewan Architectural Heritage Society Vintage Building Award in 1998 for Adaptive Reuse.
PHOTO COURTESY SAHS

"The school house light fixtures in the addition are close replicas of the original ones that were common to the era," Moore said. "The furnishings included some of the original steel cabinets dating back to the early 1900s. The countertops, for example, still have their battleship linoleum. The focus of the project was to bring back the attention to the material and workmanship evident in the early years of the past century."

Moore was named the Moose Jaw Citizen of the Year in 2000 and was a finalist the same year for the Saskatchewan Women of Achievement Award. For outstanding contribution to the conservation of Saskatchewan's Built Heritage, Yvette received the Saskatchewan Architectural Heritage Society's "Vintage Building Award" for Adaptive Reuse of a community landmark. In December 2002, she was presented with the Golden Jubilee Medal in honour of her artistic achievements and community involvement.

Born in Radville, Saskatchewan, Moore grew up on her family farm. That's where she developed her passion for the beauty of the prairies and lifestyle that she vividly portrays in all of paintings. Her work reflects everyday events to historical architecture.

Yvette Moore paints with a passion for detail that extends beyond an attempt to simply be realistic. Her paintings are acrylic portrayals of pattern, texture, colour and emotion. Painstaking attention to the things that are normally taken for granted— grain patterns in old and new wood, wistful strands

of curled hair, or the stitches in crocheted lace— never obscures her primary purpose of creating an intimacy between the viewer and image.

Yvette is also a writer. *A Prairie Alphabet* has sold more than 300,000 copies since it hit the book shelves in 1992 while *A Prairie Year,* published in 1994, has sold more than 100,000 copies. *Heartland: A Prairie Sampler* has sold more than 15,000 copies and was a finalist in the 2002 Saskatchewan Book of the Year Awards.

Moore's patience and attention to detail helped her convert the Land Titles Building into a unique business environment with panache and style.

The building was the last one of 11 surviving land registration facilities in the province to have retained its original function until 1998. Others had been closed or converted to other purposes by then, such as the Regina Land Titles Building that became the Saskatchewan Sports Hall of Fame and Museum.

Rapid growth in the Moose Jaw area after the turn of the century was the reason the Land Titles Building was constructed. During peak times, people would line up for several blocks to register their land claims. Moose Jaw's population increased from 1,558 in 1901, to 6,249 in 1906, to 13,823 in 1911. The city's population growth and evolution into a key regional commercial and administration centre justified the construction of the Land Titles Building.

Architects Storey and Van Egmond designed the building while Navin Bros. of Moose Jaw won the construction tender. The cost to complete the building was $35,920.

Although the building features the highly contrasting brick and Tyndal stone as facing materials and the round-arched window form of the earlier provincial land titles buildings, its overall design was more Classical Revival in its inspiration. Fireproof materials were used in construction because of the building's planned use.

The concrete construction, with brick and stone exterior, was extended into the interior with plaster mouldings, keystones, beams, and wall finish. The interior doors and windows were faced with copper, one of the most unique and intriguing features inside.

The ceiling height is 18 feet, adding to the elegant and breath taking grand atmosphere of the building. In 1922, the building was enlarged along the street façade in a manner that replicated the form and decoration detailing the original structure. The brick on the original east wall was carefully removed and reused on the front. On the new east and north walls, T. P. Moka brick from the brick plant in nearby Claybank, Saskatchewan, was used.

The Moose Jaw Land Titles Building, located at 76 Fairford Street West, was declared a Municipal Heritage Site in 1997.

Almost 100 years old, the structure's solid building materials continue to ensure its longevity.
Photo courtesy Saskatchewan Heritage Foundation

RED CROSS OUTPOST
Paddockwood

Anita Shaw is proud to say her Paddockwood home was the first Red Cross outpost in the British Commonwealth.

Built in 1920, the two-storey wooden building now is located 4.4 kilometres east of Paddockwood on the main grid road. The community is 35 kilometres north and another 18.4 kilometres east of the City of Prince Albert.

Shaw moved into the former medical centre in 1998, when she moved from northern Saskatchewan to begin a fresh start on her life.

"This building and area appealed to me," Shaw said. "It was a part of history that I wanted to maintain while starting a new business."

The former delivery room in the Red Cross outpost now is a spare bedroom. The reception area, or alcove, is the office for Shaw's business, Frost Creek Water Hauling.

"The emergency room is my dining room," she explained. "My living room was a ward for patients."

Helen McCaslin, who now lives in Regina, was among the thousands of Red Cross outpost patients at Paddockwood.

"My interest in the building is that I was born there on February 16, 1942, during a big snowstorm," McCaslin said. "My mother-to-be and my two-year-old sister were made comfortable in the roomy back seat of the 1932 Chevrolet."

She said a team of horses was hitched to the car, and her father and uncle then shovelled "every inch of the three miles or so to get to the 8 Mile Road" that would take them to Highway 2 into Prince Albert.

"But I was coming too fast, so they stopped at the Red Cross outpost, that was then located on Eight Mile Road," she said, referring to the fact that years later the building was moved from the secondary road to its current location. "Another woman died that night giving birth to a baby boy."

Red Cross nurses provided medical treatment for people in rural areas of Saskatchewan decades before medicare and, in some areas, even before hospitals were established.

Ruth Shewchuk was the nurse appointed by the Red Cross to close the Paddockwood outpost in 1948, ending a 28-year career of medical service to the area.

"To my knowledge, the outpost at Paddockwood was the first to be established within the British Empire," Shewchuk told the Saskatoon *Star Phoenix* after being honoured for her nursing work by the Canadian Red Cross in 2003.

"So many communities depended on our service."

Shewchuk had mixed feelings closing the outpost on July 30, 1948.

"The outposts were medical lifelines in the rural areas. The community provided the building, and most had a large Red Cross painted on its roof," she recalled. "Ours had a three-bed ward, a case room, patient reception area, nursery, and an alcove off the dining area."

The Red Cross would supply staff and equipment, while volunteers from the community would form an "auxiliary force" to help. "Supplies were brought to us by a team and dray. Sometimes you had a nurses' aide and sometimes you even had a cook and cleaner."

There were significant challenges for the nurses, Shewchuk said. "You didn't have a doctor available in the community. You couldn't be reached by telephone after 10 P.M. and you didn't have a vehicle," she said. "We got around the best we could by Bennett buggies, sleighs, cutters, trucks, and tractors."

Nurses had to deal with a wide range of medical problems, from delivering babies in people's homes to setting broken bones.

"You also have to remember that during the 1920s and 1930s the roads were gravel and nothing like the pavement we have available today," Shewchuk reflected, noting that nurses referred very serious injuries to a doctor in Prince Albert.

"One time, a little girl came to the outpost with a broken clavicle. I stabilized it as best I could so her dad could take her all the way to Prince Albert on an open tractor. I later got a phone call from the doctor in Prince Albert saying he was sending the girl back in the same condition I had sent her. I guess I had trussed her down so well that the bone set itself."

Anita Shaw says she often gets persons dropping by her home who have either personal memories of the former Paddockwood outpost or have heard stories about it from their parents and grandparents.

"I like it," Shaw said. "I've tried to keep the building up as best I can and I enjoy hearing their stories. I feel proud to live in a building that means so much, to so many people."

A distinctive red and white cross painted on the green roof is now covered by shingles. The building, which is not a heritage site, has been moved twice since the Red Cross Outpost closed in 1947.

First, it was relocated about two kilometres east of Paddockwood. Then, in 1979, the building was move to where it now stands, 4.4 kilometres east of the community. A small cairn marks the location of the original Red Cross Outpost along Highway 2.

Transportation took many forms and was time-consuming in remote areas of Northern Saskatchewan. PHOTO COURTESY CANADIAN RED CROSS

Being a Red Cross nurse in an outpost was an often lonely existence that required dedication and a 24/7 work ethic. PHOTO COURTESY CANADIAN RED CROSS

LAND TITLES BUILDING
Regina

Saskatchewan's first land titles building also became the first property designated a Provincial Heritage Site in 1978.

The adaptive reuse of the building serves two purposes. It is the permanent home of the Saskatchewan Sports Hall of Fame and Museum. In addition, it is one of a trio of Administration Centres for Sport, Culture and Recreation that SaskSport has in the province.

Provincial sports organizations ranging from basketball to tennis share office space in the building, along with more than two dozen not-for-profit groups, including air cadets, the Kids Help Phone, and the Sport Medicine & Science Council of Saskatchewan.

The Regina Land Titles Building was designed by architects Darling and Pearson, and constructed between 1907 and 1909. The distinctive architectural style is highlighted by the Romanesque arched windows and decorative entablature above the projecting brick columns.

All of the land title records for the Regina district were stored in the building from 1910 until it closed in 1977. Following a year of renovations, the building reopened in 1979 with its dual purposes.

The Saskatchewan Sports Hall of Fame had been established on Oct. 31, 1966, to honour outstanding Saskatchewan athletes, championship teams, and sport builders. However, there was no permanent home for the Hall of Fame until the provincial government opted to convert the former Regina Land Titles Building for reuse.

"Without a home we could not display the sports memorabilia of Saskatchewan," said Cas Pielak, who was inducted in the Saskatchewan Sports Hall of Fame as a baseball builder in 1989 and then served as the chairman of the Hall in 2000. "We needed a place for people to see the richness of the sports history of Saskatchewan."

There are 167 athletes, 115 builders and 86 teams from more than 40 sports who have been inducted into the Saskatchewan Hall of Fame.

Provincial, national and internal champions from virtually every walk of life in the sports world have been honoured.

Inductees have included Johnny Bower, Gordie Howe, and Bryan Trottier in hockey, Reggie Cleveland and Terry Puhl in baseball; as well as the Richardson family curling legends led by Ernie Richardson.

Women are also represented. The late Sandra Schmirler, whose women's foursome won the first gold medal ever awarded at the Olympic level in 1998, is an inductee and so too are Mary "Bonnie" Baker and Arlene Noga, who played in the All American Girls Professional Baseball league. The character played by Gina Davis in the movie *A League of Their Own* is believed to have been based on Baker.

Nominations are received each year for athletes, builders, and teams to be inducted into the Sports Hall of Fame. These supplement the pre-existing nominations on file. All nominations are reviewed by a committee that prepares an "inductees slate" for the Board of Directors of the Saskatchewan Sports Hall of Fame to consider. Directors can either ratify the slate or send it back to the volunteer committee for revision.

The Saskatchewan Hall of Fame and Museum occupies about half of the first floor of the three-storey, brick building just south of Victoria Park and across the street from the historic Hotel Saskatchewan.

Pielak, who served as president of Saskatchewan Baseball for 2 years before being elected President of Canada Baseball for 10 consecutive years from 1975 to 1985, said there are advantages and disadvantages for the Hall of Fame and Museum to be located in the historic Land Titles Building.

"On one hand, it's great to be located in the former the Land Titles Building because it's part of the history of Saskatchewan," said Pielak. "On the other hand, it's very costly for the upkeep of the building. But, all in all, it has been a great building for the Saskatchewan Sports Hall of Fame and Museum."

Pielak believes a special fund should be established to preserve and protect the building. "I did not realize that this was the first building designated a provincial heritage site. As such, we should make this more known, and a building fund should be started to maintain this building," he said. "I am sure that there aren't many people in Saskatchewan that know this building was the first building designated as provincial heritage site and, if they did, they would support to maintain the building."

The museum is the official repository for the Saskatchewan Roughrider collection, so something from the Canadian Football League team can always be seen at the museum. In addition, there is a wide range of apparel, equipment, photographs, and trophies from other sports rotated throughout the year.

The Saskatchewan Sports Hall of Fame and Museum is open Monday to Friday during the winter, and seven days a week between the Victoria Day and Labour Day weekends. Donations are accepted.

The majority of space in the building is offices operated by SaskSport, the nonprofit federation working with more than 12,000 provincial sport, culture, and recreation organizations.

SaskSport administers the Saskatchewan Lotteries program, that includes national games such as Lotto 649 and Super 7. It's a partner as well in the Western Canada Lottery Corporation that offers regional games such as Scratch 'N Win tickets.

The SaskSport Administration Centres provide volunteer groups the opportunity to work together and share resources and ideas. There are a variety of services available at the Centres including administrative support, printing services, and office and meeting space.

"SaskSport members coordinate sporting activities and distribute funds to member clubs, teams, and athletes in communities throughout the province," said Pielak, president of SaskSport from 1974 to 1975.

"These organizations provide professional guidance, ensure safety, provide insurance, set rules, raise money, acquire sponsorships, and train athletes, coaches and officials."

The sport section of the Saskatchewan Lotteries Trust funds more than 6,000 local, zone, and provincial sport organizations that provide numerous programs and services such as community skills clinics, high-performance athlete training, sport science and medicine services, and coaches certification programs.

He also said these organizations host more than 100 major sporting events in the province each year, which have a significant impact on the local economy.

"As well, sport organizations initiate programs that are directed at increasing participation by under-represented groups such as youth at risk, people with disabilities, Aboriginals, women, northern residents, the economically disadvantaged, and seniors," Pielak explained. "Through the efforts of these organizations, more than 300,000 Saskatchewan residents are registered members of provincial sport organizations and thousands more participate in community-based recreation programs."

The renovated former Regina Land Titles Building continues to serve a dual role for the community by providing a valuable link from the past to the future. Achievements and history of sport in Saskatchewan can be celebrated within the building, while only a few metres away, groups build for the future from within the SaskSport Administration Centre.

The Land Titles Building is located at 2205 Victoria Avenue in Regina.

UNION STATION
Regina

Maintaining the aura, ambience, and decor of a railway station has helped Casino Regina to attract two million visitors a year and become Saskatchewan's number one tourist attraction.

More people now visit the casino each day than arrived and departed from Union Station in a week when passenger train service was at its peak in the west.

Casino Regina is a highly successful financial and heritage partnership between the Government of Saskatchewan and the Federation of Saskatchewan Indian Nations.

Casino Regina opened in 1996 and built on the railway heritage of Union Station in everything, from its advertising compaigns to the tasteful blend of old and new furnishing.

Constructed from 1911 to 1912 by the Canadian Pacific Railway, Union Station was designed to accommodate both the CPR and the Canadian Northern Railway, which later became Canadian National.

A major expansion 20 years later added a new rotunda. Despite restricted funds, construction materials used in the 1931 expansion were superior to those used in the 1911 construction. The original station was faced with Ashlar stone, while Tyndal limestone dominated the new construction. The renovation project was designed to make maximum use of local and regional suppliers.

Bass relief pilasters, lacy iron canopies, medallions, and stone detailing gave the building a simple elegance. With its high arched ceiling, the grand concourse had relief medallions, while finely carved stonework featured contemporary Art Deco light fixtures manufactured entirely in western Canada by the Canadian Electric Plating Company.

The seats in the waiting room, specifically designed for the station, were manufactured in Regina. The flooring in public areas was done in terrazzo, and marble was installed in the high-traffic areas such as entrances and stairways.

In 1995, the casino project received a Saskatchewan Architectural Heritage Society Vintage Building Award for Adaptive Reuse.
PHOTO COURTESY CASINO REGINA

Once the hub for train transportation in Regina, the structure sat vacant for a number of years before being redeveloped.
PHOTO COURTESY SASKATCHEWAN HERITAGE FOUNDATION

Marble-surfaced counters, brass fixtures, and lettering also added to the station's stateliness. A staircase of white marble connected the main passenger lobby to the offices above. The waiting rooms were finished with white polished oak.

The beauty from Union Station was tastefully preserved during the interior restoration to become the casino.

The main entrance to Casino Regina is through the grand concourse. Now, instead of spotlessly-clean terrazzo floors, visitors pad along on wall-to-wall carpet.

An island of four blackjack tables and three roulette wheels fill the grand concourse. High above the gamblers, one can clearly see the nicely retouched medallions and stonework. The ceiling was repainted to highlight the plasterwork. It used to be pale green colour. Ceramic plate designs in the corners are of buffalo and cattle create a prairie atmosphere.

On the west wall of the lobby, the hand-painted Arrival/Departure wooden timetable reminds visitors of the station's past. People read how The Owl would arrive from Saskatoon at 5:10 A.M. or that The Canadian would depart for Vancouver at 9:40 P.M. daily.

Tucked just to the side of the timetable are the white marble stairs leading to the casino's offices on the second and third floors. Some offices still have the railway décor on the doors and within.

Walking north from the timetable, the ambience begins to shift closer to the change counter,

which was the original 1911 ticket counter. The clunking of coins hitting the bucket at the bottom of electronic slot machines drowns out the music system from the concourse turning the corner past the 25-cent Playboy machines.

Casino Regina has 803 slot machines and 35 table games to choose from, including blackjack, roulette, Let It Ride, Caribbean Stud Poker, Red Dog, and Casino War. In addition, the casino claims Canada's number one poker room.

The $37-million renovation was done in conjunction with Heritage Regina. "We entered the project with some misgivings but our over-riding concern was the preservation of a very important Regina building," wrote Nick Russell, Chair of Heritage Regina, in a 1996 booklet entitled *The Story of Regina's Union Station.*

"The Gaming Corporation from the first saw the heritage aspects of the building could be used constructively, rather than viewing them as an impediment to development. The resulting collaboration has been challenging, exciting, and productive."

"Heritage purists will be upset that certain aspects of the old station have not been preserved. And the heritage groups have certainly had to make compromises," Russell wrote. "But the bottom line has always been saving the building. In the end, because the developers have poured millions of dollars into this building, Union Station has been given a guaranteed extension of its life."

Although Union Station had some glory times, its popularity began to fade as train travel was surpassed by airlines and automobiles. VIA Rail bought Union Station from the CPR and spent $300,000 to refurbish the waiting room and washroom area in 1984. But due to government cuts, Union Station, as well as 17 other passenger routes in Canada, were closed. The last VIA train pulled out of Regina on January 16, 1990.

So the Casino Regina project was a second chance for Union Station.

The casino still proudly distributes the 40-page booklet, *The Milk Train, The Silk Train* and *The Skunk* for free to visitors who want to learn more about the history of the 617-foot-long building.

It provides a glimpse into the lives of people with links to Union Station such as George Orton, who served with the Royal Canadian Air Force in the Second World War.

Orton recalled posters advertising Victory Bonds lining the wall as he boarded the train at Union Station in March 1943 for Halifax, where he caught a ship to England.

"My parents and my five brothers and sisters saw me off at the station. The station was quite crowded because there were Air Force and Army personnel leaving at the same time. We weren't on a troop train, but most of the passengers were men leaving for war," Orton said.

"At that time you didn't walk out the door and cross the tracks. You went underneath a tunnel and came up to whatever track you needed to get to your train."

The entrance to that tunnel is closed today, but it is visible at the bottom of the stairs to the washrooms at the north end of the main lobby.

"Nobody, except passengers and employees, could go beyond the doors and go out to the platform, so they said their goodbyes in the rotunda. It was very emotional," Orton recalled. "I was 19 years old and in a sense we were excited because we were going to another country."

After the war, Orton worked in the CPR freight sheds for 38 years, 20 of those as a supervisor.

Union Station's monumental style testifies to the importance of railways in the development of Saskatchewan. It is also a textbook example of adaptive reuse of a heritage property.

Union Station, located at 1880 Saskatchewan Drive in Regina, was designated a Provincial Heritage Site in 1999.

VICTORIA PARK BUILDING
Regina

Housing the popular Copper Kettle Restaurant, the building garnered two Lt.-Gov. of Saskatchewan Heritage Architecture Excellence Awards in 2003.
PHOTO COURTESY BANADYGA MITCHELL PARTNERSHIP ARCHITECTS

Business conducted within the Victoria Park Building since 1929 has ranged from clothing to cuisine, bowling to beer, and now even sushi is available in the heart of downtown Regina.

The two-storey building, which was restored in 2002 to its original appearance, was one of a number of low-rise, retail-office blocks designed by architects Storey and Van Egmond and built in Regina during the mid- to late-1920s.

It has been known, however, by its primary tenant for the past 40 years, The Copper Kettle Restaurant. The main ground floor entrance, which also provides access to the second-storey office and basement levels, is embellished with stone.

The entrance features a recessed, round-arch opening outlined with cable or rope moulding, and a peaked panel that sports the building's name. The pilasters, that decline the building bays, are capped with decorative peaked elements that project upward and outward from the larger pressed-metal parapet cap. There is also a series of glazed-tile panels, arranged in a diamond pattern above each of the second-storey windows.

Mac & Mac Ltd., a men's clothing store and one of the original tenants, occupied the space in 1947 Scarth Street for 50 years. Vic Bowling Alleys was located in the basement from 1930 to 1978.

The original façade exhibits a distinguished mix of Tyndal stone and Claybank brick appropriate for its prime location, among the many elegant buildings facing Victoria Park. Unfortunately, the façade was covered over and post-war renovations to the ground floor detracted from the original character.

The Copper Kettle Restaurant is a Saskatchewan business success story that reflects the entrepreneurial enthusiasm of a family of immigrants.

Robert Gardikiotis moved to Regina in 1963 and bought the lunch counter at Aren's Drugstore the following year. Originally from a small village near Athens, he had met his wife, Ann, when she had returned home to visit relatives in Greece from Regina. They met, fell in love, and married.

He and a brother had operated a confectionary type business in Greece before moving to Canada. His wife had worked at a restaurant in the downtown area prior to their marriage, and he began looking for business opportunities for them to grow together.

so he first bought the lunch counter in the back of the drugstore and then expanded it to a full-scale restaurant when the owner made a career move.

"The Bay had approached Grant Argue to run the pharmacy in the new store they were opening in Regina," Gardikiotis recalled. "Grant was really excited because he was going to be working just 8 hours a day instead of the 18 hours a day he had been putting in as the owner and pharmacist."

Naming the new restaurant was a problem until Robert spoke with a friend who had returned from a trip to the United States. "He had been visiting New York City and came back with stories about eating at a restaurant there named The Copper Kettle," he said. "I liked the name so much that I borrowed it for my Regina restaurant."

Over the years, Gardikiotis has rejuvenated his business and the Victoria Park Building with major renovations in 1968, 1975, and 2002.

For his most recent efforts, the Saskatchewan Architectural Heritage Society (SAHS) bestowed two Heritage Architecture Awards of Excellence upon him in 2003 for exterior restoration and interior renovation.

Banadayga Mitchell Parntership Architects and Gabriel Construction of Regina also were recognized for the work they did on behalf of Gardiokiotis.

Gardikiotis and his wife made a point of having their daughters and son work with them in the restaurant over the years. "I wanted them to learn how to make a dollar," he said. "The restaurant business demands lots of hours. This way we could spend time together and they could learn to deal with people."

Gardikiotis has expanded market penetration by operating three distinctively different restaurants under the one roof of the Victoria Park Building.

The Copper Kettle features Greek and Canadian food. O'Hanlon's is an Irish pub that was rated the number one location for Guinness beer consumption in Manitoba and Saskatchewan in 2003, and Miccis, is a Japanese sushi restaurant.

A well-known Regina architectural firm, Pettick Phillips Partners Architects Ltd., now is the main tenant on the second floor with more than 6,000 square feet of office space.

Gardikiotis began converting the former bowling alley in the basement into a 30-stall underground parkade.

The Victoria Park Building is located from 1945 to 1953 Scarth Street in downtown Regina.

STRATHDEE BUILDING
Regina

The Strathdee Building, built as a grocery warehouse more than 70 years ago, has been used as a furniture store and then was converted in recent years into a multi-purpose facility with condominiums, a retail mall, food court, and the Bushwakker Brew Pub.

"The building was intended to be seen as the 'Cadillac' warehouse in Regina with five storeys, decorative architecture, and massive post and beam structure," explains Bev Robertson, owner of the brew pub on the first floor. "It still is among the biggest and handsomest warehouse buildings in Regina today."

A laundry on the site had been destroyed by the tornado that tore through the capital city in 1912. Construction of the warehouse began in early 1913 and was completed in March of the following year.

An annex was added during construction because demand for the services to be provided by the building grew during construction. The exterior of the building combines red brick and Tyndal stone.

The building, which measures 110 feet by 100 feet, now is considered the cornerstone of Regina's Old Warehouse District.

"Railway cars would be unloaded at the rear on tracks that ran next to the building," Robertson said. "An army of workers moved goods to the six large floors for storage from the basement to the top floor that was before the days of palate jacks."

Owners of stores in the smaller communities surrounding Regina would buy supplies wholesale, such as dried bean, cloth, and flour, then haul their goods away by truck.

The building is named after James Strathdee, a Scottish immigrant from Winnipeg, who came to Regina in 1914 to manage the property for the original owners.

Robertson said that at some point in the early 1930s Strathdee was returning from Calgary by motor vehicle and was involved in a serious accident near Swift Current.

Strathdee, although he sustained head injuries, managed to recover but with a diminished capacity and role in managing the facility. A few years later, he was found dead along the railway tracks near the building. Police ruled the death a suicide.

Over the years, the economic climate changed as patterns of distribution shifted.

Eaton's, the Canadian retailing giant, used the building as a warehouse for several years. The Saskatchewan Liquor Board had offices and storage in the building for another period of time. It became Regina Modern Furniture and then the Strathdee Mall and Bushwakker Brew Pub, home of what is said to be the largest and most significant judging of amateur beer in Canada.

Many who live in the upper floors of the warehouse or who work in the businesses there believe the building is haunted by Jim Strathdee

Dave Meldon, an antique dealer, tells the story of working late one night, turning off the lights, and heading for the stairwell. Shops on the third floor are made secure by closing and locking a large, wrought iron gate.

After locking the gate and turning out the nearby light, he noticed that he had missed a small three-position light that could still be seen glowing faintly at the far end of the floor.

"Hey, Jim, can you turn out that light for me," Dave yelled.

Before he could turn to leave, the light went from low to medium. He froze. Then the light went to high and then off.

Others in the building claim to have seen the apparition, out of the corner of their eye, pass them as they walk down hall ways.

The Strathdee Building, located at 2206 Dewdney Avenue in Regina, was designated a Municipal Heritage Site on July 3, 1990.

PRINCE EDWARD BUILDING
Regina

The Prince Edward Building, a stone post office constructed in 1906, now is the home of Canada's only permanent theatre-in-the-round, the Globe Theatre.

After the Post Office moved its offices to South Railway Avenue in the 1960s, the building served as Regina's City Hall until 1976.

"We were hired in 1979 by the City of Regina to find a way to accommodate the Globe Theatre at no ongoing cost to the city," explained Kevin Boyle of Roberts Properties Inc.

"The Globe wanted the use of the main floor but our proposal put them on the second and third floors so that the city could receive some income leasing space to commercial tenants on the main floor."

The Globe Theatre had been a $1-per-year tenant of the Merchant's Bank Building, which the city had owned, but it was sold to SaskTel so land could be assembled for the creation of the Cornwall Centre, the province's largest downtown mall in the late 1970s.

Changes to Old City Hall included installing a new elevator and windows plus a water sprinkler system at a cost of $1.3 million by the company then called H. A. Roberts Group.

The company managed the building for a number of years on behalf of the city until it was purchased by Art Fennell.

"In 1995, when Fennell experienced financial difficulties, Roberts Properties bought the building at a sheriff's sale in partnership with Fred Soofi, who, at the time, ran Alfredo's restaurant, located on the south end annex that linked the building with the adjacent Northern Bank Building," Boyle said. "We own the building to this day."

The main floor continues to be used as a mini-mall. Tenants include a cafeteria style restaurant, jewellery, and women's fashion stores.

"The public and the tenants tend to call the building the Old City Hall even though it was only a temporary home for the city and was built as a post office," Boyle said.

"The late George Bothwell used to phone me on a regular basis to complain about the inappropriate name for the building and chided me for allowing this incorrect use. When in 2003, with our permission, the city renamed the building to honour Prince Edward, I had a pang of guilt knowing how upset George would be."

Bothwell was involved in public life in Regina for 65 years as a newspaper reporter, insurance agent, an advertising agency manager, and as a public relations consultant. He was a member of the Regina Public Library Board for more than 30 years, serving from 1962 to 1970 and then again from 1973 to his death in 1996.

Bothwell was a staunch supporter of cultural heritage as shown to citizens through the built environment.

He was a member of the Plains Historical Society from 1978 to 1990, was the first chairman of the Regina Municipal Heritage Advisory Committee in 1980, and was elected as the first President of Saskatchewan Architectural Heritage Society in 1987.

The Globe Theatre, which now comfortably occupies the second and third floors of the Prince Edward Building, was founded in 1966 by Ken and Sue Kramer.

The Globe, Saskatchewan's first professional theatre company, has grown to become the province's largest arts organization.

The unique 20 foot by 20 foot stage set in an intimate 409 seat theatre offers exciting challenges to artists and designers and strikes a dynamic relationship between actors and audiences.

The Globe season consists of six Main Stage productions offering a blend of contemporary theatre as well as classic favourites. The Globe also programs a three-show Shumiatcher Sandbox Series that showcases new work and emerging artists through its three-show Shumiatcher Sandbox Series.

"On the outside, the Prince Edward Building is a beautiful reminder of the Regina's rich history," said Susan Parkin, marketing director of the Globe Theatre. "Inside, the space reflects the growth and success of our theatre company." The building marks both tradition and new accomplishments, she said.

"Newcomers to The Prince Edward Building are always amazed by the beauty of the building, both inside and out," Parkin said. "Our long-standing Globe supporters have great memories of the building and often share with us their reflections on the changes on the changes to the landmark and to Regina's downtown."

The Prince Edward Building is always a positive topic of conversation, she said. "It continues to be a busy centre of activity and demonstrates the vibrancy of Regina's arts community," Parkin maintained.

The Prince Edward Building, located at 1801 Scarth Street across from the main entrance to the Cornwall Shopping Centre, was named a Municipal Heritage Property on February 15, 1982.

From Post Office, to City Hall to the Globe Theatre Company, the structure remains an icon in downtown Regina.
PHOTO COURTESY SASKATCHEWAN HERITAGE FOUNDATION

LITTLE CHIEF SERVICE STATION
Saskatoon

The Little Chief Service Station, built by the Texaco Oil Company in 1929, continues to serve the community today as a police sub-station.

The small but eye-catching building on the northeast corner of 20th Street West and Avenue D was an early landmark on Saskatoon's west side.

Originally known as West Side Service Station, the name was changed to Little Chief Service Station in 1943.

The station was built at a time when the automobile was becoming popular and 20th Street West was a shopping and service hub for residents of Saskatoon, as well as for people living in neighbouring communities and on area farms.

"The Saskatoon Police Service was delighted to be able to transform the Little Chief Service Station into its latest role," said Russell Sabo, the city's police chief.

"It's a community-based police station that houses a local reporting office, a community liaison office as well as meeting space for both the police and the public. As an integral part of our community policing initiative, the Little Chief Community Station continues to be a friendly, welcoming place that serves the changing needs of the community."

Frank Carr, who managed and operated the station between 1947 and 1980, helped to preserve much of its history. "This station was a vibrant part of the neighbourhood and a busy place," he recalled years later.

Carr and two other mechanics serviced a wide range of commercial, farm, and private vehicles in two garage bays.

During the 1950s and 1960s, Carr recalled that many farmers who lived west of Saskatoon patronized 20th Street businesses.

"They would leave their vehicles for servicing at the Little Chief, then head down the street to do their shopping at the likes of Adilman's or Lehrer's department stores," he said. "The Victoria Cafe, on 20th Street West near the Adilman's store, was a popular lunch spot."

As time changed the face of 20th Street West, the diminutive Little Chief Station has remained one of its most enduring and endearing landmarks.

With its white stucco, wide overhanging eaves, tile roof, and parapet walls, the Little Chief Station is as good an example of Spanish Colonial architecture as one is likely to find in Saskatchewan. Despite the fact that Spanish Colonial is a well-loved style and was once a popular architectural style for service stations, this is the only commercial example of it in Saskatoon and one of just two examples in the entire province.

The building was built according to a standard design used at a time by the Texas Oil Company. It was a Texaco outlet and has sported the company's logo and its red, white, and green colour scheme throughout most of its history. Design and colour were intended to attract motorists' attention. To ensure it was equally as attractive at night, there were lights every three feet under the eaves, plus lights on every fence post and on the parapet above the repair bays. There also was a light standard at the pump island and lights on the distinctive Texaco sign pylon.

According to land titles records from 1929, the corner lot at 344–20th Street West was valued at $3,500. City of Saskatoon records from the same year show a building permit issued to construct a building valued at $10,000. It seems a small price to pay by today's standards considering the Little Chief Station's architecture continues to contribute so much to the commercial character of 20th Street West.

In 2002, the Little Chief Service Station underwent extensive renovations in preparation for its

latest role in serving the community as a community-based police sub-station.

The City of Saskatoon, through its Heritage Conservation Program, provided guidance and financial assistance for the renovation. All work—from replacing the flat roof over the garage bays to repairing and repainting the parapet, column extensions, and exterior stucco—was carried out with careful attention to preserving the building's original architectural style.

Additional work such as replacing the original garage doors with fixed, partially glazed door panels eased the conversion of garage space into office and meeting space. Site design, landscaping, and the refurbishing of the original Texaco pylon sign help retain the historical appearance of the grounds while allowing the property to blend easily with nearby residential areas.

The Little Chief Community Station was designated a Municipal Heritage Site in 2003.

Saskatoon Architect Maurice Soulodre was tasked with adapting this once boarded up building
PHOTO COURTESY MAURICE SOULODRE ARCHITECT LTD.

The Adaptive Reuse project was recognized with a Lt.-Gov. of Saskatchewan Heritage Architecture Excellence Award in 2004
PHOTO COURTESY MAURICE SOULODRE ARCHITECT LTD.

LAND TITLES BUILDING
Saskatoon

The former Land Titles Building in downtown Saskatoon, constructed during the building boom of 1909, is the oldest provincial government building in Saskatoon and has been the offices of the Brayford Shapiro law firm since 1994.

During its tenure as a land titles building from 1910 to 1959, only four individuals served as registrar. Gust Fournier, who was an assistant registrar, was probably the most interesting character who worked in the building.

He came west at the age of 17 and worked for a number of years at Batoche, including during the era of the Northwest Resistance of 1885. From there, Fournier worked for the Massey Harris Company and eventually ended up working with the provincial government, starting in 1909.

Fluent in French, Cree and English, he was an extremely valuable staff member during a busy period of history. In 1909, Fournier worked at the Battleford Land Titles Office and then moved to

Saskatoon, Humboldt and back to Saskatoon for the opening of the new building.

By 1910, the land titles staff in Saskatoon was handling on average 100 claims per day. Every day, during the boom years, the staff would open the door to a large crowd of men who were waiting to get in and make their land title claim. Many of the claims then changed hands on the steps of the building in land swaps.

From 1959 to 1994, the building was home to a variety of provincial government departments. The interior was renovated with each subsequent department arrival.

In 1994, the building was bought by lawyers Mark Brayford and Dan Shapiro. Yet, long before ever purchasing the site, Mark Brayford had his assistant mark a file "Land Titles Building" in hopes that some day he would purchase it.

Under the guidance of architect Darrel Epp, the interior of the building was gutted and renovated. Many key architectural features that had been hidden were discovered and highlighted. The renovation allowed for modern function but also restored it to its former grandeur.

"The potential reuse of this building was easy to see despite the unfortunate modifications due to function that had happened over the years," Brayford said.

"Unfortunately, in the last half of the century the community at large was not cognizant of the fact that heritage buildings could become fully functional. It is a sad commentary on how buildings are built today that none of them will see a century of use."

Despite hectic work hours, he does remember to look around and appreciate the uniqueness and permanence of the Land Titles Building.

Storey and Van Egmond, the architects who designed the Land Titles Building in Saskatoon, are credited with designing more than 40 schools and government buildings through the province as well as the Saskatoon Court House.

Contractors were Smith Bros. and Wilson who also built the Hotel Saskatchewan in Regina, the Bessborough Hotel just down the block from the Land Title Buildings, and did a large amount of work on the University of Saskatchewan campus.

A major addition in 1911 increased the size of the building by two thirds of its original capacity.

Three other buildings in the province bear similar style to this building. One of the features that set this building apart from the others is the fact that a good portion of 21st Street was built during the boom years in Saskatoon, and this is one of many fine buildings that remain.

Because it was a land titles building, the structure was built of solid brick masonry. The core and inside walls are cement. This was done to prevent fire from destroying the records and has made the building extremely stable.

This 55 by 35 one-storey building has strong symmetrical lines and incorporates a number of classical elements in the building design from the Romanesque Revival period.

The addition a year after design does not distract from the building because it carried over all the design elements and merely turned the building from an L to a T shape.

This was the most elaborate of the four Provincial Land Titles Buildings constructed soon after Saskatchewan entered Confederation, and a great deal of money was spent on a stylish interior.

Arched windows had decorative keystones cut around them and the marble staircases and wainscoting showcased an elaborate wrought iron handrail. The 17-foot plaster ceilings and the rolled tile windows allow each room to feel big even if the dimension of the room is not.

Today, the former Land Titles Building still conveys the strength, permanency, and good order as the architects had intended by housing law offices.

The building, located at 311–21st Street East in Saskatoon, was designated a Provincial Heritage Site in 1985.

The Brayford Shapiro law firm have had their offices in the former land titles building since 1994.

T. C. DOUGLAS CHURCH
Weyburn

During the Great Depression, the Calvary Baptist Church in Weyburn is where T. C. (Tommy) honed his skills for five years as an orator, developed his social gospel, and then moved into the political arena from the pulpit.

Douglas went on to become a member of Parliament and served as premier of Saskatchewan from 1944 to 1961, during which time his administration pioneered many programs that have been adopted throughout the world, including government-paid medical care.

Constructed by volunteers in 1906, the church was moved from the corner of Coteau Avenue and Third Street in the downtown area to its present location on South Hill in Weyburn's Heritage Park in 1985.

It was reopened in 1991 as the T. C. Douglas Calvary Centre Theatre for the Performing Arts Concerts and recitals as well as the annual Weyburn Music Festival are held in the building, that was the only place Douglas served as a minister.

Mayvis Goranson, a member of the Douglas Centre Founding Committee, said there were two reasons the community wanted to maintain the heritage of the building.

"We felt very strong about preserving the tiny clapboard building because it was indicative of what people did in 1906. This building represents the story of what you can achieve when you work together," she said. "A lot of our heritage is disappearing across the prairies. How many of the little schools, churches and hospitals remain standing today? This represents that era for us very well."

Goranson said the second reason was to commemorate the impact Tommy Douglas had on the community, the province, and Canada.

"He came to Weyburn just as the Great Depression was beginning," she said. "Here was a young man who had a vision of how people could work together who became a Canadian statesman."

Born in Falkirk, Scotland, in 1904, Douglas immigrated to Winnipeg with his mother and sister to join his father who had come to Canada the year before.

The roots of his passion for politics and desire to provide health care for everyone likely stems from a personal incident soon after arriving in the Manitoba capital. He was diagnosed with osteomyelitis in his right leg, which he almost lost because his family couldn't afford the best or most immediate treatment.

Douglas, when he was 18, decided he wanted to become a minister. During the winter of 1929, he and his best friend, Stanley Knowles, were invited to the Calvary Baptist Church on a trial basis. They preached on alternating Sundays, but it was Douglas who the congregation decided to keep and asked him to return to Weyburn after his ordination in 1930.

"They looked us both over and finally decided to call me," Douglas wrote in one of his memoirs. "Later, when I became a CCF politician, some of the deacons were thinking that probably they'd made a mistake and that they should have taken Knowles. But eventually Knowles became a CCF politician too and they'd been stuck either way." Knowles served as a Member of Parliament from Winnipeg from 1942 to 1984.

The arrival of Douglas in Weyburn coincided with the beginning of the Great Depression and severe drought across the region. He worked closely with young boys in the community as well as organizing relief programs and trying to help keep the community together.

The Baptist Church became the scene of uplifting theatrical productions, including an ambitious Christmas pageant and a sunrise Easter service. It was where his daughter, Shirley, made her debut as an actor.

In later years, Shirley married Canadian actor Donald Sutherland and their twins, Rachel and Keifer, continue to work in the arts and entertainment industry. Keifer, star of the television series "24," has attended special functions to honour his grandfather at the Weyburn centre in recent years, said Goranson.

Douglas, who told people to just "call me Tommy," witnessed family courage, hardship, and poverty. "This period was probably more difficult than any other time to be a minister of a church," he wrote. "I buried a young man at Griffin and another one at Pangman, both young men were in the thirties with young small families. They died because there was no doctor readily available and they hadn't the money to get proper care."

Douglas helped organize and then became president of the Independent Labour Party in 1932. The party began to raise awareness of social politics, then evolved a few months later into the Farm Labour Party, which advocated, among other things, hospital care for everyone on an equal basis, unemployment insurance, and universal pensions.

The social democratic movement continued to gain momentum when the labour parties from four western provinces merged to create the Co-operative Commonwealth Federation (CCF).

Douglas lost in his bid to win a seat in the Saskatchewan provincial election of 1934. While pondering his political future, he was told by the Superintendent of the Baptist Church in western Canada he'd have to pick between politics and the pulpit.

The ultimatum did not stop Douglas from running again. He was elected to the House of Commons in 1935 with four other members of the fledgling CCF.

In 1942, although still a member of Parliament, Douglas became leader of the CCF party in Saskatchewan.

The CCF under Tommy Douglas swept to power in 1944 on the election slogan of "Humanity First." He promised 70 percent of government spending would be on social services. The Douglas brand of socialism depended on political and economic democracy.

During his first term, the Douglas government paid off the provincial debt, created a province-wide hospitalization plan that was the first in North America, and brought electricity to rural Saskatchewan residents.

Douglas stepped down as the premier and provincial leader of the CCF in 1961 to become federal leader of the New Democratic Party, the successor to the CCF. He served as federal NDP leader for 10 years, though he lost his home riding in Weyburn and had to seek a safe haven in a NDP stronghold in British Columbia.

The Douglas footprint in the sands of time can be seen across decades not only in Weyburn and Saskatchewan but across Canada and North America as well.

His government introduced the first government-run medical care insurance plan, public automobile insurance, rural electrification as well as other innovative social programs.

The feisty Scot was a man small in physical stature but large in heart. He died in 1986 at the age of 81 and is remembered daily in the Calvary Baptist Church from where he launched his social gospel and political career that continue to touch the lives of people even today.

The Calvary Baptist Church, located on Signal Hill in Weyburn, was designated a Municipal Heritage Site in 1987.

LANE HALL
Wilcox

L ane Hall, a two-storey, wood-sided former bank building in Wilcox, became the home and office for almost two decades of the founder of the residential school that now bears his name: Athol Murray College of Notre Dame.

Remarkably, the bland-looking building also held some of rarest books in the world in its vault until the school's Alberta alumni raised money to build a temperature-controlled museum in 1992.

From humble beginnings in shacks and abandoned railway cars, Notre Dame College rose out of the prairies 50 kilometres south of Regina to become the educational institution it is today because of Athol Murray's determination, intelligence, high ideals, and above all—an unwavering belief in God and the primacy of the spiritual.

Born on January 9, 1892, Athol Murray (better known as Père or Father) was educated in the classics and the liberal arts at Loyola College and Laval University in Montreal. He studied law at the University of Toronto's Osgoode Hall.

Ordained in 1918, Père was sent to Regina in 1922 "on loan" from the Diocese of Toronto. One of his first acts was to start an athletic club for boys. When he was appointed to St. Augustine's parish in Wilcox in 1927, 15 boys followed him—the original Hounds.

Père had a positive influence over thousands of people in his lifetime. He was courageous and bold. He received the Order of Canada, our country's highest honour, in 1968, was inducted into Canada's Sports Hall of Fame in 1972 and into the Hockey Hall Fame in 1998. He died in 1975.

Wendel Clark, Curtis Joseph, Vincent LeCavalier, and James Patrick are among more than 100 former Notre Dame players who went on to play in the National Hockey League.

The population of Wilcox doubles during the school year. Notre Dame has a residential population of 330 students in Grades 8 to 12. In addition, some of the junior hockey players who have completed high school can take courses from University of Regina professors.

A former bank building was the first home, office and classroom for Father Athol Murray.
Photo courtesy Athol Murray College

Some of the rarest books in the world were once kept in the vault.
PHOTO COURTESY ATHOL MURRAY COLLEGE

"My first year here at Notre Dame was in 1958," recalls Jim Williams. "In that year, Père lived in the front room or office of Lane Hall. His entire home was there in that tiny structure, perhaps 14 feet by 14 feet. The man was extraordinary."

Lane Hall was different then, he said.

"In this humble structure one could take a three-year university course and finish with a Bachelor of Arts from the University of Ottawa," Williams said. "Père and a small handful of other splendid teachers taught here at the university level. It was great to study in Lane Hall because of its imposing atmosphere. The classrooms were mingled with the 14,000 books of the library."

Père Murray often used his legendary oratorical skills to encourage individuals to donate books and money to support the school.

A bronze plaque by the front door provides a glimpse of the roots of the school:

Notre Dame of Canada
LANE HALL
Memorial Library
Commemorating its American Donor
Klondike Adventurer and Famed
Sportsman Harry "Bill" Lane
of
San Diego

Lane bought the former Bank of Commerce Building in 1938 for Père. It was the first real building used by the Notre Dame students.

The walls inside the Lane Hall held pictures of Franklin Delano Roosevelt, a gift to Père from the American president's wife, Eleanor, and a painting of British Prime Minister Winston Churchill, Grey Owl, and Alexander of Tunis.

The outer room of the bank was cleared away to make room for class desks, chairs, and tables. The walls were lined with volumes of western civilization.

The Greeks and Romans were well represented by the Laocoon, Dionysius, The Thinker and Socrates. Representing the 'West' was the bust of U.S. President Abraham Lincoln.

Above the books were plaster cast reproductions of the Parthenon Frieze, a gift to Père Murray from a friend in Boston. When Père's father died, the family library was shipped to Wilcox.

A former Chief Justice enhanced the library with law books and the magnificent medical collection of Dr. John Ulrich of Regina was also a valuable donation.

Laura Lee Davidson, a Baltimore writer, knew Père through a doctor at Johns Hopkins, a university and teaching hospital. She possessed Confederate General Robert E. Lee's personal library, and, when she heard of Athol Murray's struggle to establish a library, she arranged to ship the entire collection by rail to Wilcox.

Père collected, from unknown sources, medieval manuscripts of the 13th and 14th centuries. Some were hand lettered and illustrated on sheepskin and pigskin.

Other precious books include the following treasures: John Peter Schoehher's 1462 *Chronicles of the Kings of France*; *The Convivia* of Franciscus Philelphus of 1477, a rare copy; a 1482 *Golden Legend of the Saints* with marginal notes that indicate the copy was read by Ignatius Loyola while convalescing from a leg wound received at Pamplona in 1521; and a three-volume Frankfurt edition of Martin Luther's Bible in German, written about 1535.

On rare occasions, Père invested in the future of his students with a crafty purchase. He bought the *Nuremberg Chronicles*, printed in 1492, for a mere $600.

The majority of the art, books, and curios Père acquired during almost 50 years now are on display in the pyramid-shaped Archives / Museum Building that the Alberta alumni of the College built in 1992.

"For myself, this building (Lane Hall) is our most historic structure on campus," Williams said. "Lane Hall is the last of the old Notre Dame buildings so it is the most historic structure on campus, representing the days of the shacks."

Today, some high school classes are still held in Lane Hall, which still houses the university library.

Lane Hall is located at 14 Main Street in Wilcox.

COMMERCE

"The building . . . was for many, many years the way SGIO was portrayed throughout the province."

–Jim Crighton, who worked at Saskatchewan Government Insurance Office (SGIO) from 1948 to 1984

Saskatchewan's economy has grown from family farms to family fortunes and from small locally owned cooperatives to multi-million dollar Crown corporations over the past 100 years.

Agriculture, once the sole engine of economic growth, now is a large piece of an intricate machine driven by oil and gas production, uranium and potash mining and a recent spurt in value-added processing and manufacturing.

For decades, there were more people living in rural parts of the province than in the larger cities such as Saskatoon, Regina, Moose Jaw and Prince Albert. However, more people now live in Saskatchewan's largest cities than on all the farms and in all of the other communities combined.

In the early years of the province, settlers sold or bartered the crops they grew or the cattle they raised on their farms with fellow producers or merchants in the nearby settlements. As the population of the province grew, reaching almost one million people in the 1920s, so too did the system of trade.

Throughout Saskatchewan, groups of like-minded people banded together or cooperated to conduct business.

The Saskatchewan Wheat Pool began operations in 1924 with 45,725 members. The cooperative became the symbol of the province's agricultural roots and changing economic fortunes.

It grew to become one of Canada's largest cooperatives, with sales topping $2 billion annually, but changed its corporate structure in the 1990s to a publicly traded company with shares listed on the Toronto and New York Stock exchanges.

Its head office, located in a Regina building constructed as a department store in 1913, remains a symbol of the province's agricultural roots.

A few blocks away is a six-storey building that became the symbol of the country's first publicly funded automobile insurance program for almost 30 years. Built over a three-year period ending in 1914 for the Canada Life Insurance Company, the building was the headquarters for the Saskatchewan Government Insurance office until 1979. Its white terra cotta façade is one the most striking designs in the province.

Meanwhile, the backbone of commerce in the towns, villages and hamlets across Saskatchewan continues in small, family-owned businesses affectionately called "mom and pop shops."

A 200-kilometre drive southwest of Regina brings the tradition into focus. Branded into a wooden sign above the entrance to the store owned and operated by Gail and Ron Aust is a reflection of their marketing savvy that has kept their business operating in Big Beaver for almost half a century: IF WE DON'T HAVE IT, YOU DON'T NEED IT.

Saskatchewan's economy—even the parts that haven't changed—can be seen in the buildings in which people do business every day.

AUST'S GENERAL STORE
Big Beaver

"If We Don't Have It You Don't Need It" is branded into wood above the door to Aust's General Store in Big Beaver, about 200 kilometres southwest of Regina.

It's more than a slogan. It's a friendly invitation for townsfolk and travelers to cross the threshold into a turn-of-the century atmosphere.

Big Beaver is nestled in the rolling hills on the edge of the Saskatchewan badlands. It's a part of the province where cattle and cowboys are more common than cars.

The store, which covers about 4,000 square feet, has a little bit of everything, ranging from nylons to nails and vegetables to veterinary supplies.

"Our store is made up of three old stores attached to each other," explains Gail Aust. "We refer to them as the Corner Store, the Main Store, and the Hotel-Store-Café."

All were built as two-storey wooden structures about 1928 when Big Beaver's population was a booming 300 people. The top floors now are used for storage.

In 1959, Roy and Lena Aust purchased the business of Harold March, who owned the Main Store, and bought the Corner Store. The couple also bought the old hotel-store-café from Roger Sabanski.

All of the stock from both stores was moved into the new Aust's General Store, or what used to be called the Main Store. The Corner Store was turned into a feed and hardware area, while a local couple operated the third business as a hotel and café.

"In 1968, we connected the two stores and moved dry goods, paint, and veterinary supplies in this area," she said.

"Beside the post office, we also have three coffee booths where the locals come to drink coffee, play cards, and visit. Many are the problems that have been solved and stresses that have been relieved around the card tables. In the city, one has a psychiatrist. Here we just come to Aust's Store."

She said her husband Ronnie Aust was 16 when his parents bought the store.

With the exception of the 10 months he worked for Safeway in Regina, he has spent the last 45 years working in the general store.

"He has clocked up thousands of hours working here and made millions of miles hauling our own supplies from Regina," Gail said.

"If we don't have it you don't need it" should read: "if we don't have it, we'll get it—if it's at all possible."

Ronnie and Gail were married in May, 1965. "So I have been in the store for almost 40 years," she said. "Our children were raised going to the store everyday. When Chad was hardly two years old, he sat on the floor filling egg cartons from the boxes of eggs the farmers brought in to sell. He never broke an egg!"

Nicole would sweep and dust for hours but was so shy that she would hide in the sugar bin if someone teased her, Gail said.

"We bought the store from Ronnie's parents in 1976 and still continue to make a living, thanks to our supportive community," she said. "We also have more and more tourists come through in the summer months."

Staff turnover is not a problem in the business. Marsie Chartrand worked at the Aust General Store for 25 years and their most recent employees, Rhonda Anderson and Brenda Vancuren have been with them for 14 and 7 years respectively.

"In more than the 76 years, this old store has seen many changes and many people pass through its doors," she said. "We have had articles written about us in magazines, newspapers, and appeared on television shows. The store has come through the Dirty Thirties, the Drought of the 1980s, and hopefully it will survive Mad Cow."

After a cow on an Alberta ranch was diagnosed in May 2003 with "mad cow" disease, all Canadian beef was banned from being imported into the United States. The result was a dramatic drop in beef prices. Federal and provincial governments established emergency programs to help the industry cope, but farmers and ranchers were forced to sell off their herds.

Meanwhile, Aust's General Store, on the edge of cattle country in southwestern Saskatchewan, manages to survive on a steady stream of small orders and the loyalty of local people. It is not a heritage property.

"I've never had a street address," explains Ron Aust. "I've always said we're on the corner of Main and Only—Main Street and the only avenue we have in Big Beaver!"

To get to Big Beaver from Regina, take Highway 6 south to the junction of Highway 13, then go west on Highway 13 to the junction of Highways 13 and 34, which is north of the Town of Bengough. Then you take Highway 34 south to its junction with Highway 18. Big Beaver is one mile west of Highway 34 and one mile north of Highway 18.

The sign above the store's entrance explains what's available: If we don't have it you don't need it.
PHOTO COURTESY GAIL AND RON AUST

BRICK PLANT
Claybank

Bricks made from clay in the Dirt Hills of Avonlea can be found in the Chateau Frontenac Hotel in Quebec City, on board steam locomotives, in Second World War warships, and even at the NASA launch pad at Cape Canaveral in Florida.

The first record of clay deposits in the Dirt Hills was made in 1886 by Tom McWilliams, a local homesteader, when he applied to the federal government for permission to mine the clay.

He had found a rare and rich deposit of refractory or heat resistant clay. Refractory clay is well suited for manufacturing fire bricks, which in turn are used in fireplaces, and to insulate boilers, furnaces and any area where extensive heat is generated.

Over the years, the brick plant in Claybank was operated by a variety of companies:

• Moose Jaw Fire Brick and Pottery Company (1904 to 1912)
• Saskatchewan Clay Products (1912 to 1916)
• Dominion Fire Brick and Pottery Company (1916 to 1954)
• Dominion Fire Brick and Clay Products (1954) Ltd. (1954 to 1971)
• A. P. Green Refractories Ltd. (1971 to 1989)

The Claybank Brick Plant was a successful Saskatchewan-based small industry, specializing in the production of refractory or heat-resistant brick from 1914 to 1989.

The plant is a remarkably intact example of an early 20th-century brick making complex. All the key structures erected during the site's development from 1912 to 1937 and much of the original brick making equipment survive.

Changes in technology forced the plant to close after almost 75 continuous years of operations. Although some modernization of the plant was made over time, most of the brick plant still demonstrates the effective use of 19th-century brick manufacturing technology.

The Claybank Brick Plant was donated in 1992 to the Saskatchewan Heritage Foundation by A. P. Green Refractories Ltd., the last company to make brick at Claybank.

The community has embraced the project, formed a Claybank Brick Plant Historical Society, and works closely with the Heritage Foundation and Parks Canada to preserve the site and deliver interpretation by providing tours of the kilns and buildings. Annual Heritage Day celebrations, on the last Sunday of June, are a focal point for the community to share their enthusiasm for the past for future generations.

Stories from former brick plant workers, families, and friends continue to be collected by the society to preserve and promote the heritage of the facility.

Ron Clarke recalled a visit to the plant with his father in 1958 when he was just 12 years old. "I can remember, as if it was only yesterday, that finally I was going to see how men made blue clay into brick. Seeing all the others who worked there, people that I almost knew from supper-time talk, were suddenly to become real," he said. "I was going to experience first hand the blending of cinders, wet clay, diesel, and sweat, a smell I did not find at all offensive, just different from oat sheaves and horses."

He said that understanding the process of making fire brick was secondary to exploring the cluster of squat, circular kilns, and the expanse of sheds and shops nestled below an outcrop of clay deposits that towered in the background.

"Everywhere I went the ground and all around radiated heat," Clarke said. "Heat waves shimmered between and above the kilns. The place reverberated, seemingly touched by a huge inferno hidden somewhere below. For the first time, I became aware that heat was an integral part of mak-ing brick and that between the cycles of firing kilns and letting them cool, the place was a veritable sauna where men worked and sweat."

At the end of the day, he had an appreciation of the men who worked so hard for a small company at the base of the Dirt Hills.

"The brick plant provided a living and, for many, a life-long career. Those who worked there were a proud lot," Clarke said. "As I left that night I carried dad's lunch pail. The same one he used for 38 years."

J. Cameron Worcester worked as the chemist at the plant in the 1940s. "The time I spent at Claybank was a time in another era, pastoral, peaceful. We were all young, happy to have jobs after the mass unemployment of the 1930s," Worcester said.

"No computers, no labour unrest, little violence, no children shooting children. Time did not control our lives, but, when we had a job to do, we did it, conscientiously and to the best of our abilities."

The Claybank Brick Plant, named a National Historic Site of Canada in 1994, is on Highway 339 just 15 kilometres west of Avonlea or 1 kilometre east of Claybank—turn south at the Claybank Brick Plant Road sign. Avonlea is about 80 kilometres southwest of Regina.

A great deal of "horsepower" was used in this 1950s photo of the Dominion Fire Brick and Clay Products Ltd. Plant near Avonlea, Saskatchewan
Photo courtesy Garth Pugh

SASKATCHEWAN WHEAT POOL HEAD OFFICE
Regina

The Saskatchewan Wheat Pool Head Office, located in a building constructed as a department store in 1913, has been the symbol of the province's agricultural rural roots and changing economic fortunes since 1925.

The C. W. Sherwood Department Store owned the building until 1916 when it was sold to the Regina Trading Company. The building was used for a variety of purposes, including being employed as a military supply depot during the First World War.

In 1925, the Saskatchewan Wheat Pool rented the top two floors and bought the building the following year for $200,000.

The Saskatchewan Wheat Pool was created by a special act of the Saskatchewan Legislature in 1923 and incorporated as the Saskatchewan Cooperative Wheat Producers Ltd.

Known simply as the Pool, the cooperative began operations in 1924, with 45,725 members.

"There's a picture of those who attended the first delegates' meeting standing in front of the

Pool building," recalled Jim Wright, who worked for the Pool for almost three decades until he retired in 1986. "My father was one of those guys."

Wright's father, Percy, was one of the organizers in north east Saskatchewan who signed farmers up to join the cooperative in 1924. Percy Wright went on to serve the area as a member of Parliament.

Jim Wright followed in his father's footsteps with the Pool. A farmer in the Tisdale area, he was elected a delegate to the cooperative's annual meetings in 1947, then joined the Pool staff as field man in 1957. Wright worked his way up the corporate ladder.

In 1962, he became the supervisor for all field activities at the Pool headquarters and three years later moved into the corporate offices as the assistant secretary to the Pool board of directors.

Wright was named corporate secretary in 1967, a position he held until his retirement in 1986. "We were involved in a lot of policy issues

SASKATCHEWAN WHEAT POOL

by ourselves and through the various organizations we supported," he said.

"The Pool was a major business in Saskatchewan. In those early days, it was quite influential with the provincial government because of the organizational structure of sub-committee and committees that covered the province."

Recruitment was among Wright's early duties with the Pool. "One of our jobs was to eye out young farmers who should get involved in our organizational structure," Wright explained. "I thought Garf Stevenson was the kind of farmer that could help the Pool. So I encouraged him to get more active."

Stevenson, who operated a mixed farm near Whitewood, about a 150 kilometres east of Regina, took Wright's words of wisdom to heart. Stevenson had been elected to his local Pool committee in 1953. He became a delegate to the Pool's annual meetings in 1959, and was elected to the

Saskatchewan Wheat Pool Board of Directors in 1968, and the executive committee in 1971.

He was elected a vice president in 1981 and then was elected president in 1987, a position he held until he retired from the Pool in 1993.

"When I think back to 1924 when the Pool was founded, it wasn't an easy task getting around in our district," Stevenson said. "I've heard people took the Canadian Pacific Railway to Brandon from Whitewood, changed lines there and took another train to Rocanville to hold membership meetings. Each district was comprised of two rural municipalities, so it was quite difficult getting around in those early days. But they survived and we're better for it today."

The Pool began to have an impact on the entire province. "Our library served the whole province," he explained. "The field men took gas generators with them in the early days and showed films after their district meetings. It became an integral part of

Gargoyles adorn the ornate exterior of the head office.
Photo courtesy SAHS

the way people lived in rural Saskatchewan for many, many years."

Stevenson said the Pool also had a huge economic impact on the City of Regina and the province.

"We employed 400 to 500 people in Regina and we had an elevator in virtually every small town, employing 4,000 people at 1,000 locations at our peak," he said. "You also have to remember that the Pool elevator agent often was one of the better paid people in these small communities as well, so that had a big impact."

Over the years, the Pool grew to become a multi-billion-dollar enterprise with holdings in grain handling and distribution, and terminals in Saskatchewan and the major Canadian sea ports. The Pool also did commodity trading as well as publishing its own weekly newspaper *The Western Producer*. The Pool was involved in oilseed processing, fertilizer production, flour milling, and livestock marketing.

"We became very active and influential internationally through our membership in Canadian Federation of Agriculture and the International Federation of Agricultural Producers," Stevenson said. "I can recall that we had almost day-to-day conversations directly with the premier of Saskatchewan or sometimes even the most senior members of the federal cabinet in Ottawa about agriculture issues."

For Stevenson, however, his fondest memories are from policy debates. "I always thought that one of the most unique features about the Pool was how you could get 100 delegates into one room, talk and argue about a subject for hours, then shake hands at the end of the day. It was democracy in action," he said.

A few years after Stevenson and Wright left the Pool, the company underwent a fundamental change.

In 1995, the Pool had $4 billion in revenue, had rationalized grain operations to 400 country elevator locations, and operated 16 farm service centres and 22 livestock marketing centre. The Pool held interest in 22 affiliated companies.

About 65 percent of the farmers who held shares in the Pool converted their equity into a new $12 share offering. The Pool's public share offering began on April 2, 1996.

Within less than a decade, however, the stock rose to a peak of more than $20 then plummeted to under $1 before creditor refinancing was arranged. Several divisions were sold and hundreds of elevators were closed.

The Pool head office building, however, remains a symbol of past and future generations of Saskatchewan farmers.

It is the last remaining department store from the pre-Second World War era in downtown Regina.

The heritage character of the property rests in the façade, that extends 125 feet along Albert Street and 162 feet along Victoria Avenue. To this day, some farmers unfamiliar with the urban sprawl of Regina still ask for directions to new businesses and homes by getting directions from the Saskatchewan Wheat Pool head office by asking: "Where is that from the Pool?"

The terra cotta gargoyles on the building are rare architectural elements in Regina. Another unique feature is that the footings were dug 18 feet below grade, apparently to accommodate an extra two storeys above the three-storey structure.

David R. Brown and Hugh Vallance of Montreal, who also designed the Torwest Building on Hamilton Street and the Saskatchewan Revenue Building on Smith Street in Regina, were the architects.

Initial renovations were carried out to the interior in 1926 by Hipperson Construction of Regina. In 1963, the building was stripped to the shell to accommodate new services and computer facilities.

The first floor, over the years, was leased to various companies including Bothwell Motors, the provincial Department of Natural Resources, and the Bank of Montreal.

The Saskatchewan Wheat Pool Head Office, located at 2006 Albert Street on the southwest corner of the intersection with Victoria Avenue, was declared a Municipal Heritage Site on December 5, 1983.

NORTHERN CROWN BUILDING
Regina

The Northern Crown Building, which opened one year after Saskatchewan became a province, is Regina's oldest downtown commercial building.

The five-storey structure with the Classical Revival façade has become a symbol of effective multiple use for a heritage property.

In fact, a photograph of the Northern Crown Building was the image used on posters commissioned by the provincial government in the 1980s to promote heritage buildings throughout Saskatchewan.

Alfredo's—a pasta restaurant and wine bar—is on the main floor; Colliers International, a commercial real estate company; and RIS, a computer tech company, occupy the second floor while all 2,600 square feet of the third floor has been developed into one of the first condominium-style lofts in the downtown core of the city.

"Regina is a little bit behind other cities, I think, in the development of downtown lofts," said

Frances Olson, a shrewd and successful former real estate company owner. Frances Olson Realty Ltd. was renowned for its magenta signs and exclusively female real estate agents.

Olson and her husband, Ralph, had retired to Mexico but were looking for, as she said, "some place to live downtown near everything" in Regina when they started seriously thinking about returning home to Saskatchewan. "I absolutely love living here. I like living downtown because there's everything I want almost literally out my front door," she said.

The Northern Crown Bank Building is only a few steps away from the Cornwall Centre, the province's largest downtown mall. It is the second last structure along the F. W. Hill Mall, a pedestrian-only mall bordered by 11th and 12th Avenues.

"There's lots of shopping and outdoor restaurants to enjoy in the spring and summer," Olson said, noting there's an air of excitement throughout the day from "the young people" on their lunch

Features on the front of the Northern Crown Building are so well-defined that it has appeared on posters to illustrate architectural heritage.
Photo courtesy Saskatchewan Heritage Foundation

"The Northern Crown Bank Building is so architecturally different from the newer office buildings in downtown Regina," Denise said. "It's a beautiful building to live in."

William M. Logan was the general manager who opened the Northern Bank Building in 1906. The building was designed by Blair and Northwood, official architects for the Northern Bank in Winnipeg. Their design appeared in the August 8, 1906, edition of the *Winnipeg Telegram* and described the Regina building as "one of the handsomest structures of its kind in the west."

After the building was completed it became a prestigious business and office location in Regina.

The already well-known architectural firm of Storey and Van Egmond maintained their offices on the top floor of the Northern Bank Building from 1907 to 1911, when they relocated to Regina's newest high rise building, the McCallum-Hill Building, one block south.

Other prominent early tenants of the Northern Crown Bank Building included: W. W. Hilton, architect; The Saskatchewan Building Construction Company; various doctors, lawyers, and insurance and real estate agents; and, the Regina Printing Company. The printing operation, under various names over the years, was to become the longest tenant of the building, remaining there until 1978.

The Northern Bank, known after 1908 as the Northern Crown Bank, utilized the premises until 1918, when a merger resulted in closure of the office and a transfer of all records and some staff to the Royal Bank of Canada.

From 1918 to 1923, the Imperial Canadian Trust Company continued the banking function in the Northern Bank building, but in 1924 moved out. The ground floor was converted for use as a barber shop and confectionery/tobacco store.

Those businesses, as well as a jeweler's store, constituted much of the ground-floor business operations for the next 50 years.

The Northern Crown Building has gradually been vacated over the past two decades as the building's interior deteriorated, and new office space in Regina became more attractive.

and coffee breaks from the downtown-based businesses and offices. "Flowers in the spring and summer and Christmas-style lights in the winter make it a very beautiful place to go," she said.

"What I really like about it is the amount of sunshine the windows let into my home is incredible," Olson said. "My loft covers the entire third floor, some 2,600 square feet. The elevator opens right into my home and there's parking beneath the building."

Len and Denise (Olson's daughter) Currie along with Fred Soofi purchased the building in the mid 1990s to redevelop the first and second floors into commercial condo space and the third to fifth floors into residential condos. The Curries are designing and redeveloping the fourth- and fifth-floor residential condos.

One of the last professional tenants, architect Clifford Wiens, maintained his offices of the fifth floor from 1960 to 1970.

The 1990s brought renovation and innovation to the Northern Crown Building, which is enjoying a return to its former prestige.

Renovations have blended modern décor while maintaining the classic charm and features of the original building.

The exterior structure has not been altered, maintaining the Roman Ionic columns and capitals, the Norman arch windows, and the sandstone lintel. The offices on the second floor have been designed with professional elegance utilizing glass walls for the large offices. There is a charming bridge overlooking the main floor, with an atrium lined with the original brick walls and windows.

The Northern Crown Building, located at 1821 Scarth Street in Regina, was designated a Provincial Heritage Property on January 13, 1989.

CANADA LIFE ASSURANCE BUILDING
Regina

A six-storey building constructed over a three-year period ending in 1914 for the Canada Life Assurance Company was the symbol of the country's first publicly funded automobile insurance program for almost 30 years.

The headquarters for the Saskatchewan Government Insurance Office was located in the building until a new 18-storey head office opened almost literally across the street in 1979. To coincide with the move, the government changed the name to Saskatchewan Government Insurance or SGI. Today, the business is known as SGI Canada.

Now called the Reed Stenhouse Building, the structure was an inspiration of Montreal architects Brown and Vallance. Its white terra cotta façade is one of the province's most striking designs.

The building is graced with a number of ornamental images, including the Canada Life Assurance Company's logo—a pelican feeding her young. It is one of Saskatchewan's most impressive early 20th-century buildings.

"The building, itself, had been there the year of the Regina cyclone, and because it was undamaged it became a symbol of stability," said lawyer John Green. "It was also one of the centres of business activity in Regina. There were many companies and private firms which had offices there as well as some government departments. So it was just natural when SGIO started up offices in downtown Regina to occupy that building."

A cyclone with a wind velocity of 500 miles per hour struck Regina's downtown and more prestigious residential districts. After the winds had died down, the cyclone had claimed a total of 28 lives, rendered 2,500 persons temporarily homeless, and caused over $1.2 million in property damage

John Green was one of the key figures in SGIO history. He began his career at SGIO as the legal advisor for the fledgling company, specifically to help solve the growing problem of compensation for auto accident victims. He later became one of the architects of the Automobile Accident

Insurance Act (AAIA). Before joining SGIO in 1945, Green was practising law in Saskatoon.

AAIA ensures that all Saskatchewan drivers receive basic auto insurance coverage automatically when they purchase their vehicle registration. As the pioneer of compulsory auto insurance in Canada, Saskatchewan's system was studied by several other provinces.

Green was considered an expert in this area and assisted both the Insurance Corporation of British Columbia (ICBC) and the Manitoba Public Insurance Corporation (MPIC) to develop no-fault insurance programs. He went to Manitoba for a short time to help form the plan for partial no-fault in 1969. Then, he went to British Columbia for six months to help draft legislation in 1972 to 1973. He was made a member of the Order of Canada in 1980.

Over the years, Green played a key role at SGI, serving as legal advisory, General Counsel heading up the litigation, and general manager, a position now called president.

Jim Crighton began as a junior clerk in 1948 in the SGIO head office and rose to become an executive officer of the Crown Corporation. He retired in 1984. "SGIO had grown to the point where it needed more room than the space allocated for it in the Saskatchewan Legislative Building," Crighton said. "They were looking for a prestigious building and that's how they chose the Canada Life Assurance Building."

SGIO got an instant storefront presence in downtown Regina and a visual image that was emblazoned on advertisements, letterhead, and insurance polices for the next 30 years.

"The building became a graphic image for SGIO," Crighton said. "I assume the government, in their desire to have a presence in downtown Regina, wanted a grand looking building for their head office. It was for many, many years the way SGIO was portrayed throughout the province."

SGIO moved into building in February 1946 and occupied half the ground floor. The high-vaulted ceilings of the main floor had been built to impress people who came there to do business. SGIO handled fire, casualty, and auto insurance.

There were some problems with the building. During the first two years, employees working in the

back of the head office building, including Green, had to go outside and around the corner to the front doors to see their coworkers in the front office. In 1948, an opening between the areas was created. Crighton said the building "was like a hot box" to work in during the summers.

Eric Pelzer, who joined SGIO in 1963 and continues to work with the Crown corporation today, worked on four floors of the first head office.

"The basement, which was the file storage area, became known by all the staff as "The Dungeon" because it was very crowded and dreary," Pelzer said.

The Canada Life Assurance Building, located at 2201–11th Avenue on the corner of 11th Avenue and Lorne Street in downtown Regina, was declared a Provincial Heritage Property on April 5, 1978.

Canada's first publicly-funded automobile insurance program utilized the building as a marketing visual for almost 30 years.
Photo courtesy Saskatchewan Heritage Foundation

CANADA BUILDING
Saskatoon

A bronze statue of a young boy selling newspapers outside the Canada Building, an eight-storey 'skyscraper' built in 1912, symbolizes Saskatoon's entrepreneurial and political heritage.

Unveiled in 1972, the statue depicts an encounter between Prime Minister Wilfred Laurier and John Diefenbaker, a future Prime Minister of Canada, as the enterprising boy sold his daily newspapers.

"Most of us living in Saskatoon have heard the story about Diefenbaker selling Laurier a newspaper and talking politics with the Prime Minister at that time," explained Jack MacDonald, a chartered accountant whose office was in the Canada Building from 1960 until 1978. "Whether it's true or not, I'm not really sure."

Oral histories of Saskatoon say the encounter between Diefenbaker and Laurier inspired Diefenbaker to enter politics. Born on September 18, 1895, in Neustadt, Ontario, Diefenbaker went on to become Canada's 13th Prime Minister, serving from June 21, 1957, to April 22, 1963.

When Diefenbaker died on August 16, 1979, according to his funeral plans, his body was shipped from Ottawa to Saskatoon by train for burial.

The Diefenbaker newspaper story is part of Saskatoon folklore. "I knew Dief and it's the type of story that he was fond of telling," said MacDonald. "The point, however, is there's a monument there today for future generations to picture the encounter in their mind of the two people."

The Canada Building was considered among the most prestigious commercial real estate locations in Saskatoon for more than 50 years.

"Our firm of Fewster Kirkpatrick MacDonald Ayers, Chartered Accountants, moved into the Canada Building in 1960," MacDonald said. "We merged with Price Waterhouse in 1968. We then needed more space and took over the sixth floor," he said. "By 1978, we again required more space and would have remained a tenant but the landlord was unable to meet our requirements."

Ownership of the building changed hands several times, but it was always a well run and maintained building, according to MacDonald.

MacDonald remembers that many smaller offices for dentists, doctors, and insurance brokers created a unique ambience in the main floor coffee shop and in the elevators, which for many years required operators to run.

"I came back from lunch one day and one of the female elevator operators looked sad and asked me if I'd heard the news," he said. "What news? I asked her. 'President Kennedy has been shot,' she replied. I think everyone our age can tell you exactly where they were that day and what they were doing."

Rnold Smith, who owned and operated Buy Rite Furniture from 1967 to 1980, remembers visiting a dentist in the Canada Building as a school boy. "I also remember my mom telling me a story about sitting beside Mrs. Thode flying back to Saskatoon one day and reading in the newspaper that her husband had just bought the Canada Building," Smith said. "My mom said Mrs. Thode's reaction was that 'she always knew her husband had money somewhere' and then laughed."

Sid Buckwold hired MacDonald to be his consultant on the purchase of the Canada Building from Hec Thode. Years later, Buckwold served as mayor of Saskatoon and eventually was appointed to the Canadian Senate.

The Canada Building was an entrepreneurial venture by Allan Bowerman, who originally planned to construct a four-storey structure. An economic boom in Saskatoon resulted in Bowerman opting to double the size of the building during construction from 1912 to 1913.

When completed, Bowerman said the building was the largest between Winnipeg and Vancouver, a claim he clung to for many years.

Bowerman became a self-made millionaire. He was a postmaster and businessman who was a member of the first Saskatoon town council from 1903 to 1905. He made a fortune in real estate, then had the Canada Building foreclosed upon in 1922.

James Chisholm and Sons of Winnipeg were the architects that designed the building that is 115 feet tall. It measures 140 feet by 75 feet and features a red granite base from Scotland and grey Norman brick from Ohio.

The eighth floor of the building is set back and ornamented with massive fluted columns and surmounted by an elegant denticular cornice. Each corner has the molded beaver motif in place.

The interior of the building was also suitably appointed, with the main floor having terrazzo marble floors from Italy and with four varieties of marble wainscoting for the entrance walls. Maple flooring and American oak trim appointed all other office floors, and the café was finished in Elizabethan style, with oak wainscoting and ornamental plastered ceiling and mosaic tiles.

A massive iron and glass marquise was suspended in front of the main entrance by chains secured into life-size ornamental buffalo heads.

The full basement housed the impressive electrical works—the most up-to-date on the continent at the time.

Completed at a cost of $475,000, the Canada Building for many decades was recognized as the undisputed financial centre of Saskatoon.

Today, the Canada Building, located at 105–21st Street East in downtown Saskatoon, serves exactly the same function that it did in 1913—commerce-sharing space in a grand building.

WEYBURN SECURITY BANK
Weyburn

For almost 100 years, people in the Weyburn area have conducted their banking in a building with an impressive white terra cotta façade that has been owned by three different banks, including the only one to operate with a Saskatchewan Charter.

The head office of the Weyburn Security Bank was constructed over a two-year period ending in 1911. The bank received its Saskatchewan Charter as an outgrowth of the Weyburn Security Company, founded in 1902.

At its peak, the Weyburn Security Bank was the headquarters of 32 branches across southern Saskatchewan. However, poor economic conditions of the Great Depression forced the bank's sale in 1931 to the Imperial Bank of Canada.

"It came out of a clear blue sky," said William McConachie, who was a teller at the Weyburn Security Bank the day it became part of the Imperial Bank of Canada. "We were told the bank had been taken over and these men showed up to teach us a new routine, with different forms, while the bank was open to serve customers that day."

His 36-year banking career took him to four provinces for the Weyburn Security Bank, the Imperial Bank of Canada that acquired the Weyburn bank, and then the Canadian Imperial Bank of Commerce that was formed by another bank merger.

McConachie said the Weyburn Security Bank had offices on the second floor for its own lawyers. Extra office space, for a while, he said, was rented to a dentist.

"I worked six days a week—Monday to Saturday afternoons," he said. "We were open at 9 each morning. We did everything manually and balanced our ledgers once a week."

McConachie was sent from time to time to deliver $5,000 cash to grain elevators in surrounding towns where the managers there paid farmers from their deliveries. "We always worried about getting robbed, but we never did," he said.

The road to creating the Weyburn Security Bank began in 1899, when six businessmen from Minnesota and South Dakota formed a Canadian investment company in the newly founded settlement of Weyburn.

The company bought 50,000 acres of land, brought in settlers and branched out into the lumber business. In 1902, the year Weyburn was incorporated as a village, the Weyburn Security Company was formed to take over all the business of the Canadian Investment Company, except the original land. The company then expanded into real estate, general business, mortgage loans, and banking.

As Weyburn grew, incorporating as a town in 1903, the Weyburn Security Company opened branches in nearby Yellow Grass, McTaggart, Halbrite, and Midale.

The next eight years brought a tremendous influx of settlers, and the company expanded even more. A new manager, H. O. Powell, was brought in from South Dakota, and branches were opened in Griffin, Colgate, and Radville. A new head office building was constructed in Weyburn.

The company's shareholders soon came to realize that the bank would have to have a Charter if it was to compete effectively with Chartered banks coming into Saskatchewan.

It applied for and was granted a charter under the name Weyburn Security Bank in 1911 and shortly thereafter began issuing bank notes in denominations $5, $10, and $20. The notes were sent to the branches, where the manager countersigned them before placing them in circulation.

The notes were readily accepted as currency. In the peak year of 1925, there was $858,910 worth of notes outstanding. The aggressive business style of the Weyburn Security Bank ruffled the feathers of many competitors.

When the Weyburn Security Bank opened a branch at Leoville, later renamed Assiniboia, the Union Bank of Canada protested. It had advertised that it intended to open branches all along the Canadian Pacific Railway. The Union Bank felt the Weyburn Security Bank had usurped its position.

The complaint fell on deaf ears of federal regulatory officials, and by 1921 the Weyburn Security Bank had 24 branches 250 miles east and west and 100 miles north and south of Weyburn.

It was on a roll, taking over several branches from other Chartered banks. In 1921, the Union Bank of Canada complained to the federal minister of finance that the Weyburn Security Bank was paying four percent on deposits, which was higher than the rates paid by other Chartered banks. The finance minister ignored the complaint.

By 1929, the Weyburn Security Bank had 33 branches, assets of more than $6 million, and paid a semi-annual dividend of 3.5 percent.

Then the Weyburn Security Bank was hit hard by a drought and Great Depression because farming was the only industry in the region where the bank operated. By the summer of 1930, farmers who had previously deposited money wanted only to borrow money. In November 1930, the Imperial Bank of Canada offered to buy the Weyburn Security Bank; shareholders were quite happy to accept the proposal.

On May 1, 1931, the Imperial Bank, which until then had no branches south of the Canadian Pacific Railway mainline, assumed responsibility for all assets and liabilities of the Weyburn Security Bank.

The building was restored in 1987 by the Canadian Imperial Bank of Commerce, that has operated a branch in the former Weyburn Security Bank building since the early 1960s.

The former Weyburn Security Bank, located at 76–3rd Street in Weyburn, was designated a Provincial Heritage Site on November 24, 1982.

Constructed in 1911, three different banking institutions have served Weyburn area customers. PHOTO COURTESY SASKATCHEWAN HERITAGE FOUNDATION

EDUCATION

"The bricks used to construct this magnificent building made the physical structure, but it was the people inside who really made this institution."

–Ed Bitz , at the 75th anniversary celebration of
School Sisters of Notre Dame boarding school in Leipzig

Saskatchewan people have always appreciated the value of education. Early settlers ensured that schools were among the first buildings constructed in their communities, and, in some cases, classes were taught in the languages those settlers spoke, such as German, French and Russian.

Growth of the education system in the province can be attributed to the tireless efforts of missionaries who were ministers, monks and nuns.

Schools not only provided each community with a sense of pride, but with a tangible asset around which to build a settlement into a hamlet, a hamlet into a village, a village into a town and a town into a city.

The University of Saskatchewan Campus, for example, took shape when the province was less than a year old and the population had grown just large enough to call Saskatoon a town—a far cry from the hub of commerce and innovation it exudes today as the province's largest city.

Sir Wilfred Laurier, then Prime Minister of Canada, made the trek west from Ottawa to attend the ceremony when the cornerstone for the College Building was laid in 1910. The College Building continues to this day to be the key structure at the east end of an elliptical green space known as "The Bowl" and stands as a distinguished landmark on campus.

The architectural style and materials used to construct the building were chosen to provide almost an instant validation of credibility.

The turrets and stonework of the chemistry building, the other key landmark in "The Bowl," are reminders of the European architectural influence on the institution, the city of Saskatoon and the province. Both buildings would not look out of place on the campus of any Ivy League school on the eastern seaboard of the United States or Oxford or Cambridge in England.

Schools in smaller communities, on the other hand, often became more recognized for the quality of their educators than for the architectural style of the building.

Benedictine monks have been teaching elementary, high school and subsequent university classes at St. Peter's College in Muenster since the day they personally completed the facility themselves in 1921 because a contractor had walked away from the project. In the west central community of Leipzig, the School Sisters of Notre Dame operated a boarding school for almost half a century. To this day, French remains the primary language of education at College Mathieu, a residential school in Gravelbourg in southwestern Saskatchewan.

Saskatchewan's heritage—and its people's belief in the future—can be seen within the bricks and mortar of schools and university buildings.

COLLEGE MATHIEU
Gravelbourg

College Mathieu is named in honour of Olivier Mathieu, the Archbishop of Regina at the turn of the 20th century.
PHOTO COURTESY COLLEGE MATHIEU

The Pavilion, a wood and brick building completed in 1918, was the first home for College Mathieu in Gravelbourg, which evolved to become the home-away-from-home for students attending the French residential school.

The building that measured 84 feet by 40 feet has been used for a variety of purposes over the decades. Between 1931 and 1946, the Pavilion became "Le Grand Séminaire de Mazenod" or a seminary for the education of future priests.

From 1946 to 1968, it was renamed "Le Pavillon des Arts," a residence for Arts and Science students, including within its walls chemistry and physics laboratories.

Since 1968, the Pavilion has been, and is still called, the Boys' Residence.

"The old Pav or Le Vieux Pav, as it was known then, was our home, away from home," recalled Real Forest, who attended College Mathieu from 1957 to 1965 and now is the school's Executive Director.

"We studied there. We socialized there. We slept there. Heck, that's even where we honed our oratorical skills with the weekly Saint Edward's Academy speeches in English and the Académie Saint Pierre, the speeches in French."

Forest said College Mathieu is very unique because it now is the only French residential high school in western Canada.

At the turn of the century, Olivier Mathieu, the Archbishop of Regina, dreamed of building a private school for his parishioners of French Canadian origin. His dream became a reality in 1918 when "le Collège catholique de Gravelbourg" opened its doors for the first time to French Canadian youths. In 1920, the Oblate Fathers accepted the responsibility to continue the program started by Mathieu, which they assumed until 1976.

During those 58 years, the Oblates changed the name of the institution to Collège Mathieu, offered a Bachelor of Arts program, built a gymnasium, and a library, and administered an industrial arts program.

In 1976, due to a lack of vocations, the Oblates decided to transfer the College to a corporation consisting of Fransaskois lay people.

Today, College Mathieu still has the mandate to offer a quality French and Catholic education. It offers a complete academic program that is complimented with religious, cultural, and recreational activities.

"Through these programs, we offer a complete education to students, prepare them to take an active role in society, and help them acquire the necessary knowledge to continue their education at the post-secondary level," Forest said.

On May 14, 1988, College Mathieu lost two buildings to a fire: its old military hangar, which served as a gymnasium, and its main building, which housed among other things, the administration offices, the classrooms, the girls' residence, and the cafeteria.

"College Mathieu has been in existence as a functioning college since 1918, offering full Bachelor of Arts degrees up until 1968," Forest said. "For the first two years of operation, College Mathieu was affiliated with Laval University, and then with the Ottawa University in the ensuing years."

In its earlier history, the college also offered divinity courses for seminarians, who assisted with dormitory duties and the teaching process.

One of the original instructors was a priest, Louis Pierre Gravel, who was the founder of the town that bears his name: Gravelbourg.

Louis Marchand, lived in Gravelbourg, but was a student at College Mathieu from 1952 to 1960. "When I went there it seemed like it was at its peak with about 250 students," said Marchand. "It was a family life. We did everything together, all the time, as they now say 24/7."

Marchand is still close with many of his classmates. "We're still holding class reunions 45 years later. We meet every five years," he said. "That's what College Mathieu meant to us."

Marchand credits the dedication of the priests who worked long hours for very little pay to keep College Mathieu operational for many, many years. "The Oblate priests were incredible," he said. "For $10 per month and a can of tobacco they not only taught us our studies, but were involved in sports and arts programs as well."

Marchand, a retired public school principal, now works part-time teaching math and physics to grade 11 and 12 students at College Mathieu, where his six daughters and one son were also educated.

Richard Chabot, who attended College Mathieu from 1968 to 1973, teaches immersion French, social studies, art and physical education at the school today.

"Attending College Mathieu taught me lifetime skills, responsibility for myself and toward others, the value of sports, plus the opportunity of making numerous lifetime friends from boarding at the Pav," Chabot said. "It's a learning experience I cherish to this day!"

For Henri LePage, his memories bring a song to his heart from the eight years he was involved in various choral groups while completing his high school education and earning a Bachelor of Arts degree.

"Once my voice had stabilized in my late teens, I was chosen as one of three to sing the "Proper" of the then-Latin mass with a group called The Schola," LePage said. "I was also in the general choir called Les Alouettes."

LePage was chosen in 1963 to be a member of a group of eight, appropriately called L'Octopus, which gave concerts in Edmonton, Prince Albert, and Winnipeg as well as more than a dozen small Saskatchewan centres. Six members of the group eventually returned to College Mathieu as teachers. LePage and another member alternate conducting choir at mass each Sunday.

College Mathieu no longer caters to only students with a French Canadian origin. "The school's mission was, and still is, to offer students a French-language, Catholic-oriented education," Forest said. "However, many students are from non-French cultural backgrounds, taking advantage of the excellent bilingual immersion inherent to the College Mathieu education program."

He said College Mathieu began a diversification strategy in 2001 with the introduction of a hockey residential school. "Keeping to its Francophone heritage," Forest said, "the College is currently recruiting hockey students from French communities worldwide."

The Pavilion Building, located on the College Mathieu Campus at 308–1st Avenue East in Gravelbourg, was designated a Municipal Heritage Property on November 5, 1981. Gravelbourg is about 150 kilometres southwest of Regina at the junction of highways 58 and 43.

SCHOOL SISTERS OF NOTRE DAME
Leipzig

The School Sisters of Notre Dame operated a boarding school in the small west central Saskatchewan community of Leipzig for almost half a century, and their legacy lives on in the hearts and minds of the students they taught.

Ed Bitz, who attended the school from 1937 to 1948, spoke on behalf of former students at the 75th anniversary celebration of the Leipzig convent in 2002.

"The bricks used to construct this magnificent building made the physical structure but it was the people inside who really made this institution," he said. "The School Sisters of Notre Dame were the ones who taught us about respect for older people. They taught us how to introduce people, greet people, how to walk and sit. We were taught about compassion, integrity, religion, honesty, and politeness."

Being educated by the School Sisters of Notre Dame was different from the school systems of today, Bitz said.

"We didn't have a football team, a basketball team, or a volleyball team. We didn't have field trips with days off," he said. "Oh, yes, our field trips consisted of marching in pairs from the elementary school to the church for choir practice during noon hour or marching to the church for benediction or Stations of the Cross. Those were our field trips."

About 550 former students, sisters, priests, friends, and relatives reflected their fondness for the school and convent by attending the 75th anniversary celebrations.

The Leipzig convent and school was set up by the religious order in response to request from Oblate priests who had appealed for help to provide education to the children of German settlers in the area.

The first four sisters arrived in Leipzig on August 26, 1926, from their headquarters in Waterdown, Ontario, to establish their new mission in western Canada.

Four sisters arrived in Leipzig in 1926 to begin teaching children of German settlers in the area.
PHOTO COURTESY HELEN KOBELSY

Until the convent and boarding school were constructed, classes were held in the two-room public school offered by the Catholic School Board.

Hilda Delaney was among the 60 students divided into two classes when the school began on September 20th.

"What a difference pupils noted in their schooling. The teacher was standing and teaching all day," recalled Hilda who was 12 years old at the time. "No sitting at her desk while we mostly read books from the library. We were given homework, weekly or monthly tests. We had Saturday morning class. We realize how little we had been taught in former years."

She said that by the end of the year all the pupils in grade 8 that her teacher, Sister Cajetan, recommended for the departmental exams passed.

A bunk house a short distance away was where the 15 girls, 7 boys and 1 sister slept the first year.

Work on the convent and boarding school, designed by Edmonton architect Archbishop Paul Desrocher, began the following spring. Top soil was cleared on May 31, concrete was poured for the foundation on July 14, and the first bricks were laid on August 8. The roof was completed on October 9th and the first fire in the furnace was lit on November 1.

The School Sisters of Notre Dame moved into their four-storey, 40-room red brick convent on Christmas Eve while the boarders were celebrating with their families at home.

Helen Kobelsky was determined to finish her high school education at Leipzig after completing grade 9 and 10 by correspondence. "Lack of money could have been a deterrent, but gallons of lard paid for the monthly tuition of $4," she recalls. "I boarded at my sister's home. A new bike resulted in a dislocated wrist so it was horse and buggy in summer and rides with neighbours in the winter."

Helen continued her education after graduating from Leipzig by becoming a teacher, and then she became a member of the School Sisters of Notre Dame. She returned to Leipzig where she taught her nieces and nephews in elementary school.

As the School Sisters of Notre Dame began to expand their roots into other Saskatchewan communities, the Leipzig convent became more important for educational and religious purposes. Sisters who had established mission houses in Revenue (1927), Handel (1944), and Wilkie (1957) held summer retreats at Leipzig.

The convent closed in 1969 and was sold to Henry Friesen five years later. He used the building as a private residence, after being married in the convent chapel. The structure went through a number of owners until 1992, when Ronald and Mary Kolenosky purchased the 20,000 square foot building for use as a bakery and residence.

"We are still using the water system that was put into use for the first time in 1927. It's good water and extremely plentiful, as we can use it 24 hours a day 7 days a week," says Mary Kolenosky. "We have lived in the convent since 1996 and are pleased to call it home."

The School Sisters of Notre Dame began a relationship with the Archdiocese of Regina in 1981 as religious education consultants and coordinators of the five deaneries. They have also served as parish administrators in Beechy, Bengough, Oxbow, Wolseley, and Viscount.

To get to Leipzig, travel 129 kilometres west of Saskatoon on Highway 14 to Landis, then continue on Highway 14 six kilometres northwest to the Pascal Road turn off. From there, drive 10 kilometres west to the St. Joseph Statue, designating the first mass of the St. Joseph's Colony in 1905 and turn south five kilometres to the Leipzig sign. The Notre Dame Convent, which became a Municipal Heritage Site in 1994, is one kilometre east of the sign.

WEISSENBERG SCHOOL
Lemberg

No children have attended the Weissenberg School near Lemberg, the oldest separate school still standing in Saskatchewan, for more than 40 years, but their footprints in the sands of time are huge.

Robert H. Mann, who was the last secretary of the school board and whose grandfather served as the school's first secretary in 1900, recalls his parents talking about a crucifix being removed from the school in 1929.

The crucifix controversy was publicly debated by Premier James Gardiner and Dr. John H. Hawkins, a Saskatchewan organizer of the Ku Klux Klan (KKK).

Gardiner, who was the member of the Legislative Assembly for the area, defended his Liberal government's support of freedom of religion. Newspaper reports indicate more than 1,000 people attended the three-hour debate in the nearby Lemberg hockey rink.

In 1928, the KKK claimed a Saskatchewan membership of 75,000 people. At a Klonvakation in Saskatoon only months before the 1929 Saskatchewan general election, KKK members voted to abolish separate schools, stop teaching the French language in schools, and suggested that all schools should be completely nonsectarian. So the debate over removing the crucifix from the Weissenberg separate school was historically significant.

Gardiner's Liberals won 28 of 63 seats in the legislature on June 9, 1929, but it wasn't enough to form a majority government because the Conservatives under James Anderson had taken 24 ridings with 6 independents and 5 Progressives winning as well.

Gardiner waded into the Lemberg debate knowing he didn't have the electoral support to continue to be premier, but he did not waiver in his support for displaying religious icons, such as a crucifix, in schools. He won the debate with the KKK organizer, but two months later Anderson formed a coalition government and was sworn in as premier.

Anderson became a one-term wonder. In the subsequent 1934 provincial election, the Liberals under Gardiner had a massive landslide, capturing 50 of the 54 seats to return to power. Gardiner left for federal politics the following year. Prime Minister Mackenzie King needed a new federal minister of agriculture and asked Gardiner to leave provincial politics to join him in Ottawa. Gardiner agreed and resigned as premier on November 1, 1935. The following January, he was elected the member of Parliament for Melville. He was reelected federally five times.

The Weissenberg School, from its construction before Saskatchewan became a province of Canada to its closure in 1964, was frequently making news.

Settlers began arriving in the region, 30 kilometres southwest of Melville, in 1893 from the Weissenberg area near Lemberg in Austria. Their heritage resulted in the naming of the school and the community. In 1899, they got permission to build a lumber school under the name of Weissenberg Roman Catholic Public School No. 49, to be built a half mile east of Lemberg.

A year later, the settlers decided to build a school from fieldstone rather than from lumber. This fieldstone school, measuring just 27 feet by 21 feet, was built in 1900 by William Sebastian Hanowski and Peter Reiger.

However, as Lemberg grew to more than 500 people the Weissenberg School became too small, so a public school was built. Two school boards were established and both claimed the tiny Weissenberg stone building and furnishings. Bitter feelings in the community were punctuated with a letter writing campaign to Premier Walter Scott by a group of 50 Roman Catholic families.

Finally, in the fall of 1907, the two school boards agreed that the Catholic ratepayers would pay their taxes for 1907 to the Lemberg Public School in lieu of ownership of the stone school built in 1900. It then became Weissenberg Roman Catholic Separate School District #17.

As the number of children grew, the stone school became too small. In 1922 a bigger one-room school was built of lumber and the old stone school was used as a residence for the teachers, who were nuns and lay people until its closure in 1964.

George Mildenberger was only 19 when he was hired to teach at the Weissenberg School. "Teachers had to wear white shirts, a suit and tie," he recalls. "That was where I learned to wash clothes on a wash board and had to haul water from an outdoor pump in the school grounds to do all of my cleaning."

Mildenberger was paid $1,500 per year when he started in 1949 and was allowed to live in the former stone school.

"The only string attached was that I had to maintain the heat in the school for the children," he said. "My stone residence was damn cold! It was heated by a wood and coal burner. When I sat between the burner and the wall I would burn on one half and freeze on the other half of me." Mildenberger said he would get dressed under the covers before getting out of bed each morning.

In 1950, he was paid extra to reshingle the stone building's roof. "When I make the trip back to Lemberg from Indian Head, where I now reside, I still take pride in the fact the shingles on it today were the handiwork of myself over 50 years ago," Mildenberger said.

Joseph T. Cyca remembers going to the Weissenberg in 1922, his first year of school, by horse and buggy in the fall and spring, and horse and cutter in the winter.

"The horses were kept in a barn within the school grounds," Cyca said. "We'd have to water and feed the animals at lunch."

A favourite pastime for the boys, he said, was snaring rabbits in the bushes within the school grounds. Rabbit skins could be sold for five or six cents each, Cyca said.

A declining population led to the 1964 closure of the Weissenberg School, but the legacy of the tiny stone school continued in the chapters of history books for years to come.

To get to the Weissenberg School, declared a Municipal Heritage Site in 1989, drive 26 kilometres west on Highway 10 from Melville to the Junction of grid road 617. Then, drive south about 13 kilometres into Lemberg.

ST. PETER'S COLLEGE
Muenster

St. Peter's College in Muenster, which Benedictine monks completed themselves in 1921 because the New York company contracted to do the work went bankrupt, has become the only rural university college in Saskatchewan.

The four-storey, red brick building with a metal roof is an educational icon and a regional landmark. It is visible above the evergreen tree tops that line the gardens and fields of St. Peter's colony, established in 1903, two years before Saskatchewan became a province.

In fact, the college can easily be seen from Mount Carmel, some 30 kilometres away, and dwarfs the nearby grain elevators of Muenster and Humboldt, 8 kilometres to the west.

"The school was established to provide Catholic education to boys at a time where there were no publicly funded separate high schools as there are today," explained Bill Allen, who attended high school and his first year of university classes at St. Peter's from 1960 to 1965. "Parents paid tuition for their children to attend St. Peter's as well as paying taxes to support the public school system."

Allen, now a vice-principal at Riffle High School for the Regina Catholic School Board of Education, noted that system changed in 1964 when the provincial government extended funding to Catholic high schools as well as elementary schools.

St. Peter's popularity as a residential high school began to dwindle in the 1960s when the education system in the province became more standardized and high schools were built in more communities across Saskatchewan. Students simply began to stay in their own hometowns to receive high school education.

As a result, St. Peter's ended its high school program in 1972 and then formalized its relationship as a junior college with the University of Saskatchewan. St. Peter's College is a member of the Association of Benedictine Colleges and Universities (ABCU) and the Association of Catholic Colleges and Universities of Canada (ACCUC).

Benedictine monks have taught at St. Peter's College in Muenster since before Saskatchewan became a province.

St. Peter's College provides university education for men and women through programs in the liberal arts and sciences, and preprofessional studies leading to baccalaureate, masters and doctoral degrees.

As an affiliate of the University of Saskatchewan, St. Peter's College offers classes that are academically integrated as well as programming unique to the college. The goal of St. Peter's College is to enable students to progress as academic, social, and spiritual leaders.

Small class size is a distinct factor in the success of the St. Peter's university students. Approximately 40 sections of instruction are offered in agriculture, business, fine arts, humanities, social sciences, and the natural sciences. Students, depending on their area of study, are able to move well into their degree programs through St. Peter's.

Classes are offered via face-to-face instruction, as well as Web-based, televised, multi-mode, and the traditional correspondence models. Learning is enhanced by Internet, a local area network, and digital technology, as well as a library established more than 100 years age and now containing more than 40,000 titles.

St. Peter's Abbey, founded in 1903, was the first established by the Order of St. Benedict in Canada. For more than 100 years, the Benedictines have served the surrounding communities with educational and spiritual expertise.

Many students attribute their success and life's work to values learned while attending St. Peter's. For example, Bill Allen's passion for politics, social justice, and education is a direct result of the experience of being educated at the Muenster school.

"St. Peter's had a great effect on me and many others who went there and came away with a tremendous passion for social justice and great respect for education and learning," said Allen. "Thus, my life's work first in politics and secondly in education."

Allen served two terms as a member of the Legislative Assembly from 1975 to 1982 and then was the president of the New Democratic Party's Saskatchewan section for five years ending in 2000.

"The Benedictine community has always been supportive of movements that support change that helps people," he recalled. "Whether it's the plight of farmers in Saskatchewan or the poor in their mission in Brazil, we, as students, were nurtured in an atmosphere that fostered the notion that Christians cannot be indifferent to injustice in the world."

Allen and several of his fellow graduates were so moved by their encounters with Father Albert Ruetz, known lovingly as the Bear, that they nominated him for a Saskatchewan Award of Merit for his service as a math teacher at St. Peter's for 50 years.

"St. Peter's is like a part of my family," explained Brenda Friestadt, who grew up in Muenster and opted to take her first year of university classes at St. Peter's. "The [Benedictine] monks serviced our communities by way of placing parish priests in the surrounding towns. In every community they served, they became involved. I don't think it is just coincidence that the area surrounding the Abbey has been very successful and is culturally a wondrous thing."

Friestadt was among 7 of the 10 children in her family who attended St. Peter's.

"These men of the cloth [Benedictines] had a great effect on the people they came in contact with," she explained. "Their service and their example of work and prayer were inspirations to all, as was their love of all things cultural."

Having the junior college in her home town helped ease the transition from high school into university, Friestadt said.

"It was just a natural progression. I wasn't sure what I wanted to do and first-year university was right at my doorstep," she said. "If I wanted to try out a year of university, why would I go to Saskatoon and spend extra money on classes, not to mention housing, when it was available to me here?"

Smaller class size was also an attractive incentive for Friestadt. "I knew I wouldn't get lost in the crowd," said the woman who has returned home to St. Peter's as the administrative assistant to the president, dean, and financial officer.

Another major step in the evolution of St. Peter's came in 1997 when the Centre for Rural Studies and Enrichment was established. It is the only research and development office in the province dedicated to the issues and needs of rural residents.

St. Peter's College, located on the south side of
the Village of Muenster, was named a Municipal
Heritage property on August 6, 1996.

COLLEGE AVENUE CAMPUS
Regina

A trio of red brick buildings constructed in the Collegiate Gothic style, which stretch for five blocks and mark the northern edge of Wascana Park, is known as the College Avenue Campus of the University of Regina.

The Old Normal School or Fine Arts Building is a key element of Regina's historic College Avenue streetscape and marks the northeastern corner of Wascana Park.

This was the first normal school constructed in Saskatchewan, where students were trained to become teachers. The building has had a history of occupants and uses that reflect much of the cultural, educational, and military past and development of Regina and Saskatchewan.

Of particular architectural note is the still remaining central entrance tower with its impressive Tudor-arch portal, narrow vertical leaded glass windows, and crenellated parapet.

"Over the years I have run into so many people with wonderful stories and great memories of this building," said Bill Henderson, who was the founding chairman of the Saskatchewan Heritage Foundation and now specializes in restoration of heritage buildings for Prairie Restoration Ltd. "This, more than any other building in Regina, has nurtured the cultural development and training of many generations of Saskatchewan's artists and teachers through most of the 20th century."

Henderson, a past president of the Saskatchewan Architectural Heritage Society, has fond memories of the building from the days when it still served as the University of Regina's Fine Arts Building.

"At the end of each academic year, the building would be filled with frenetic activity of arts students finishing their art projects and the enthusiastic preparations for the graduating class art exhibition," he recalled. "It was a hive of creativity."

Storey and Van Egmond were the architects of the building constructed in 1913. It was originally designed and used as Regina's Normal School from

1913 to 1915 and then after the First World War from 1918 to 1940.

The building was used as the headquarters and to billet members of the 195th Battalion from 1916 to 1918. It did double duty as the first home of the Provincial Museum of Natural History from 1916 to 1940 and from 1945 to 1969

During the Second World War, the Royal Canadian Air Force (RCAF) held its Initial Training School in the building from 1940 to 1944. Then, after the war, a pair of provincial government departments occupied the building.

From 1946 to 1969, it served as the University of Saskatchewan's Teachers College campus building. From 1970 to 1997, it was the University of Regina's Fine Arts Building. During the 1990s the building was poorly maintained. It fell into further disrepair when it was left vacant from 1997 to 2001.

In 2002, all but three sides of the exterior shell and the central entrance tower were demolished and then reincorporated into a new $23 million sound stage funded by the federal and provincial governments.

Normal School/Fine Arts Building, now known as the Saskatchewan Film Production Studios, is located at 1831 College Avenue on the corner of the intersection with Broad Street.

* * *

The Conservatory College Building is the middle and most prominent of the three Collegiate Gothic-styled buildings that comprise the Regina College Avenue Campus. It is arguably the best example of the Collegiate Gothic style in the city.

Until 2001, the three buildings were connected with utility tunnels, allowing people to walk underground from basement to basement.

The middle building has provided studio and classroom facilities for a wide variety of fine arts programs and continuing education courses for the general public.

"The building has many prominent architectural features," Henderson said. "Most well known is the principal, six-storey Gothic tower with its fine studios and its crenellated battlements at rooftop." He added that possibly one of the least recognized but significant architectural features of the building is the steeply tiered, three-storey lecture hall with its original seating and finishes still intact from 1912.

James H. Puntin was the architect of the building constructed for use as the Methodist Church's Regina College.

The Duke of Connaught, then Governor General of Canada, laid the cornerstone for the Regina College Building. It became a residential and day school for high school students until 1926.

The Collegiate Gothic styling was often used in educational buildings and armouries, reminiscent of Tudor times.
PHOTO COURTESY SASKATCHEWAN HERITAGE FOUNDATION

A long tradition as the home of the Regina Conservatory of Music began in 1912 and continues to the present day.

In 1914, the west wing and main tower were constructed for use as a women's dormitory for the out-of-town students. There were plans to build a matching tower and dormitory wing for male students, but these were never implemented.

The building served as junior college for the University of Saskatchewan from 1926 to 1934 and then became the centre of its Regina Campus in 1959. It remained the central University of Regina Campus until the new main campus was established in 1961.

Today, it serves as home for the University of Regina Centre for Continuing Education as well as the Conservatory of Music.

The University of Regina Conservatory College Building is located at 2155 College Avenue.

* * *

Darke Hall is the third and smallest of the Regina College Avenue Campus buildings. It is graced with a bay gothic-arched entranceway flanked by two towers.

The front façade features extensive leaded glass window bays illuminating offices and music studios located in the two towers and the gallery above the main entrance.

This well-proportioned Collegiate Gothic building design makes a pleasing focus point at the Cornwall Street intersection with College Avenue.

James H. Puntin was also the architect for the building.

Darke Hall was originally known as the Music and Art Building when it was erected in 1928. The backstage area was enlarged with an addition in 1929.

It came to be called Darke Hall after the former mayor, prominent local businessman, and philanthropist Francis N. Darke, who had this music hall constructed as a gift to the citizens of Regina.

Francis Darke's former family home still stands on the opposite side of College Avenue, facing Darke Hall. Over the years, Darke Hall has been the venue for numerous recitals, music competitions, theatrical events, lectures, and debates. It is well appreciated for its excellent acoustics and inviting atmosphere.

The building underwent an extensive structural stabilization and architectural restoration in 1986. The basement was redesigned to accommodate soundproofed music practice rooms, now intensively used by university music students.

Darke Hall is located at the intersection of College Avenue at Cornwall Street.

Darke Hall is a sought-after venue for music recitals, lectures and debates because of its excellent acoustics.
Photo courtesy Saskatchewan Heritage Foundation

THORVALDSON BUILDING
Saskatoon

The turrets and stonework of the Chemistry Building on the University of Saskatchewan Campus are reminders of the European architectural influence on the institution, the City of Saskatoon, and the province.

The building was officially opened on August 22, 1924, and was renamed in 1966 to honor chemist Thorbergur Thorvaldson.

Walter Murray, the university president, made a point of mentioning an interdisciplinary project in his 1924 annual report into decay of concrete involving Thorvaldson, head of the Department of Chemistry, and C. J. Mackenzie, dean of Engineering.

The deterioration and failure of concrete structures had been a growing cause for concern throughout western Canada. Research at the University of Saskatchewan determined that sulphates in alkaline groundwater were causing the deterioration. For the next decade, Thorvaldson and his graduate students researched means of prevention.

The results of their work changed the manufacturing of commercial cement and significantly increased the durability of concrete structures.

In his 1952 annual report, President W. P. Thompson noted Thorvaldson's "remarkable capacity as a scientist" and praised his contributions to the west. "Many of the problems solved by his [Thorvaldson's] wide knowledge and experimental ability have been directly related to economic improvement, and the value of his research could be computed in amounts considerably greater than have been spent on the construction and maintenance of the University during its entire history," Thompson wrote.

"He has built up a Department of Chemistry that has carried the fame of the University of Saskatchewan wherever his students have gone."

Sketches drawn for the Chemistry Building were completed in 1913, but plans were halted because of the First World War and then lack of funding.

Growing out of an architecturally-plentiful campus, the Thorvaldson tower has been a classroom home to thousands of chemistry students through the years.
PHOTO COURTESY UNIVERSITY OF SASKATCHEWAN

Construction by local contractors, Shannon Brothers and Bennett and White, took three years, ending in 1924.

Colin Tennent, University of Saskatchewan Architect, noted that the building was designed by David R. Brown, of the architectural firm of Brown and Vallance, located in Montreal, who was responsible for the College Building and numerous other early buildings on the university campus.

"This neo-Collegiate Gothic building features crenellated turrets, relief sculptures, and tall central towers," Tennent said. "Vaulted ceilings, brick wainscoting, arched doorways, and windows give an impression of a castle-like structure on campus which has been used repeatedly for movie productions."

The trim is an Indiana limestone and local grey or fieldstone. Smith Brothers and Wilson were responsible for the quarry supply of local grey stone. James Wilson, a businessman and pioneer of the Saskatoon district, advised the University of Saskatchewan Board of Governors to use the local grey stone.

Large deposits of glacial limestone proved to be hard, durable, and clean with some variety in colour. Picks, shovels, and dynamite were used to remove the limestone from the deposits. Skilled stonemasons then created the blocks for the Thorvaldson Building. Stonemasons were often in short supply, and the company recruited from Scotland.

The interior of the building features brick wainscoting and tile floors in the hallways.

The building was designed to have a second identical wing on the north side, but this never occurred because the Great Depression and the Second World War, put a halt to all capital expansion on campus for decades.

The entrance faced away from "The Bowl," an elliptical green space on campus, and toward the entrance of the university. The interior of the building had been designed specifically to meet the needs of teaching and research in chemistry. The first floor was almost all classrooms and two laboratories.

The second floor housed laboratories featuring acid-proof lining on all fume vents as well as countertops and cupboard facings from New York granite. The second floor was also home to the auditorium and lecture theatre. This impressive room features a tile dome ceiling rising 68 feet from the floor and had extraordinary acoustics for the period. The curved rows of wooden seats and steep gradient allowed all attendees excellent access to hear and see the lecturer.

"One of the features of the dome is the focusing of sound from one area of seating to another, giving the impression of someone speaking from an empty seat" noted Tennent.

The second wing finally opened in 1966. The three-storey addition was designed by John B. Parkin in a very modern style and provided classrooms, undergraduate and research laboratories, offices, and a library.

In 2003, the third addition was officially opened. The four-storey addition echoed the campus' original architectural style and the neo-Collegiate Gothic façade harmonizes well with the original splendid building. A portion of the 1924 structure underwent extensive renovation during the construction of the Spinks Addition, which cost $30 million compared with the $733,000 bill for construction of the original building.

Today, along with its two modern contemporaries, the Thorvaldson Building continues to be the home of an excellent educational department. It is poised for the new millennium with access to facilities that are unique, nationally and globally.

The Thorvaldson Building is located at 110 Science Place on the University of Saskatchewan Campus in Saskatoon. It is north of College Drive and west of Higgins Crescent.

COLLEGE BUILDING
Saskatoon

The College Building was the first building completed on the University of Saskatchewan Campus in Saskatoon and continues to be a landmark of education decades later. The cornerstone was laid by Sir Wilfred Laurier, prime minister of Canada, on July 29, 1910.

"Overall the University of Saskatchewan Campus is the best example of in-situ Collegiate Gothic architecture in Canada and the College Building stands centre stage," explains Colin Tennent, the university's current resident architect within the Facilities Management Division.

"This style was chosen by the Board of Governors who took a fact-finding, three-month long trip through Canadian and American universities. They came away with a style that declared the university's links to a European past and chose a Canadian architectural firm to design the building."

Originally called the College Building, it has been home to various departments over the years,

and was most recently the centre for the university's administration office.

Constructed at a cost of $297,000, the College Building is one of 15 buildings on campus designed by architects Brown and Vallance of Montreal, a prominent national firm of that era.

The College Building is the key structure at the east end of an elliptical green space known as "The Bowl" and stands as a distinguished landmark on campus.

"There are those who say that this is arguably the most important building in the province after the Provincial Legislative Building in Regina because it is the central symbol of the provincial university and the most handsome building on campus," he said.

The neo-Collegiate Gothic building features exterior gargoyles with prairie motifs such as gophers and rams. This classical Elizabethan building displays unique prairie touches such as the locally quarried grey stone and exterior carvings.

The College Building is undergoing a multi-million dollar restoration under the federal government's Historic Places Initiative.
PHOTO COURTESY SASKATCHEWAN HERITAGE FOUNDATION

The assembly hall seated 600 upon completion and was used for convocations until the 1970s. In the early years, it was also used as a dance hall and registration room.

The Elizabethan shape of the building combined beauty and utility necessary for an early campus building that served many functions.

The interior halls have a wainscoting of terra cotta tile and the frieze is decorative tiles inlaid with the names of all students who fought in the First World War. This includes John G. Diefenbaker, who went on to become Canada's 13th Prime Minister, and his brother. Great care is being taken with these tiles during the restoration of the exterior hall.

Murray Adaskin, a renowned Canadian composer, was head of the Music Department from 1952 to 1972.

"My personal opinion is that there is no finer hall of equal size in Canada," Adaskin said, referring to the acoustics of Convocation Hall.

Tennent added that Convocation Hall has a sky light that was covered over at some point in time. "This will be opened again to allow for natural lighting," he said. "The original interior lights were removed in the 1950s and replaced by satin brass lights designed specifically for the space."

The fall 2001 edition of *Green and White,* the University of Saskatchewan alumni periodical, published a narrative by Mary Jean Roy, a 1973 graduate, entitled "A Family Affair."

"My mother, Inez Holding, graduated from the University of Saskatchewan in 1917 with a Bachelor of Arts degree," Roy wrote in the article. "I have lived in Saskatoon since 1958 and one time, when she was already getting old, she was visiting so we went into Convocation Hall."

She said her mother recalled dances in Convocation Hall where the university president, Walter Murray, and his wife chaperoned. "If a couple was dancing too closely together, getting a bit too affectionate, Mrs. Murray would tap the young man on the shoulder and ask that he behave more appropriately!" Roy said. "The students in those days wore academic gowns to classes daily, so they really had to own them."

She still has her mother's gown, ensuring that her children and grandchildren and friends have worn it to their own convocations. "My son, Roy Sydiaha, wore it to receive his Bachelor of Music exactly 75 years after Inez," Roy said. "It's a beautiful gown—the names of all those who have worn it are recorded inside the gown."

A controversy has bubbled on the campus over the past decade about the future of the College Building because of serious structural issues. The future of the structure has been in jeopardy because of the financial implications.

The university's facilities management team, including Tennent, the university architect, has been adamant that the College Building is too important to the whole campus to allow for its demolition. "The University of Saskatchewan recognizes the importance of the heritage buildings that we are the stewards of," Tennent said.

A $20.7-million rehabilitation, begun in 2001, will result in the structural deficiencies being corrected. Convocation Hall, which Tennent refers to as the "jewel" of the project, is being restored to its original glory. Great care and effort are being taken with this section of the building as well as the interior hallways. An addition on the southeast corner is also under way, that will tie in with the new Administration Building.

The College Building, located at 105 Administration Place on the University of Saskatchewan Campus in Saskatoon, became a Provincial Heritage Property in 1982 and was named a National Historic Site in 2001.

NUTANA COLLEGIATE
Saskatoon

Students who have attended Nutana Collegiate in Saskatoon during the past 90 years reflect the growth of the tiny community into the province's largest city as well as the changing demographics of the inner city neighbourhood.

Notable alumni include: John Diefenbaker, the 13th prime minister of Canada; Ray Hnathyshyn, the 24th governor general of Canada; Sid Buckwold, mayor of Saskatoon for 11 years before becoming a senator; and author Max Braithwaite, who wrote *Why Shoot the Teacher?* and *The Night We Stole The Mounties' Car,* for which he was honoured in 1972 with the Stephen Leacock Award for Humour.

George Genereux was just a 17-year-old student attending Nutana Collegiate when he won a gold medal at the 1952 Olympic Games in Helsinki for trap shooting. For that accomplishment, Genereux was awarded the Lou Marsh Memorial Trophy as Canada's Outstanding Athlete. He was forced to retire from competition at the age of 20 because of rheumatoid arthritis,

became a doctor like his father, and focussed his efforts on medical research.

In the past two decades, Nutana has been on the leading edge of educational reform, providing a unique blend of instruction as well as support services for students and parents through the school.

Agencies and groups now linked through Nutana range from the Saskatoon Health District and the Saskatoon Tribal Council to provincial departments of justice and social services.

Former teachers and students recognize the shift in focus at Nutana, yet fondly remember the time they were touched by the aura of the building originally named Saskatoon Collegiate Institute.

Gordon Kincade taught English, journalism and social studies at Nutana from 1967 to 1984. "I think those were among the glory years of the collegiate," he recalled.

"We had excellent teams in basketball, football, soccer and track and field. Students won academic

Designed by the prolific Regina architectural firm of Storey and Van Egmond, the highschool featured exaggerated dormers over the front entrance.
<small>Photo courtesy Saskatchewan Heritage Foundation</small>

awards, including Governor General Medals, and had winning teams on 'Reach for the Top'."

An outstanding staff enabled success for students, Kincade added. "All one needs to do is look at the graduates of Nutana to see a Who's Who of leaders in all fields of endeavour, including the arts, business, politics, professions, sports, and the trades," he said.

Bill Cooke, now director of education for the Saskatchewan Rivers School Division No. 119, a public school division in and around Prince Albert, was a student at Nutana in the early 1960s.

"I believe Nutana is important to the city and the province because it has stood the test of time and rolled with society's changes," he said. "It is one of the oldest schools in the province and has shifted from an academic and athletic focus to one that is reflective of the community it serves today."

Cooke said that, in hindsight, his fondest memories of Nutana were of an idyllic life. "We believed, at the time, probably as most high school kids do, that our school was the best, that Nutana 'Ruled the World,'" Cooke said. "I still believe that Nutana serves its clientele very well."

Glenn Reeve was born in Regina, grew up in Grenfell, and taught for four years in Melville before starting a 20-year career at Nutana as a history teacher in 1966.

"It was an incredible honour for me to be there because I was fully aware of the history of Nutana," he said. "When I attended the University of Saskatchewan, I became aware of Nutana because of all the Nutana graduates on campus who were easily identified walking around with their famous double-blue jackets."

Reeve recalls an incident at Nutana that reflects the emphasis, at that time, on academic achievement. "I remember a guidance counsellor coming into the teachers' staff room one day almost in tears because he had just figured out that only 63 percent of the graduating class had gone on to university, which was a new low for Nutana," he said. "Today, most high schools would cherish that number. Nutana has changed over the years to serve a different clientele."

Nutana's roots run deep into the history of the community. The city was created in 1906 by the merger of the pioneering settlements of Nutana, Riversdale, and Saskatoon. It was a time of unbridled optimism. Saskatoon had 6 doctors, 6 lawyers, 3 dentists, 2 veterinarians, 6 banks and more than 30 real estate offices. Saskatoon grew from 3,000 people in 1906 to 28,000 in just five years.

When the four-storey, red brick building opened in 1910, Nutana became the first secondary school in the new city.

It also was the home for the University of Saskatchewan—until their buildings were completed—and the Normal School where teachers received their training.

Regina architects Edgar Storey and William Van Egmond, who played an integral role in the construction of many key educational and institutional buildings at that period of time, designed and supervised construction of Nutana. The total cost was $84,555.

In 1919, the students' council began a Canadian art collection in memory of the 29 alumni who died in the First World War. It is recognized as the first significant art collection in Saskatoon and now consists of 56 oil and water paintings, 3 acrylic paintings and 30 wood cuts.

There were 95 collegiate students on the opening day, but attendance mushroomed to 940 students by 1927. Overcrowding became a familiar theme of Nutana during its first 50 years.

The first major addition came in 1930 when a new gymnasium was added on the northwest side of the building at a cost of $33,000. Almost a quarter of a century passed before more major renovations were done.

A flat-roofed, two-storey structure contained the memorial library, three classrooms, an audio-visual room, washrooms, as well as female and male teachers' rooms. The cost was $238,000. The exterior was constructed with brick, to match the 1930 expansion, and terra cotta tile.

In 1964, the gymnasium was converted into three classrooms and a new gymnasium was built that measured 95 feet by 149 feet and was 36-feet high.

A dental clinic was added to Nutana in 1982 and social programs for students became more prevalent.

Today, Nutana is a symbol of pride for alumni and the community as the school provides a focus for a new generation of students living in the inner city on the east side of the South Saskatchewan River that knifes its way through Saskatoon.

Nutana Collegiate is located at 411–11th Street East in Saskatoon

CENTRAL SCHOOL
Swift Current

Thousands of students have attended Central School since it opened in 1914 on the hilltop overlooking Swift Current, but there have been only six principals.

"I find it truly remarkable that in the 90-year history of Central there have been only six principals," said Keith Ahrens, who was principal at Central from 1989 to 2001. "I think it's a testament to the building itself that teachers and principals didn't mind staying there for many, many years."

Ahrens spent more than half of his 31-year career within the public education system in Swift Current at the elementary school. He taught grades 6 and 7 at Central from 1970 to 1975 before returning 14 years later to be the principal.

"The fellow who was the principal ahead of me was there 18 years," he said. "You don't see that kind of loyalty to a location and a dedication to that individual by a school system like that very much anywhere in Saskatchewan."

Rapid growth and buoyant optimism in the early 1900s required that a school be constructed in Swift Current.

Designed by architects Reilly, Dawson, Bancock and Reilly, and built in 1914, Central School helped symbolize the emergence of Swift Current as a city in its own right.

There were 12 classrooms in addition to rooms for wood- and metalwork for the boys and what was called "domestic science" for the girls. An auditorium doubled as a gym.

Central School's size, hilltop location, and Western Canadian Classic Revival architecture have made it a familiar landmark for generations.

The range of grades has changed over the years starting with grades 1 to 8, evolving to kindergarten to grade 7, and now with its current student complement of children from kindergarten to grade 5.

"Central School is unique because it dispels the myth that rural and urban don't mix in

Saskatchewan," said Ahrens, who opted to begin selling vehicles for Regier Honda in Swift Current after retiring from his educational career.

"There's a unique agreement or a type of 'grandfather' clause that allows the children or grandchildren of former students who lived on farms around Swift Current to attend Central School." That means regardless of where these children live in the nearby surrounding farming area, they can chose to attend Central School.

"I was teaching fourth-generation students when I was there," Ahrens said. "That meant that the great-great grandparents of the children were among the original homesteaders and they sent their kids to Central!"

Ken Yee taught at Central from 1974 to 1984. "To me it was the school that I really wanted to teach at. It was what I always thought a school should look like," said the former vice principal. "The red brick structure with a sculptured parapet and the gargoyles which greeted me every morning made my teaching experience special."

Yee said the high ceilings, which are almost 12 feet high, gave the reverberating echo of all the "learning" that had gone on in the past and continued in the present.

"The marble hallways added to the aura of what a school should be, but financially cannot be any longer," he said. "When I went to teach at Central it shouted to me: 'This is what a school should look like.' "

Donna Rezansoff, another former teacher, said Central was and always will be her favourite school building.

Built in 1914, Central School helped boost the image of Swift Current as a key community in southwestern Saskatchewan.
Photo courtesy Swift Current Museum

"Besides being visually beautiful, it was the perfect school building—strong, secure and perfectly proportioned for school programs," she said.

Boh Ciona has fond memories of the school, students and staff.

"The thing that most impressed me about Central School was the interior and exterior architecture, the marble floors, wooden railings on the stairs, as well as the old-fashioned drinking fountains which we used when I first came to teach at the school," said Boh Ciona.

His wife, Diana, was the first Kindergarten teacher at Central. "I was teaching in the basement in the same classroom that I had done my practice teaching in 10 years earlier," she said. "My principal was Ken Lewis. I had played with his kids when I was quite young."

Diana will never forget the fire alarm located outside her Kindergarten classroom. "When it rang many of my children would stand and just cry and be unable to move," she recalled. "The alarm was very loud. It had been used as a warning signal for our city in the early days. Later, the alarm was muffled so it wouldn't scare us so much."

Central School, located at 121 Dufferin Street West in Swift Current, was declared a Municipal Heritage Property on May 6, 1985.

Though thousands of students have passed through it doorways, the school has had only six principals since opening.
Photo courtesy Saskatchewan Heritage Foundation

ENTERTAINMENT

"This is an example of people working with city hall, not fighting city hall."
–Gary Hyland, Executive Director of Arts In Motion, which helped turn the
Capitol Theatre into the Moose Jaw Cultural Centre

A measure of the maturity of a community comes from its ability to rest and relax together. Gathering to celebrate the end of a harvest or simply to enjoy time away from the tough day-to-day grind has always been an important activity for Saskatchewan people, whether it was a regular Saturday night dance, an opportunity to see live entertainment such as vaudeville act or stage play, or taking in the latest movie release.

Growth and, to some extent, the importance of a community to a particular region can be measured by buildings constructed specifically for the purpose of entertainment.

Progress followed a distinct pattern. First, settlers built their own homes, either on their farms or in the smaller settlements, villages and towns. Then, they invested their own labour and money to construct a place to worship. Schools and government buildings such as town halls or municipal offices followed soon after.

The next obvious growth of a community was into the entertainment sector—private clubs, dance halls and movie theatres.

Many of the early entertainment destinations across Saskatchewan have succumbed to a wrecking ball or neglect, but people in several communities in recent years have rallied to preserve, protect and promote their heritage. Renovations to former movie theatre buildings in Arcola, Moose Jaw and Saskatoon have led to a revival of a neighborhood or an infusion of excitement and activity into the community. The trio of success stories is providing hope to others, including those in the southwestern city of Swift Current who want to save the former Lyric Theatre from being erased from the Prairie landscape.

Meanwhile, several generations of Saskatchewan people have literally been able to kick up their heels at Danceland in the tiny central community of Manitou Beach. People who have enjoyed a two-step at Danceland sing the praises of the dance floor that has been built upon layers of horse hair and provides less stress on the feet, ankles, knees, legs, hips and backs of the dancers.

Renovating or maintaining buildings for entertainment purposes have given a second life to not only the structures but to the communities as well.

MAC MURRAY THEATRE
Arcola

A movie based on the W.O. Mitchell book, Who Has Seen the Wind, *premiered in the Mac Murray Theatre.*
PHOTO COURTESY ADRIAN PATON

Several groups in the small Town of Arcola, almost 200 kilometres southeast of Regina, have combined forces to preserve, restore, and then operate the Mac Murray Theatre, complete with a flashing-light marquee reminiscent of the glory days of theatres.

"I've been going to movies since I was six years old and it's very important for Arcola to have the Mac Murray open," said Ida Brownridge, who was born in 1921. "It has become a very important part of the community. We don't need any more things taken out of rural Saskatchewan. We have lost too much over the years."

Joe Hengen, who was mayor of the town of 540 people when the restoration project began, agrees with Brownridge. "The theatre provides another form of recreation for people of Arcola and the surrounding area," said Hengen, who served as the Mayor of Arcola from 1991 until 2003. "It has become just as important to the community as any other form of entertainment such as the rink."

The former teacher and principal said people enjoy their movie going experience. "People like it because it's special to see a movie on the big screen rather than just renting DVDs to watch in their homes," Hengen said.

The Optimist Club of Arcola negotiated a unique arrangement with the town, which apparently acquired the building for back taxes.

"The Optimist Club rents an apartment upstairs and uses this space for executive meetings and for storage for Optimist Club equipment such as minor baseball equipment in the off-season," explained Glen Lawson, the service club's president. "The town maintains the building, although the Optimist Club has renovated and redecorated much of the theatre, including the lobby and concession area."

A balcony was converted into a new projection room, while about half of the 400 seats were designed to provide more leg room for customers.

"Renovations included wainscoting and other upgrades so that we came more in line with heritage buildings in the community," said Lawson, principal of Arcola High School. "Our last upgrade included repainting the exterior of the building and refurbishing the awning. The building now fits in better with adjacent brick heritage buildings."

John R. Meals built Arcola's first theatre on the ashes of his hardware store that burned in 1912. He named it the Princess Theatre.

"It was in operation for quite a number of years but like many businesses it was forced to close and was dismantled in the late 1930s," explained local historian Adrian Paton.

"When the men came back from the Second World War, it was felt that Arcola needed a theatre. The community banded together and built a new Princess Theatre in 1948. It was first operated by the community then later sold to private owners."

He said that in the 1980s the Princess was suffering the same fate as other theatres on the prairies. "The owners were forced to close the doors and offered the building for sale, but there were no takers and the building sat idle for a time," Paton explained.

Two retired Arcola residents—Ed Hanna, a machinist and automotive dealer for over 50 years and his brother-in-law Mac Murray, an area farmer—set out to change the situation.

"Ed did much of the legwork but unfortunately passed away before the deal was completed. Mac Murray went ahead and purchased the theatre and donated it to the Town of Arcola," Paton said. "That's when the name was changed to Mac Murray. The town and the Optimist Club then combined to operate the theatre."

The Optimist Club of Arcola operates the theatre on Friday and Saturday nights from October to May. Other uses for the building over the last few years have been community drama, high school drama, and town meetings to organize the rebuilding of the community rink.

In addition, the community holds its annual Remembrance Day service in the theatre. The Town of Arcola pays the utilities on the building and does some maintenance.

"About six years ago, the Optimist Club approached the Students Representative Council (SRC) at the high school to help with the theatre," Lawson said. "The students help with the concession work and cleanup. In turn, the Optimist Club gives the SRC a sum of money used to help pay for the school yearbook."

The service club has established six crews that include a captain to organize work, a projectionist, and other members to help the students. "In addition, there are others in the community that volunteer some time even though they are not members of the Optimist Club or the SRC," Lawson said. "Each crew works only five or six weekends throughout the year."

He said the original goal of the service club of reopening the theatre was to provide entertainment for youth and adults in the community.

"I think the theatre is important for many reasons," Lawson said. "It provides entertainment, is a gathering place and another asset for this area. Many people look forward to the movies beginning in the fall."

Arcola theatre goers get to see top-rated movies only a few weeks after being released in major centres throughout North America.

"Like many smaller theatres, we book eight or so movies at a time and get an advertising mat printed and mailed to area communities," he said, explaining how the service club markets the movies. "We like to have a couple of children's shows, family shows, and general interest movies."

During the winter of 2003–2004, the theatre screened movies that included *Lord of the Rings: Return of the King* and *Agent Cody Banks: Destination London*. The controversial film by Mel Gibson, *The Passion of the Christ*, was also shown at the theatre in Arcola.

The theatre building was also featured prominently in the 1977 Canadian movie, *Who Has Seen the Wind*, based on the book by author W.O. Mitchell. The movie was filmed in Arcola, premiered in the community, and had a 25th anniversary showing in the same theatre.

"The Mac Murray Theatre is a chance for a group of people to work together on a major project that makes this town a better place to live," said Lawson, noting there are only 25 members of the Optimist Club of Arcola.

Students from the local high school raise money for school projects by working at the theatre now owned by a local service club.
PHOTO COURTESY ADRIAN PATON

BUILDING OUR FUTURE

"For many of us, there is a sense of accomplishment when we have a good weekend or finish some project in the building."

The Mac Murray Theatre is located at 110 Main Street in Arcola.

DANCELAND
Manitou Beach

Vic Murray didn't realize how much his life would change when he and bunch of friends took the short drive into Manitou Beach from the nearby community of Young more than 50 years ago.

"Everybody came to Danceland on the weekends," he recalled years later. "I noticed this girl wearing a red plaid skirt that was quite good doing the jitterbug. So I asked her to dance. That's how it all began."

In 2003, Vic and Irene Murray celebrated their 50th wedding anniversary, appropriately, with a celebration surrounded by friends and family in the same place they met—Danceland.

The Murrays not only fell in love with each other, but with the unique dance hall that has featured live bands since it opened in 1928. They owned and operated Danceland for 11 years until 1996.

"There were no babysitters back then, so mom and dad often brought the younger kids too," Vic said. "There was no admission charge. People could come and listen to the music and visit. If you wanted to dance, you bought tickets for 10 cents each or three dances for a quarter."

Danceland backs onto Little Manitou Lake. Manitou Beach is nestled in a glacier-scooped valley on Highway 365, five kilometres north of Watrous. The community is 116 kilometres southeast of Saskatoon and 185 kilometres north of Regina.

The resort community was established because of the density and mineral content of Little Manitou Lake. Anyone can float in the lake and it's literally possible to lie on your back and read a newspaper or book without getting the pages wet.

Danceland was financed by Wellington White of Moose Jaw, who then leased it to Guy Watkins, a blind musician, and the Art Harmony Seven who were the first and main band in the hall for many years.

How Danceland was built is what has made it a popular destination for musicians and people who love to dance for more than 75 years.

A layer of horse hair beneath the maple floor, assembled without the use of any nails, is one secret

A six-inch layer of horse hair beneath the maple floor makes Danceland a popular destination.

to the success of Danceland. The cushioning helped prevent strain and fatigue in an era when endurance dancing was popular. Another key factor is the way the rafters and support beams were designed to enhance the flow of music throughout the building.

When Danceland was built there were only three other unique dance floors on the continent. It is believed to be the last remaining dance hall of its kind in North America.

"Walter Ostanek, the Polka King of Canada and a professional musician who has frequently played Danceland, says the two best acoustic halls he ever played in were Carnegie Hall in New York and Danceland," says Mildred Strueby, who has owned the facility with her husband Arnold since 2001.

Danceland is 130 feet long by 110 feet wide with a dance floor 62 feet by 80 feet. Running down each side of the building are wings, or areas for tables and guests.

Across the north end of the dancing area is a horn-shaped bandstand designed to project the dance music forward into the hall. Behind this bandstand is a resting and viewing area glassed in, so that patrons can look over the waters of Little Manitou Lake.

The large curved roof and the side wings play important roles in the quality of the sound produced by the bands. The curved roof is supported by nine trestle-style beams. Open areas within the beams mean that the sound is not forced to rebound but can flow throughout the hall. Lumber was hand cut into 2 by 4 pieces from larger pieces of Douglas fir planks and then securely nailed into cross member sections, 15 for each beam. These beams are a vital component in the design of the building, providing the flexible strength required in the building and contributing to its outstanding acoustics.

The roof is supported by braced upright posts, each sawn from single fir timbers, thus leaving the sides of the dance area open so that the sound will flow to the wings of the building and viewers will have unobstructed viewing of the dancers.

The dance floor rests upon a supporting cushion of coils of horse hair and in turn upon a sub-floor resting on raised beams. There are no nails in the dance floor boards. Each board is double tongue and groove maple held in place by the board next to it.

Construction of the floor began in the centre of the hall. Eleven men worked to complete the floor by clamping boards together, progressively working outwards. When the outside dimensions were reached in all four directions, restraining boards were put in place. These then formed the beginning of the floor for the waiting and business areas surrounding the dance floor.

"Danceland has changed many times to accommodate the music the patrons prefer and it has come around almost full circle to the original delight of dancing," says Marilyn White of Watrous. "We are a generation that appreciates our heritage more and more. This building speaks of our heritage and the initiative that it took our ancestors to come up with such a building."

White has fond memories of Danceland. "When the music starts and the hall comes alive, it is like a welcoming friend who is always ready to accept you in," she says. "I am proud to have had a chance to see and frequent Danceland over the years and hope it is there for our children's children to appreciate."

Danceland, which was insulated in 1996, now is open on weekends 12 months of the year. Admission is $10 to $20 per person, depending on the band.

"Danceland was and still is a romantic place to be," says current co-owner Mildred Strueby. "Danceland truly holds a prominent place in the history of Manitou Beach and of this province Saskatchewan."

Danceland is located at 515 Lake Avenue in Manitou Beach.

CAPITOL THEATRE
Moose Jaw

The Moose Jaw Cultural Centre has been created by renovating and refurbishing three buildings with a rich history.

The Capitol Theatre, built in 1916, is the centrepiece and is flanked by the former Army & Navy Store and A & B Casual Clothing buildings.

A coalition of Moose Jaw arts groups called Arts in Motion (AIM) initiated the project and worked with the city to assemble the property.

"We had a unique opportunity to preserve and protect the heritage of community while establishing a centre for artists in Moose Jaw," said Gary Hyland, Executive Director of AIM. "This is an example of people working with City Hall, not fighting City Hall."

The Moose Jaw Cultural Centre, which opened its doors in April 2004, is a venue for live theatre, with a seating capacity of 443. The Grand Opening Gala event was held on June 19 of that year.

In addition, there is a gallery for emerging artists, board room, wood workshop, two studios for arts and crafts, a pottery area, offices for arts groups, an artist-in-residence office, and work space, as well as administration offices.

"Establishing the Moose Jaw Cultural Centre was the first step," said Dawn Luhning, a member of the centre's fundraising committee. "To maintain the building and ensure we are able to sustain operations for years to come will require the individuals, companies, and organizations in the community to invest their hard-earned dollars with us."

The Capitol Theatre is the key piece of the project from a historical perspective. "People in Vancouver are justly proud of their salvaged Stanley Theatre, which dates back to 1930," said Hyland. "In Edmonton, there's the renovated Roxy, which opened in 1940. Yet, here in Moose Jaw, we have the Capitol Theatre, which has been operating continuously on the city's Main Street since 1916."

The Capitol Theatre, was designed by Calgary architect James McTeague in 1913 as the Monarch Theatre, but due to the First World War the origi-

The Capitol Theatre is but one of many heritage buildings granted a new lease on life by the 35,000 residents of Moose Jaw.
<small>PHOTO COURTESY MOOSE JAW CULTURAL CENTRE</small>

nal theatre was never completed. The Allen Theatre chain took over the building and made changes to the original plans.

By the time the theatre had its grand opening on August 19, 1916, the Allen Theatre in Moose Jaw was the largest theatre in Saskatchewan. The 910-seat theatre operated under the Allen name until 1922 with a policy of showing films up to October 1 and then hosting road shows from Winnipeg's Walker Theatre as well as the vaudeville circuit.

The Theatre operated under the Allen name until 1922. At that time the name was changed to the Capitol Theatre.

In 1929, the theatre was renovated for sound and became Canada's 21st theatre in the Famous Players Chain to receive Movietone and Vitaphone equipment. It was the sixth in western Canada to have the sound improvements.

The renovations of that period were extensive and focused on modernization, including improvements to electrical and ventilation systems, new drapes, and a new stage. The theatre operated in this capacity from 1923 to 1982.

The theatre was subdivided into a 652-seat triplex in 1983 and operated that way until it closed in 2001.

The Capitol Theatre has most of the unique and great architectural features today as it did at the early part of last century.

Despite the array of operators, the age of the building, and the numerous renovations to the building, most of the standard interior features of the 1910 period are still present.

The Capitol Theatre building featured quasi-classical bas-relief panels emblazoned with cherubs and the familiar crest of the Allen Theatre Chain. There is an ornate plaster ceiling, mirrored columns, and tile floors in the lobby with marble entrance stairs and panels along the stairwells to the balcony. All but the balcony, the mirrored columns, and the marble panels have been saved, although the marble was salvaged and used to highlight the entrance to the theatre.

The most striking feature of the exterior is the decorative geometric design created with vari-coloured brick set into three large recessed panels. From above and below, white imprinted mouldings highlight the panels.

While the Capitol Theatre forms the primary venue for the live performances to take place at the new Moose Jaw Cultural Centre, the former Army & Navy Department Store next door at 225 Main Street North provides the administrative area.

The original occupant of the building was the Merchants Bank of Canada. It was constructed in 1918, designed by Storey and Van Egmond. The Merchant Bank was the main tenant until 1922.

An array of retailers and bank offices utilized the building until 1945. The Army & Navy Department Store moved into the building and remained until 2000, when the retailer phased out its Saskatchewan operations.

The building's exterior presents an excellent brick pattern. Some detailing had been lost due to renovations. The interior ambience and decoration still remains and the façade is made from the same material as the Capitol Theatre.

The final piece of the puzzle to create a location for the cultural centre was the former A & B Casual Clothing building at 213 Main Street North, on the other side of the Capitol Theatre.

The building was constructed in 1909 for Manley, Loney and Co. Real Estate, which occupied the facility until 1915. Retailers, insurance agents, doctors, dentists, and musicians were all tenants from 1915 until May 31, 2002

Moose Jaw's Cultural Centre provides a vision of the future for the arts in the community by building around the heritage of one of the few lasting images of the golden era of cinema, The Capitol Theatre.

The Capitol Theatre, located at 217 Main Street North in Moose Jaw, was designated a Municipal Heritage Property on December 3, 2001.

ASSINIBOIA CLUB
Regina

The Assiniboia Club, originally founded in 1882 by eight men who had a love of music, has survived drought, boom-and-bust economic cycles linked to agriculture and even a cyclone in 1912 to become western Canada's oldest private club.

"In the early days, the Assiniboia Club provided a stark contract to the train ride across the wide open prairie and the tent city that greeted the pioneers," said Larry Deters, president of the club in 2004. "Over the 122 years of its existence it has left visiting dignitaries of the City of Regina with a much different impression than was often their original notion."

Local business and community leaders, civic, provincial, and federal politicians along with members of the British Royal family and Hollywood stars such as Drew Barrymore have enjoyed private dining in the Assiniboia Club over the years.

The three-storey brown brick building, designed in the Queen Anne Revival style by architects Storey and Van Egmond, was constructed in 1912 by Smith and Wilson Company for $57,400. It is the fifth and final location occupied by the Assiniboia Club.

"Of particular importance is the image of the capital city having a corresponding gathering point of the kind that is provided by all other capital cities," Deters said.

The Assiniboia Club is affiliated with similar private clubs in every provincial capital, plus the Rideau Club in Ottawa and the Calgary Petroleum Club. Individual membership costs $750 per year while corporate memberships are $3,500, which can be enjoyed by six employees.

"The Assiniboia Club not only provides a centre for visiting business executives and local people, its history is full of rich and interesting stories," Deters said. "Modern day amenities are contrasted to the folklore or our past."

He said a room now reserved for Internet and satellite communications is believed to be the home of a female ghost from the turn of the century.

Food, hospitality, and even lodging were services provided over the years by the Assiniboia Club. The first president was an Anglican bishop, the Right Reverend Dr. Adelbert Anson.

The Assiniboia Club was a male-only bastion until 1988, when Dr. Roberta McKay, head of medicine at the Plains Health Centre, and Lt. Gov. Sylvia Fedoruk were voted members.

Suffering from declining membership, a stagnant economy, and more stringent tax laws regarding the ability to deduct entertainment and food as a business expense, the club closed in 1994.

The rebirth of the Assiniboia Club, and of the building itself, is attributed to Garry Huntington, a local entrepreneur who bought the building in 1996 for more than $750,000 and began an aggressive renovation effort.

Huntington, a long-time member of the Assiniboia Club, had the building's mechanical systems upgraded and interior redecorated and modernized, while retaining the distinctive architectural features of the Storey and Van Egmond design.

He turned the main floor into an upscale restaurant, Danbry's, and leased the upper two floors to the Assiniboia Club. Huntington's 1996 idea was to have the restaurant provide food and management services to the Assiniboia Club, which would share operating cost.

"Danbry's, as the landlord, is supplying all the services, not just food and beverage, which allows for a very stream-lined, cost-effective organization," said Garth Fredrickson, president of the Assiniboia Club a year after it reopened in 1998. "What the old club wanted to be was a very expensive proposition." The Assiniboia Club, for many years, had its own chef, kitchen, and serving staff as well as a full-time manager.

The renovated Assiniboia Club can seat more than 200 people for dining as well as provide private rooms for breakfast meetings and working lunches and dinners.

Evolution continued in 1999 with the election of Mary Ann Davidson, a partner with KPMG, an accounting and business consulting firm, as the first female president of the Assiniboia Club. "The club has to reflect the business community to

which it provides services," Davidson said in a newspaper interview at the time.

The Assiniboia Club is located at 1925 Victoria Avenue in Regina.

The club was founded in 1882 by eight men who had a love of music.
PHOTO COURTESY SASKATCHEWAN HERITAGE FOUNDATION

BROADWAY THEATRE
Saskatoon

People of all ages have cried, laughed and sat spellbound watching live entertainment, foreign films, and black-and-white classics such as *Casablanca* at the Broadway Theatre in Saskatoon since 1946.

The Broadway Theatre also provided the cornerstone around which the renaissance of the Nutana neighbourhood in south Saskatoon began to flourish almost 40 years later.

"Being involved with this theatre for so many years has been an enlightening experience because of the amount of dedication shown by so many individuals working together to keep the doors open," said Phyllis Cameron, who has worked as a projectionist and concession stand operator at the Broadway Theatre since 1979. "This building has a heart. It is maintained by the hearts of all the people that believe in its mandate."

Cameron's first experience with the Broadway Theatre came in 1969 when she saw her first foreign film there. "The movie was the 1969 Academy Award winner for Best Foreign Language Film, *Z*, by director Costa-Gavras," she recalled "This film opened my youthful innocent eyes to political reality and lessons that have never been forgotten."

Cameron is proud of the niche the Broadway Theatre provides to the people of Saskatoon and the Nutana neighbourhood.

"Since almost all other cinemas are part of mega-chains showing American blockbusters, theatres like the Broadway are integral in getting the opportunity to watch movies made in our own country," Cameron said. "There would be no lack of cultural identity for Canadians if only more of us would go out to watch the wonderful movies made here."

Susan Pederson-Bradbury is extremely enthusiastic when she talks about her love affair with the Broadway Theatre

"Like many people who grew up in rural areas outside of Saskatoon, I did not become fully acquainted with the Broadway Theatre until I began attending university," she said. "So as my post-secondary schooling began, so did my film education—an eclectic syllabus of silver screen classics, notable repertory films from all corners of the world, independent oddities, and the weekend kids' matinees."

The Broadway was a natural place for first dates and nights out with friends, Pederson-Bradbury said. "The most delicious experience though was a dark and solitary couple of hours with only myself, a silent cadre of fellow film-lovers, and the magical, flickering images dancing on the screen," she said. "How many 30-somethings can boast that they saw *Casablanca* and *Singin' in the Rain* for the very first time on the big screen?"

The Broadway Theatre, she added, is the only place in Saskatchewan where you can hear 17th-century string instruments and modern jazz, dress up like nuns and alien transvestites for a mass sing-along, or catch a world-class play straight from Edinburgh Fringe Festival.

The Broadway Theatre was constructed in 1946 for Isber F. Shaker, who was Mayor of Hanna, Alberta, at the time, and owned a series of independent theatres in the west.

The Art Deco design of the post-Second World War era is reflected in the seamless exterior made of brick, tile, and concrete. At the time, it was an ultra-modern building with state-of-the-art electrical, sound, and projection capabilities, most of which still function today. It had a 700-seat capacity and boasted the largest neon marquee between Winnipeg and Edmonton when it opened.

The building is 50 feet wide by 125 feet deep and features futuristic ceilings and wall designs as well as a parabolic floor.

The first movie screened at The Broadway Theatre was *Shine On, Harvest Moon,* a biographical look at a Nora Bayes and Jack Norworth, a pair of 20th-century stars of Broadway in New York City.

The 1984 rejuvenation of the Broadway Theatre became one of the early boosts to the revitalization of the whole community of Nutana. This was the first area in Saskatoon to embrace its history and market itself on it.

The Broadway Theatre is the only medium-sized theatre in Saskatoon and as such fills an important niche in that city's ability to host many cultural events. It broadens the cultural and artistic fibre of the entire city by bringing unique and varied entertainment. The Broadway Theatre brings people to Broadway Avenue.

The 2002 restoration to the exterior building brought the façade and the marquee back to its original magnificence. The interior has had significant infrastructure upgrades. The auditorium and basement have been renovated to improve stage and behind-stage activities, and new seats have been installed for patron comfort.

The 560-seat theatre now is open daily with a wide variety of live and film entertainment attracting more than 50,000 patrons each year. All enjoy real butter on the popcorn!

The Broadway Theatre, located at 715 Broadway Avenue in Saskatoon, was designated a Municipal Heritage Site on April 14, 1997.

THE LYRIC
Swift Current

Joey Donnelly never saw a movie or a vaudeville act at the Lyric Theatre but is among a group of Swift Current people convinced the 1912 building should be saved.

"I think the Lyric could be used to draw people to the downtown area," he said. "There are many people in this province who think: Let's get rid of it then ask questions later. I think there's a better way."

Donnelly, a teacher's assistant, thinks residents of Swift Current could learn from how the Capitol Theatre in Moose Jaw and the Broadway Theatre in Saskatoon have continued to play a vital role in each of those cities entertainment industries. "The Lyric has been used by every generation in Swift Current," Donnelly said. "This is an important building for our history and for our future."

The Lyric Theatre was built in 1912 for $50,000 by a partnership of several local businessmen. It was sold to the Allen Theatre chain in 1918 and in 1926 to the Swift Current Amusement Company. F. J. Lundholm was a partner in the company and took over complete ownership of The Lyric in 1928.

The Lyric hosted vaudeville shows in its early years. Change rooms for performers on the second floor were rented out as apartments after the building was converted to a movie theatre in 1918.

The Lyric was also used for other purposes throughout the years. Dances and dance classes, poultry and pet shows, and fowl suppers were regular features in the basement. It also served as an isolation hospital during the Spanish flu epidemic of 1918.

In the late 1920s, the army cadets set up headquarters in The Lyric. Bob Dahl was 15 years old in 1930 when he became a cadet. "We met in the basement of The Lyric," Dahl said. "We learned wireless communication and it was used as a drill hall when the weather was poor. There was also a shooting range."

Movies cost just 10 cents, he said, so virtually everyone his age went to the Lyric on Saturday afternoons.

Church services and revivals were held at the Lyric over a number of years by congregations that did not yet have their own building. The theatre was also used for traveling and local variety shows, Sunday musical concerts, and plays.

The Lyric was, foremost, a movie theatre. It remained in the Lundholm family until 1969 and was used as a theatre until 1981. It was remodeled and served as a nightclub under a variety of themes and owners until it closed in 2003.

Mable Bruce grew up two blocks from the Lyric Theatre. "On certain long summer evenings, Roy Rogers movies were featured," she recalled.

"Occasionally, my older sister and I were allowed to attend. This was during the 1940s and there was always a newsreel featuring stories about the war. At that time, we had my father and three uncles in the Royal Canadian Air Force (RCAF) and an aunt in the Canadian Women's Army Corps (CWAC), so we had a personal interest in those frightening news pictorials."

Ron Phaneuf, whose father was the manager at the Lyric during the 1960s and 1970s, describes himself as a theatre brat. "I remember the buzz of a big show like *The Sound of Music*," Ron said. "Big shows meant long hours, people waiting in the lobby downstairs, and line-ups outside."

He said customers were treated like guests, with staff greeting each and keeping things organized.

"The waiting room in the downstairs lobby had an Art Deco design—round corners, torch lights, and furniture of that design," Phaneuf said. "Clean-up duty after the Saturday matinee netted all the kids a free show-pass which was worth 25 cents. I sold my pass."

Donnelly became interested in the Lyric upon returning home to Swift Current from Carleton University in Ottawa. The more research he did on the building and what was happening in the city when it opened in 1912, the more excited he got about its heritage.

"At that time, Swift Current was known as a theatre district along the CPR that enjoyed four playhouses," he said. "The first to be built in 1910 was the Unique Theatre, now Jamal Contracting, followed by the Princess Royal and her rotating stage. Both closed due to the competition from the

Eagle, now Backstage Dance, and the Lyric. Those two theatres eventually merged into the Swift Current Amusement Company."

The Lyric was by far, the most impressive of all, Donnelly said. "With a seating capacity of over 400 people, the building hosted countless events, shows, and concerts," he said.

"We are living in an important time when citizens of Swift Current must decide on the fate of these heritage buildings," Donnelly added.

Memorable Swift Current buildings built during the early 1900s include the old City Hall, built as a Post Office in 1912 and converted for municipal use in 1957, which was torn down in 2003, the First United Church, the Professional Building, Carlton Hotel, which burned down in 2003, and the former Healy Hotel.

"The Lyric was special," Donnelly said. "Where else in Swift Current has one building played Charlie Chaplin shorts, hypnotists, musicals, classic films and a local punk band?"

The Lyric Theatre is located at 225 Central Avenue North in Swift Current.

The Lyric is among only a few buildings remaining in Saskatchewan built in 1912. PHOTO COURTESY SWIFT CURRENT MUSEUM

FAITH

"It was an awe-inspiring site the first time I saw the [Holy Trinity Anglican] Church from the settlement across the Churchill River. My first thought was: What was this beautiful church doing, basically, in the middle of nowhere?"

–RCMP Corporal Gary Ritchie

A common bond among the province's early pioneers was their religious beliefs. Immigrants banded together, pooling their skills and resources, to build places to worship as soon as they were able to put a roof over the heads of their families. Some buildings took a few months to complete, while others took years or even decades to finish.

From simple one-room log and timber buildings to magnificent churches of fieldstone and brick built to mirror the majestic cathedrals of Europe, symbols of Saskatchewan pioneers' religious backgrounds rose above the prairies and pine. Many of those symbols of faith and optimism are still in use today.

A common link among the religious buildings regardless of the faith they represented was the desire of the pioneers to have places to worship in an environment that reflected or reminded them of their homelands.

This is classically illustrated in the first Anglican church constructed in the province, which has become recognized as the oldest building in Saskatchewan. Literally every nail and hinge, window and door, floor plank and wall support was shipped from England to North America with the missionaries. Even the steeple at Stanley Mission was brought to the heavily treed, remote wilderness along the Churchill River in northern Saskatchewan.

Other churches, however, are only touchstones of the pioneers' deep-rooted belief in their religion and traditional values. For example, the Shiloh Baptist Church near Maidstone in northwestern Saskatchewan marks the first organized emigration into the province of African American pioneers. The one-room log building was built in 1911 by African Americans who had been born free men or who had been freed from slavery years after the Civil War.

Their southern Baptist values are reflected in the style, structure and setting of not only the one-room log church but the nearby cemetery. Both have an east–west axis to align the rising and setting of the sun. Their loved ones were laid to rest with their feet facing the east so when the sun rose each morning it would shine on their faces.

More time and effort was spent designing and completing the interiors of several churches with lavish, life-sized images of saints and religious symbols as well as intricately crafted stained glass windows.

Religious institutions in Saskatchewan continue to withstand the test of time as focal points in communities of all sizes and across all parts of the province.

Proof of the continuing bonds of faith came during the nomination process for *Building Our Future: A People's Architectural History of Saskatchewan.* About 43 percent of the nominations were in the faith category.

BETH ISRAEL SYNAGOGUE
Edenbridge

Descendents of Jewish settlers who immigrated to Saskatchewan from Lithuania in 1905 have ensured the pioneering spirit of their forefathers will be appreciated for decades to come.

Beth Israel, the first synagogue built in rural Saskatchewan, the nearby cemetery, and 40 acres of land untouched by human hands within a stone's throw of the Carrot River now are part of the Saskatchewan Wildlife Federation's Habitat Trust Fund.

"This means that no one will be able to develop any of the land," says Jim Kroshus, project coordinator of the SWF's Habitat Trust Fund. "We will continue to work with people in the area to preserve the synagogue so future generations can see one of the most remarkable religious buildings in the province."

Coyotes, white-tailed deer and red fox amble through the 40 acres of unbroken parkland, one of the last examples of untouched mature aspen forest in one of the most developed agricultural areas of Saskatchewan.

The Edenbridge property was donated to the Habitat Trust in 1989 by Charlie Vickar and his cousin Norm "Little" Vickar, sons of the two key members of the group of 56 Jewish families that settled in the area. Charlie had been an active member of the Saskatchewan Wildlife Federation for 40 years and thought the donation of the synagogue and land would preserve and protect the heritage and memory of his pioneering relatives.

"This part of Saskatchewan and all of our neighbouring communities have benefited because of the hard work, entrepreneurial efforts, and strong sense of family value of the people who built Edenbridge," says Rod Gantefoer, a Melfort businessman and member of the Saskatchewan legislative assembly since 1995.

"We all continue to benefit today from their remarkable efforts, which included hundreds of thousands of hours of volunteer time and effort over the decades. We are all better off today in this part of Saskatchewan because of the Edenbridge settlers."

Homesteading families took an indirect route to the bush and fertile land around the Carrot River North of Melfort, Gantefoer said.

"The Edenbridge colony has its history in Lithuania when a young man of 20 years of age, born in 1877, immigrated to Cape Colony, South Africa," he said in his 1996 maiden speech in the Saskatchewan Legislature.

The Boer War had just begun, but David Vickar was fortunate enough to get a job in the merchandising business.

"His first dollar earned he sent to his impoverished father and then saved so he could bring his two sisters and two brothers out of Lithuania," Gantefoer said.

"The reason for the immigration: Jewish people lived in slums, weren't allowed to own property, were not regarded as citizens, were scapegoats for every problem, were not protected by the law. They were spat upon, insulted, beaten by drunks and their homes were destroyed."

In 1905, he said the Vickar brothers saw a newspaper advertisement promoting immigration to Saskatchewan.

"They were offered 160 acres of virgin land for $10," Gantefoer said. "This group became the nucleus of what was to become known as the Edenbridge Colony."

The 56 families opted for the Carrot River parcels because its terrain was similar to their home in Lithunia. After constructing simple wooden homes for their own shelters, they pooled their efforts to establish a cemetery in their first year of settling and then worked together to build the House of Israel Synagogue in 1909. It became the only rural synagogue in Saskatchewan.

Sam and David were not only leaders of the Jewish settlers but became pillars of the community.

David served 32 years on the local school board and was the first Postmaster of the Edenbridge Post Office. He was the reeve of the rural municipality of Willow Creek No. 458 for a total of 22 years, first from 1915 to 1917 and then from 1928 to 1947, when ill health forced his retirement.

David Vickar was instrumental in introducing one of the first medical and hospital plans in the province into the area.

The synagogue, nearby cemetery and 40 acres of unbroken parkland are now part of a habitat trust fund.
PHOTO COURTESY SASKATCHEWAN HERITAGE FOUNDATION

Sam, who was six years younger than David, served as reeve of the rural municipality after David stepped down in 1947 until 1958. Sam also was a school board trustee for 31 years and a councillor of the rural municipality from 1928 to 1935.

He was a tireless worker for everyone in the community. He helped organize the Edenbridge Hebrew Farmers' Credit Union and the Edenbridge Credit Union. In addition, he helped organize the local Saskatchewan Co-op and Pool elevators and was one of the delegates to the founding convention of the Saskatchewan Co-op Elevators, which became the Saskatchewan Wheat Pool.

Sam served as a Red Cross representative during the First World War and during the Second World War he was chairman of the local war finance committee. At the Coronation of Queen Elizabeth, he received a medal from the minister of the interior for distinguished service as a public servant.

More than 20 years later, his son, Norm, became a member of the Legislative Assembly for the area and held several portfolios in the cabinet of NDP Premier Allan Blakeney, including minister of industry, trade and commerce.

Construction of a steel bridge across the nearby Carrot River in the winter of 1906–1907 was a critical event in the growth of the Jewish community. For a wage of 20-cents-per hour, homesteaders were hired. Hundreds of round trips by oxen to Star City, the nearest rail centre, brought the supplies to the site to build the bridge.

When the Post Office was opened a year later, the community needed a name. Federal government officials wanted to avoid ethnic or religious names and refused suggestions of Jewish Bridge or Israel Villa.

Eventually, the same officials allowed the name Edenbridge, likely unaware that the word *Eden* is derived from the Hebrew translation meaning Jewish, since a bridge had been erected over the Carrot River. The words were combined to name the first Post Office. It was a variation of Yiddenbridge, meaning Bridge of Jews.

Within three years of their arrival, they built a synagogue that would serve the congregation for 60 years, imported a rabbi, created a library with Yiddish and English literature, and established a commercial industry with kosher butcheries and stores. They organized drama and debating societies, Yiddish and Hebrew studies, and a youth movement called Young Judeans Club. Children attended daily Hebrew and Torah lessons.

Ultimately, the attractions of urban life lured the younger generations away, while farm mechanization made it difficult for small farmers to compete. An exodus from Edenbridge continued from the late 1930s until the synagogue closed in 1968.

"We're very proud and pleased that the significant contributions to our community will continue to live on because the Beth Israel Synagogue now is part of the Saskatchewan Wildlife Federation's Habitat Trust program," concludes Gantefoer.

The Beth Israel Synagogue, named a Provincial Heritage Site in 2003, is located about 28 kilometres north of Star City, which is about 16 kilometres east of Melfort. The synagogue is open to the public all year. There is no admission charge, but donations are welcomed.

SALVATION ARMY
Estevan

A stone church, occupied by the Salvation Army since 1949, has been the home for several different faiths in Estevan for more than a century.

"I wonder if the original builders could have imagined that someday their little stone church would see 100 years," said Becky, daughter-in-law of Captains Linda and Kirk Green, who have operated the Salvation Army Estevan Corps since 2000.

The church is the only building that faces true north and south on a lot in Estevan.

"Historically speaking, the building binds together a wide variety of people within Estevan's faith community as well as being for some a kind of anchor to the past," she said.

It is one of only two stone structures still standing in the southeastern Saskatchewan city.

It has 30-inch stone walls and, although the wooden bell tower had to be removed years ago due to wind damage, it still retains most of its original appeal.

Through the years, various changes have occurred, including finishing the basement from its original rough wood interior and installation of a lowered ceiling for heating purposes, that hides the original tongue-and-groove wood in the open ceiling.

"In addition, exterior changes have included the installation of metal soffit and facia, and upgraded windows," she said. "These changes have stopped more than 500 bats from making the upper reaches of the church their home!"

The Estevan Salvation Army Corps Church originally belonged to the Presbyterian Church. From 1892 to 1902, the Presbyterian worshippers had been gathering in their homes and in the local stone school.

However, as the number of worshippers grew, it became evident that a church building was needed. Many Presbyterian members gave of their time, resources, and assets to help build the stone structure, which was completed in 1902 and dedicated the following year with the name Westminster Church.

The walls of the stone church in Estevan, home of the Salvation Army since 1949, are almost a metre thick.

In 1920, the interior of the Trinity Church across the street was damaged by a fire. So the Presbyterians invited the Methodists to worship in their church until the damage could be repaired. Unknowingly, this was a foreshadowing of an amalgamation of the two religious organizations that would take place only a few years later.

Westminster Church also sustained an interior fire in 1921, and the two congregations soon joined together as one. The new congregation became known as the Estevan United Church, then, in 1932, changed their name to St. Paul's United Church.

They worshipped at the original site of the Methodist Church and used the Westminster Church for other activities.

Realizing the need for a larger facility, St. Paul's added an addition to its church so that all activities could be carried on in one building. This made way for the Westminster Church to be sold to the Salvation Army in 1949.

"There is something awe inspiring about a building that has seen so many changes and yet its structure stays the same," Captain Green said.

"To some it may have been a haven—a lifeboat in the storms of life. To others, it was a place of rest, peace, joy, and laughter."

The Salvation Army Church is located at 202 Third Street in Estevan.

ECCLESIASTICAL BUILDINGS
Gravelbourg

Our Lady of Assumption Roman Catholic Cathedral in Gravelbourg, more than half a football field long, was built in 1919 to allow 1,500 people to celebrate mass together and remains an icon for the French-Canadian community in the west.

"One of the things that is truly amazing is the vision people had to build such a structure for the future," explained Henri S. LePage, mayor of Gravelbourg since 1991 and a life-long resident of the community 150 kilometres southwest of Regina. "This building has been passed down to their descendents and we will continue to care and love it for future generations."

The church was built at a cost of $96,618 starting in 1918 and was completed in October 1919. It was dedicated to St. Philomena on November 5, 1919, and was named a cathedral on July 27, 1930.

However, the name was changed to Notre-Dame de l'Assomption in 1963 after the name of St. Philomena was removed from the Roman calendar by the Vatican.

Architect Joseph Ernest Fortin chose a style that combined the Romanesque and Italian Renaissance.

He also incorporated state-of-the-art architectural technology in his design, including a steel structure, steel roof trusses, a concrete foundation, and a floor slab. Many believe Fortin's design mirrored the then-recently completed Basilica in St. Boniface, Manitoba.

The Gravelbourg Cathedral is 200 feet (54.8 metres) long, 85 feet (25.9 metres) wide at the transepts, and 65 feet (19.8 metres) high with twin 175-foot (53.5 metres) high towers. By comparison, Holy Rosary Cathedral in the diocesan centre of Regina is about 175 feet long, with spires reaching 165 feet. The outside walls are made of fireproof brick, light tan in colour, trimmed with Indiana limestone.

"The cathedral dominates this community—not only because it towers over a wide expanse of prairie—but because it is a source of constant inspiration, fascinating in its most intricate details,

A style that combined the Romanesque and Italian Renaissance was selected for the Ecclesiastical Buildings in Gravelbourg.
PHOTO COURTESY SASKATCHEWAN HERITAGE FOUNDATION

More than 1,500 people can attend services in the co-cathedral.
Photo courtesy Saskatchewan Heritage Foundation

It took Charles Maillard, the second pastor of Gravelbourg, a decade to paint the interior decorations.
Photo courtesy Saskatchewan Heritage Foundation

a symphony of changing colours," said lawyer Louis Stringer. "It is at the heart of this community where people come to worship, admire or praise in their own way."

All of the interior decorations were painted over a 10-year period, ending in 1931, by Charles Maillard, the second pastor of Gravelbourg. He was a priest-painter who asked members of the community to be models for his depictions of the Stations of the Cross.

Because canvas was expensive and difficult to obtain in the 1920s in southern Saskatchewan, Maillard painted on the back of linoleum because it was moisture resistant.

"Amazingly, Monsignor Charles Maillard adorned the cathedral from end to end with his biblical representations and did so without signing one single painting because he considered himself a priest and then a painter," Stringer said.

Mayor LePage said that an unusual benefit for the community has been the cathedral has become a popular tourist attraction, with

thousands of people making the pilgrimage to Gravelbourg each year.

"Most of us who are Roman Catholics and attend mass every Sunday sometimes think the mass here has become a little mundane and don't realize what we have in Gravelbourg," said the mayor. "If I go to mass elsewhere, it's not quite the same. You feel as though there is something left out of the service."

The Cathedral, former bishop's residence, and adjacent convent are referred to as the Gravelbourg Ecclesiastical Buildings.

"The Ecclesiastical Buildings are part of a religious and educational ensemble that speaks of the courage and devotion of our ancestors who came to this area of this province with very little but willingly gave of themselves for things they valued," said Stringer.

The bishop's residence, built in 1918 next to the rising cathedral, is privately owned. It is unusual among the Franco-Catholic colonies for its stylistic sophistication.

Convent Jésus-Marie is believed to be the largest and most architecturally ambitious convent school erected in the Franco-Catholic colonies. Few of these schools in western Canada, if any, approach its scale and character.

Louis-Joseph-Pierre Gravel wanted Gravelbourg to become a centre for French-language Catholic education.

Faced with an ever-growing student body, the four-storey structure was built between 1917 and 1918 with facilities for boarding female students. The convent school was greatly enlarged in 1927 to

a total length of 300 feet and a capacity of nearly 400 students.

The convent was sold to the local public school board in the 1970s and now is home to the Gravelbourg Elementary School.

The Gravelbourg buildings stand as significant landmarks to the architectural aspirations of the Roman Catholic Church in the early days of Saskatchewan's development as a province. Franco-Catholic settlements aspired to the best architecture within their means and the Gravelbourg buildings, as a group, are of particularly high architectural quality, unsurpassed in scale and stylistic sophistication among the dozens of Franco-Catholic colonies that dot the prairies.

The key buildings are all the work of Joseph Ernest Fortin, a Montreal-trained, Saskatchewan-based architect who almost single-handedly rendered in built form the ambitions of the province's nascent Franco-Catholic community. The ecclesiastical buildings stand as the most significant example of the built heritage of the Franco-Catholic colonizers in western Canada.

When Gravelbourg became part of the Archdiocese of Regina several years ago, the facility

was designated co-cathedral rather than reverting back to its status simply as a church to show the significance it holds in the hearts and minds of people in the community.

Our Lady of the Assumption Roman Catholic Co-Cathedral, located at 116 First Avenue West in Gravelbourg, was designated a Municipal Heritage Property on March 26, 1987.

The cathedral is among three buildings that comprise the Gravelbourg Ecclesiastical Buildings National Historic Site that was designated by the Historic Sites and Monuments Board of Canada in 1995.

This rather spartan image of the Boys' Residence, circa 1917, was made into postcards at the time.
Photo courtesy College Mathieu

The former Bishop's Residence is among the Ecclesiastical Buildings designated a National Historic Site of Canada in 1995.
Photo courtesy College Mathieu

SACRED HEART
Lebret

Bishop Tache asked that a stone church be built on the shores of Mission Lake some distance away from the Ft. Qu'Appelle fur trading post.
PHOTO COURTESY SASKATCHEWAN HERITAGE FOUNDATION

People have been gathering at a Métis settlement along the shores of Mission Lake, about 65 kilometres north east of Regina, to celebrate a Roman Catholic mass since 1864.

They came first on foot and horseback and canoe, then by train and automobile to the field-stone church at Lebret on the shores of Mission Lake. A cross atop the nearby hill helps people find the Sacred Heart of Jesus Church, rectory, and Stations of the Cross. All have achieved heritage designation status. It is one of the oldest parishes in Saskatchewan.

Guy Blondeau, who has been the organist at the church, as he says "on and off for more than 30 years," believes the Lebret mission site blends with the natural scenery. "The valley is beautiful and the church is part of it," Blondeau said.

"The church has an atmosphere of its own. It is an old-fashioned design that makes it a very beautiful place to worship and an easy church to pray in."

He appreciates the sturdiness with which the church was constructed in 1925. "It was built to last for a long time," Blondeau said. "We feel that we are looking after it for the next generation."

The church is a symbol of many things for the people of the Qu'Appelle Valley around Lebret, he said. "We work, we play and we pray together," Blondeau said. "A church is the people doing things together. This church is a reminder of our past and our hope for the future."

Sacred Heart Church is so much more than a building, he said. "It's been a part of the Saskatchewan landscape for decades," Blondeau said.

Jim Laroque, 83, lives in Fort Qu'Appelle, about a 15 minute drive from Lebret, yet still attends Sacred Heart.

"This church means everything to us," Laroque explained. "We haven't had a parish priest in more than 10 years but we still go to church every Sunday. Lay people conduct lay-presided services and it's still very special for us"

Laroque, an unofficial historian for the Lebret mission site, said the Qu'Appelle Valley was the most natural route from Manitoba into southern Saskatchewan in the 1860s. Many trails to other parts of what was then called the North-West Territories originated in the Qu'Appelle Valley.

Bishop Tache, during one of his many treks throughout the territory, wrote about his view of the Qu'Appelle Valley on October 6, 1865.

"It would be difficult to express the surprise and emotion that I felt at the moment. I stopped my horse to admire the superb panorama that was unfolding under my eyes," Tache wrote. "It was one of those magnificent Fall days that our Canadian North-West can justly be proud of. Streams of lights flooded the Qu'Appelle Valley that throve on the sweet freshness of the purest air."

At the end of a four-week mission, that included administering the sacrament of confirmation, Bishop Tache kept his promise to the Métis and established a new mission at the east end of Mission Lake. Bishop Tache purposely chose the site a considerable distance away from the Hudson's Bay Trading Company post at Fort Qu'Appelle because problems surrounding the consumption of alcohol were not uncommon.

Jules Decorby, an Oblate, became the first resident priest in 1868. His house was also the first church.

After the first church burned, a second church and residence was built in 1870. The church, made entirely of wood, faced the lake so that it would be convenient for those who arrived by canoe.

In 1884, Rev. Louis Lebret was named pastor of the mission. The following year, he asked to have the name of the parish changed from St. Florent to Sacre Coeur de Jesus or Sacred Heart of Jesus.

That same year, the community began to receive mail. Father Lebret was appointed the first Postmaster and the community became known as Lebret. It was incorporated as a village under the name of Lebret in 1911, the same year the first train arrived in the community.

After the church was expanded several times, a third church made of fieldstone was constructed in 1925. It could seat 500.

It is arguably one of the most picturesque churches in the west and was blessed by Archbishop Mathieu on July 1, 1926. It was designed by Brother de Byle and built at a cost of $38,000.

"People from the area brought stones each Sunday that were used to construct their new church that still stands today," Laroque said.

"The cornerstone was laid in 1925, but there's an error with the Roman numerals. If you look closely and translate correctly it reads 2015 not 1925. Check the next time you visit."

The Gothic-style fieldstone structure features a narthex, transepts, and belfry tower with spire.

The rectory, continually in use since its construction in 1886, is one of the oldest buildings in Lebret still in use. It served as the site of the first Lebret Post Office. The wood frame structure features an open veranda with double post on pedestal support, and a simple central dormer surmounted with a Celtic-style cross. This 1929 shrine chapel and Stations of the Cross replaced an earlier 1919 chapel.

The 15-foot wooden cross, erected in 1894, at the top of the hill was replaced in 1966 with illuminated steel. The wood frame chapel features an open steeple.

The Lebret Roman Catholic Mission Site, located 65 kilometres northeast of Regina on Highway 56, was declared a Municipal Heritage Site on December 3, 1985.

The Métis community that sprang up around the church now is named for the first past of the mission, Reverend Louis Lebret.
PHOTO COURTESY SASKATCHEWAN HERITAGE FOUNDATION

SHILOH BAPTIST CHURCH
Maidstone

The Shiloh Baptist Church, a one-room log building constructed in 1911, marks the first organized immigration into Saskatchewan of African American pioneers. The nearby cemetery is the only African American cemetery in the province.

Leander K. Lane is among those trying to preserve the memories of the group now remembered as the Shiloh People, named in honour of the little log building they once worshipped in. His great-grandfather Julius Caesar Lane, was a founding member and leader of the Shiloh Colony as well as the first person buried in Shiloh cemetery.

"In my experience, I have found that most Canadians are not aware that African American pioneer settlements once existed in Alberta and Saskatchewan. The curriculum of the schools and exhibits of the museums, celebrate a pioneer stock made up of the English, German, Ukrainian, and American settlers," he said. "The unique story of the black pioneers, on the other hand, is forgotten."

Churches were used for more than just religious celebrations, Lane said. "Many of the most senior members of the Shiloh Colony had been born into, or lived during slavery. After freedom, the church became the prime social organization, around which the African American community revolved," he said.

"After slavery our ancestors remained segregated from white society and institutions. As the slaves adapted to freedom, the church or meeting house served as a community centre and school, as well as a place of refuge and worship. When they immigrated to Canada, our African American ancestors brought many of the traditions of the old South with them," he said. "A deep and abiding religious faith was part of those traditions.

Shortly after the Oklahoma and Indian Territory merged to become a state in 1907, laws were passed that discriminated against African Americans.

"Segregation, and laws to take away the African Americans right to vote, encouraged our ancestors to take serious note of advertisements for free homesteads in western Canada," Lane said.

These ads appeared in newspapers, on bulletin boards at railway stations, and other public places. The ads proclaimed: "Free Land for the Millions, One Hundred and Sixty Acres of Free Land!"

Many of the black immigrants settled in Alberta; however, a small group of families led by Julius Caesar Lane established the Shiloh Colony 29 kilometres northeast of Maidstone, in the rural municipality of Eldon.

In early 1910, these first families—or the Original 10 as they're sometimes called—settled in the school districts of Eldon, Standard Hill, McLaren, and Milleton. These districts are located in the northeast section of the municipality, bordered on the south by big Gully Creek, and the north by the North Saskatchewan River. The area is isolated even by today's standards, with only a few farms scattered throughout the area.

Western Canada became a popular immigration destination for the African Americans. The 1901 national census records a population of 61 Negroes in Manitoba, 1 Negro in Saskatchewan, and a population of 37 Negroes living in Alberta. Ten years later, in 1911, the African American population of the three prairie provinces was 209 in Manitoba, 306 in Saskatchewan, and 979 in Alberta.

Charles Wesley Speers, who had been appointed general colonization agent for western Canada in 1897, was instructed to prepare a report in late 1910 about the growing number of African American immigrants.

In a letter to J. Bruce Walker, commissioner of immigration in Winnipeg, Speers wrote that the attitude towards black immigration among other pioneers was hostile and that outright racism was expressed by many people. "It would be unwise to retard the prospective advent of 200,000 good white people on account of the admission of a limited number of coloured people," Speers wrote.

"In addition to this, the sentiment is so strong throughout the districts in which these people are settling that I am obliged to appreciate and recognize public opinion and make the recommendation that this work of bringing in numbers of coloured people be intercepted by such prohibitory means as the wisdom of the department may deem expedient."

Policy was changed, and the flood of immigrants became a trickle, with a net increase of just 60 African Americans into Saskatchewan in the following decade to total 396 people.

The one-room log building measured about 21 feet by 25 feet and, at first, was covered by a sod roof until sheathing and hand-made shingles were available.

The first African American settlers in Saskatchewan built the church.
PHOTO COURTESY SASKATCHEWAN HERITAGE FOUNDATION

Visitors to the church today can see how the settlers squared up each log to eliminate insects and rot.

The small logs, about 10 to 12 inches wide, were easier to handle and transport over poor or nonexistent roads. The white poplar logs were cut and then hauled by ox-drawn wagon from the banks of the North Saskatchewan River, located just a few miles north of Shiloh Church.

Each log of the building was squared up with an axe then joined at the corners with dovetailed joints. Many of the logs were lapped halfway to make up the length of the building. Limestone from nearby fields was burnt to make lime for the chinks in the walls.

By squaring the logs, the pioneers eliminated all bugs and rot, most of which existed under the bark and the first few inches of wood. Overlapping shorter logs to make up length, along with the full dovetailed joints at the corners, display the pioneers' technical skill and experience in log-building construction. Three small windows on the north, south, and west walls let in light.

The most striking feature of the interior is the wood benches of various styles of construction. All are original and some are obviously very old. A few of the benches are made of peeled willow branches pegged into hand-hewn logs. Some have rough plank seats, with and without, plank backs.

"It is clear that when our ancestors buried their dead, they marked the graves in a traditional fashion, originating out of the slavery of the American South," Lane said. "Making use of Saskatchewan's plentiful supply of fieldstone, poplar, and spruce trees, they constructed their place of worship and marked their graves for posterity. In doing so, our African American ancestors left us valuable clues about the traditions and beliefs they brought with them to the wilds of Saskatchewan."

Leander Junior Lane, grandson of Julius Caesar Lane, remembers his father used to take him to the graveyard during the annual spring cleanup.

"I remember the graves were always facing east to west. I also remember the body always buried with the head to the west," he recalled. "The old people said this was so the departed could face east and better observe the coming of the Lord who will arise from the east."

Slowly, people drifted away, and most of the Shiloh homesteaders had left the area by the late 1940s. "Today descendants of the Shiloh People want to ensure Shiloh Baptist Church and cemetery remain a symbol of the African American pioneer experience in Saskatchewan—one that can be enjoyed by everyone for generations to come," concludes Leander K. Lane.

The Shiloh Baptist Church and cemetery, declared a Municipal Heritage Property in 1991, is located about 29 kilometres northeast of Maidstone at NE 12–50–23 W3.

ZION CHURCH
Moose Jaw

The Zion Methodist Church, with a dome towering 77 feet above the street, was built in 1906 to meet the growing needs of the congregation in the boom times for the City of Moose Jaw.

The Methodists were the first religious group in Moose Jaw to worship with a roof over their heads—in the original Canadian Pacific Railway station. However, by 1905, the congregation had grown to over 400 people, so a decision was made to construct their own church.

Architect James Chisholm of Winnipeg was hired and A. J. Toye was awarded the general contract. The cost to complete the church, in a little more than 18 months, was $90,000, including $5,000 for pews, $6,000 for the land, $10,000 for the heating, plumbing, and electrical work, and $64,000 for the contractor. Church records indicate the pulpit, chairs, and communion table cost $189.

The interior of the Zion Church remains almost identical to its original design. It is very impressive for both its use and the octagonal central skylight. With its front entrance porch and central dome, it follows many of the architectural themes of the Roman Pantheon.

"This is one of the largest and best-quality built churches in Moose Jaw," said Dr. Rod Stutt, an architect who teaches at the Saskatchewan Institute of Applied Sciences and Technology (SIAST) Pallisar Campus in the city.

"It was built in a classical style, which makes it very distinct in this city. In addition, the location for the church was halfway between the residential area and downtown Moose Jaw at the time, which meant the church leaders had a vision for the future of the community."

Stutt said that photographs taken of Moose Jaw during its early days as a booming community reveal the church as one of the most prominent buildings in the city. "The quality of the woodwork, the care and dedication in building this church, also show how prosperous the congregation was and

The church's shallow central dome is typical of a Renaissance version of neoclassical style named Palladian.
<small>PHOTO COURTESY SAHS</small>

The church's superior acoustics have made it a favorite venue for a variety of musical and oratorical events.

their view that they were making a long-lasting investment in their future."

The church was renamed Zion United after the Methodist Church joined with the Presbyterian Church of Canada, the Congregational Churches of Canada, and the General Council of Local Union Churches to form the United Church of Canada in 1925.

"Church buildings exist for two reasons: they exist, first of all, for the very basic purpose of housing a congregation. As a congregation, we need a place to meet, a place to worship together, a place to study and fellowship together," said Lorne Calvert in a 1983 sermon when he was pastor of the Zion United Church.

"When the church family become larger than any one of our homes can accommodate, we need a common church home. Church buildings exist firstly to house the church, the people of God. But they exist also for a second purpose: by their architecture, their design and symbolism, they exist also as art to point us to God. Through their mortar and brick, through their wood and glass, they exist to lift the human spirit and speak to use, as only art can speak of our God."

Calvert was born, raised, and educated in Moose Jaw. After high school, he studied economics at the University of Regina and theology at the University of Saskatchewan in Saskatoon.

He was ordained in the United Church of Canada in 1976 and served congregations in Perdue, Gravelbourg, Bateman, Shamrock, Coderre, and Palmer. Calvert then served as minister of Zion United Church in Moose Jaw from 1979 until 1986, when he entered politics.

He was first elected to the Saskatchewan Legislature in 1986 as the New Democratic Party representative for Moose Jaw South and was re-elected in 1991 and 1995 as the member of the Legislative Assembly for the renamed riding of Moose Jaw Wakamow.

Calvert was elected leader of the New Democratic Party of Saskatchewan on January 27, 2001, and assumed the duties of premier on February 8, 2001. He was elected premier in a general election November 5, 2003.

"As a home for the congregation of Zion over the past 76 years this building has served us well," Calvert said in a sermon the year the church was named a Municipal Heritage Site. Calvert urged the congregation to reflect on the history of the Zion United Church.

"Our ancestors, in this place, have built for us a building of beauty and rich symbolism. It has stood these 76 years to manifest our God on the Main Street of Moose Jaw and to all who have entered its doors," Calvert continued.

"As now, we study its architecture and symbolism may it again speak to us our God and our calling to be God's people."

Zion United Church, located at 423 Main Street in Moose Jaw, was designated a Municipal Heritage Site on September 6, 1983.

St. Peter's Roman Catholic Cathedral
Muenster

Mass continues to be held every Sunday in St. Peter's Roman Catholic Cathedral, one of the earliest churches in the Humboldt area and the cathedral for the Abbacy of Muenster.

German-speaking Catholics, under the spiritual leadership of the Benedictines, moved to central Saskatchewan from Minnesota after the turn of the 20th century. Muenster became the educational and religious centre for the group of immigrants.

"St. Peter's is significant to the people of this area and the province because it is the central church to the area founded as St. Peter's Colony, with the Benedictine monks as the spiritual leaders," explained Abbot Peter Novecosky

Novecosky grew up in Bruno, about 25 kilometres southwest of Muenster, attended high school at St. Peter's, and returned as abbot in 1990.

Abbot Novecosky said well-known artist Berthold Von Imhoff visited St. Peter's Abbey, located then right behind St. Peter's Cathedral, on January 5, 1919.

"He [Imhoff] developed a friendship with Abbot Bruno Doerfler and offered to decorate the sanctuary of the church with 80 of his paintings, free of charge," Novecosky said.

Work began on May 12 and on June 6, Abbot Bruno wrote in a letter to Abbot Peter Engel of Minnesota: "Mr. Imhoff is doing wonderfully fine work and the people are so satisfied and pleased that they have, during the present week, contributed enough money to have the whole church painted and decorated inside [for $3,000]. When completed, the interior of our church will undoubtedly be one of the finest on the continent."

Sadly, the first church service in the freshly decorated sanctuary was the funeral mass on June 17, 1919 for Abbot Bruno Doerfler, who died unexpectedly at the age of 52.

The monastery for the Benedictines began as a log house and a log church. But, as the colony grew, a decision was made in 1907 to build a wooden-frame church 58 feet wide by 120 feet in

Twin towers of St. Peter's Roman Catholic Cathedral can be seen poking above the tree tops in Muenster. PHOTO COURTESY SASKATCHEWAN HERITAGE FOUNDATION

same design and material of the altar at the time. It is still in use today.

The Imhoff paintings in St. Peter's Roman Catholic Cathedral are considered some of the finest in Canada.

The images in the St. Peter's sanctuary represent the foundation of the Roman Catholic Church. There is the Blessed Trinity—Father, Son and Holy Spirit; Mary, the Mother of God; St. Joseph, her husband and foster father of Jesus; John the Baptist, St. Peter, and the Evangelists— Matthew, Mark, Luke and John; St. Benedict, and a variety of female and male saints as well as images of angels.

The ceiling of the church is laid out in three panels in Romanesque styling.

The first panel nearest the sanctuary is 12 feet by 16 feet and represents the Annunciation. The back panel of the same size features the Ascension of the Lord into heaven. The centre panel is cross-shaped and features the Sacred Heart of Jesus.

length with twin towers. The inside height was to be 32 feet.

Most of the work was contracted to local people. The Bonas Brothers of Muenster were hired to prepare the foundation from stones in the area, while Herman Fleske and August Wasserman, experienced carpenters, were hired in 1909 to lead the construction efforts.

With the help of several other carpenters, the building was ready for service on July 10, 1910.

The church is made completely of wood, including all the cross braces and beams that form the undercarriage and the 60-foot-high twin towers. The beams are cross-braced and held together with wooden dowels. The dome-shaped sanctuary measured 28-feet high by 34 feet wide.

The altar from the old log church was replaced by a new alter from Munich Art Co. of Milwaukee, Wisconsin, at a cost of $2,200. The firm donated a baptismal font, which was of the

The side walls of the middle nave are also Romanesque style, showing a picture of the Apostles above the pillars. The side naves are laid out in five panels on either side. In the centre of each panel is a painted emblem of the litany of the Blessed Virgin Mary.

Celebration of mass, which begins at 9:30 A.M. each Sunday in the winter and at 10 A.M. in the summer, is now about one hour.

That's quite different than when Richard Muench was growing up. "I remember special lengthy services lasting three to four hours during the Easter Holy Week," Muench said. "The mass was all in Latin and now is English."

Ray Hoffmann, another of the 325 persons who attend St. Peter's, recalled week-long retreats held each July for teenagers in the late 1940s and early 1950s.

"Two priests from the Order of the Redemption came to speak one night and the subject of their talk was: Hell," Hoffmann said. "During that evening, while the priests were giving their presentation on hell, a severe thunder storm struck the area. Lightening lit up the whole church, followed by crashes of thunder that shook the building, followed by a very heavy rain."

Hoffmann thought it created a fitting atmosphere for the evening's topic. "I have always remembered that evening and I can still tell you exactly where I sat that night," he said.

Another vivid memory for Hoffmann was the strict seating arrangements in St. Peter's Cathedral. "Young ladies sat on the northside aisle with the young men on the southside aisle," he said. "The front rows were filled with school children while the remainder of the church was for adults who bought their seats at a pew auction every five years." Those traditions have faded with time. Now, seating is on a first-come, first-served basis.

St. Peter's Roman Catholic Cathedral, located about one kilometre east of Humboldt, on Highway 5 and just north of Muenster, was named a Municipal Heritage Site on May 3, 1984.

The magnificence of the Cathedral's interior continues to draw both worshippers and tourists alike.
Photo courtesy SAHS

RCMP CHAPEL
Regina

The Chapel has been the spiritual focal point for the RCMP for more than a century.
PHOTO COURTESY RCMP MUSEUM

The oldest known building in Regina was originally constructed by John Ross, a local builder, in 1883 as a canteen for the North-West Mounted Police, the predecessors of the Royal Canadian Mounted Police (RCMP).

Damaged by fire two years later, the building was renovated for use as a chapel and since then has provided food for the souls of generations of cadets and members of the RCMP for more than a century.

The single-storey, wood-frame building with cedar shingles painted red was extensively renovated in 1924. It was moved 5 feet west and 21 feet south to align with other depot buildings. A basement was added and the exterior was stuccoed. It was expanded several times from its original 26 feet by 60 foot wood frame to adapt to its religious use and needs of a growing group of staff and recruits.

"Since its dedication as a place of worship on December 8, 1895, the Second Sunday of Advent, the chapel has been the spiritual focal point of the force," explains Chaplain Allan Higgs.

"Many rites of passage are regularly celebrated in the Chapel." These include: troop graduation ecumenical services; marriages; baptisms; celebrations of life (funerals); renewal of marriage vows; troop reunions; memorial services; and the veterans' annual church parade.

"This is a place of serenity and peace during the hectic hours and days of training," said Higgs, who has been a chaplain at the nondenominational church since 1980.

"If the walls and benches could talk there would be thousands of stories told. Chief amongst them would be accounting for all the men and women who have sat in the chapel for their graduation service and then went forward to serve the force in all parts of Canada and indeed the world."

The highest drama that takes place in the Chapel on the Square, is the annual memorial chapel service that follows the memorial parade each second Sunday of September.

"This is the day the RCMP remembers and honours those members who have died in the line of duty," Higgs said. "Family and members from all over Canada come to remember those who responded to the ultimate call."

As they assemble in the chapel, their eyes take in the many messages of the powerful stained-glass windows. Chief amongst them are the towering figures of a scarlet-coated Mountie standing in the poses of Mourning and Resurrection.

At the top of these beautifully constructed stained-glass windows are the crests of the provinces of New Brunswick, Nova Scotia, and Prince Edward Island. These windows were dedicated in 1944 to honour 13 members from the Maritime provinces who had died in the line of duty.

The unusual ecumenical function of the Chapel was best demonstrated by a wedding in 1990. "A graduate had asked if her wedding service could be conducted in French in spite of the then-chaplain only speaking English," Higgs explained. "Further conversation revealed that the groom was from the Middle East and only spoke French and Arabic. As well, the member wanted the RCMP chaplain involved in the ceremony."

The chaplain made arrangements for a friend, who was a United Church Minister and spoke French, to preside. As well, the Chaplain had an Egyptian friend teach him some words of greeting and a blessing in Arabic. "The bride and groom were thrilled with her unique wedding in the chapel," he said.

The bride saw the chaplain a few days later and presented her freshly dry cleaned dress so it could be passed on to a bride who couldn't afford to purchase her own dress in the future.

Another touching memory occurred in 1999 when John and Grace Cuthbert celebrated their 60th wedding anniversary in the chapel in which they were married. Cuthbert's entire service with the force had taken place in Regina.

"Personally, I take great pride in showing off our spiritual home because I believe its existence has a significant influence on our force being the best police force in the world," Higgs said. "At the very least, the spire points upward to something much greater than any of us."

Over the years, many members of the royal family have visited the chapel including Queen Elizabeth, Prince Andrew, Princess Ann, as well as the Duke and Duchess of York. However, none have worshipped there.

The Chapel on the Square, located at RCMP Depot Division, 5600 Dewdeny Avenue West in Regina, seats a congregation of 195 as well as a 30-member choir. It was designated a Provincial Heritage Site on May 30, 1983.

Stained glass windows were dedicated in 1944 to honour 13 RCMP members from the Maritimes who died in the line of duty.
PHOTO COURTESY RCMP MUSEUM

HOLY ROSARY CATHEDRAL
Regina

Holy Rosary Cathedral has been the symbol of Roman Catholic faith in Regina since 1913, when almost 2,000 people celebrated the blessing of the church. "It stands as an eloquent testimony to the faith, generosity, and hope for the future of Regina's early Catholics," said Reverend Louis Kubash, rector of the church since 1999.

More than 500 services are held in the cathedral each year, with more than 100,000 people attending events, including elaborate diocesan liturgies, Episcopal ceremonies, priest ordinations, state funerals, and the daily mass.

Olivier Mathieu, former rector of Laval University in Quebec and first Archbishop of Regina turned the sod on the 13th Avenue site.

Construction of Holy Rosary Cathedral had been under way for only one month when the June 30, 1912, cyclone left much of Regina's downtown area in shambles. The area near the cathedral was left relatively intact.

Winds gusting up to 500 miles per hour, ripped through the city's nearby downtown and more prestigious residential districts. After the winds had died down, the cyclone had claimed a total of 28 lives, rendered 2,500 persons temporarily homeless, and caused more than $1.2 million in property damage.

Almost 2,000 people packed the church or watched from the streetcars stopped outside on June 29, 1913, as the building's cornerstone was blessed by the Apostolic Delegate, or Papal Ambassador, to Canada.

Mathieu celebrated the first mass in the Cathedral on November 23, 1913, and greetings were given by three prominent Catholic laymen: J. O'Connor in English, W. E. A. Turgeon in French, and Frank Brunner in German.

Smith Brothers and Wilson of Regina built the Romanesque edifice designed by Montreal architect J. E. Fortin and modelled after churches in northern France for the then-considerable sum of

$135,000. The cathedral's interior was redecorated in 1928, 1951, 1968, and 1977.

Dedicated to Our Lady of the Most Holy Rosary, Regina's cathedral is one of the province's most beautiful and imposing churches. It measures 200 feet by 90 feet and features two tall, elegant spires.

A large bell, donated in 1915 by the parish Altar Guild, is in the east tower and used to toll each Sunday to call the faithful to mass as well as punctuate the conclusion of funerals.

There are many remarkable features in the cathedral. Andre Rault of Rennes, France, added 34 stained-glass windows to the church over a two-year period ending in 1950. Stories told in the windows celebrate the life of Mary, the mother of Jesus. The cost of the windows was $28,500. Other stained-glass windows include one donated by Mrs. A. E. Forget, wife of the province's first lieutenant-governor.

In the gallery above the main doors at the cathedral's north end nearest 13th Avenue is the McGuigan Organ, named in honour of Regina educator and humanitarian Sister Marion McGuigan. Built by Casavant Freres of Quebec, the organ has more than 3,100 pipes.

Another imposing image is the large ceramic mural in the apse—the curved wall at the back of the sanctuary. Lorraine Malach of Regina was commissioned in 1988 to produce the mural to mark the 75th anniversary of the cathedral. The mural depicts the Five Glorious Mysteries of the Rosary.

"Holy Rosary Cathedral is both a visible symbol of and witness to the Catholic presence in Regina and one of the city's outstanding architectural landmarks," said Rector Kubash.

The cathedral is a living faith community with many active programs for spiritual development and many active groups striving to live and develop in faith, hope, love, and community.

"Holy Rosary Cathedral has been a constant in my life," said Jim McCashin, an 88-year-old member of the parish. "It was there when I was born and through many changes in the area it still stands as a symbol of my faith."

McCashin has known every archbishop of the cathedral from Archbishop Olivier Mathieu, who turned the sod for the 13th Avenue church, to Peter Mallon, the current Archbishop.

McCashin was baptized at Holy Rosary and received his first communion from Archbishop Mathieu. He and his wife Clarice celebrated their 60th wedding anniversary at the Cathedral on February 6, 2003.

Holy Rosary Cathedral is located at 3125–13th Avenue in Regina.

KNOX-METROPOLITAN UNITED CHURCH
Regina

The Knox-Metropolitan United Church, constructed in 1906 and rebuilt after being partially destroyed by a cyclone in 1912, continues to be a symbol of the faith and hope for people in downtown Regina.

"We are downtown for a purpose," said Rev. Robert Kitchen. "We have a lot of history behind us at the corner of Victoria Avenue and Lorne Street. Our building was once knocked down in 1912, but we got back up again. We are not retreating, for we know that our ministry belongs in the downtown."

Knox-Metropolitan has a complex and intriguing present and an even more exciting future, he said.

"Our congregation comes from every neighbourhood of Regina and a few from outside the city," Kitchen said. "We are a diverse company in race, nationality, education, occupation, and just about any other characteristic. We are united in our calling to ministry and spiritual growth in the city.

Grant Armstrong, a retired judge, has been attending "Knox-Met," as he calls the church, for more than 65 years.

"When I was about 10, my best friend and I were going to Sunday School at different churches," Armstrong recalled. "I wanted to be with him and since he was the older and hence in some control, I switched to Metropolitan United. It didn't hurt that the Sunday school teacher worked for a biscuit company and some times passed out sample cookies. I am still there."

Armstrong has been involved in church affairs for some 50 years including over 30 years as chair of the board of trustees.

The church and the people are familiar to Armstrong, but he has other reasons for continuing his support.

"Since Knox United Church and Metropolitan United Church became one in 1951, Knox-Met has been the flag-bearer for the United Church in Regina, located as it is in downtown Regina," Armstrong said.

"Its continued presence there is important not only to the church but to the city because, together with the Baptist and Catholic downtown churches it adds to the sense of community."

The church was constructed by the Metropolitan Methodist congregation in 1906 to replace their second church that had burned in 1889. The 1912 cyclone that ripped through downtown Regina badly damaged the building, but it was repaired by 1913. In 1925, the congregation joined the United Church of Canada and was renamed the Metropolitan United.

When the former Presbyterian congregation joined in 1951, the congregation renamed it Knox-Metropolitan United. The cornerstone was moved from the church and placed at the entrance of the newly constructed adjacent office building and hall in 1956.

Architects Frank Portnall and J. E. Fotin used a traditional blend of Norman and Gothic styles in designing the red brick building. It features large stained-glass windows and a square tower with belfry and parapets.

Jamesina Jamieson's grandparents were among the first pioneers in Lumsden, northwest of Regina, who helped build the Presbyterian community there.

She followed her family's Presbyterian ties with the United Church when she moved into Regina. As a teenager, she was active in one of the numerous youth groups originating at Knox-Met as well as taking organ lessons in the beautiful facility. "I've always felt comfortable here," she said. "It's a hardworking congregation. I wouldn't feel at home anywhere else."

Joan Church, another long-time member of the congregation, has seen a dramatic shift in how society has viewed the role of a church in their lives in her lifetime. "I find it hard to believe how things have changed so much in Regina," said Church, 78.

"In the past, all of the activities took place in and around your church. All of the social and recreational things we did as kids and families were related to the church. Now, people have way too many destinations."

She said there used to be 800 children enrolled in Sunday School at Knox-Met.

Acoustics of Knox-Met make the church a highly prized venue. "It may not be a requirement to love music to come to Knox-Metropolitan, but it sure makes it easier," said Kitchen. "Our music program, directed by Hart Godden, is the strongest in the area, centred around a 30-member choir and also includes numerous concerts featuring our Casavant organ."

There are 14 organists practicing at Knox-Met regularly. In addition, the Regina Symphony Orchestra, the Regina Philharmonic Chorus and numerous other musical groups perform at the church. The Rotary Carol Festival, a week-long event, has been held at Knox-Met before Christmas each year since 1940.

"Knox-Metropolitan is located at the centre of the City of Regina and we have always been committed to ministry at the crossroads," Kitchen said.

For example, he said the Regina Anti-Poverty Ministry (RAPM) has had offices and staff located at Knox-Met for more than 25 years.

Approximately 50 groups and organizations hold regular meetings in the church hall. Activities include karate, Tai Chi, baton twirling, business luncheons, self-help groups, and flea markets.

"Come along and squeeze in," he said. "Knox-Metropolitan is a place bursting with life. We have been here since the beginning—the beginning of Regina, that is—and we'll be here for a long, long time to come."

Knox-Metropolitan United Church, located at 2340 Victoria Avenue on the northwest corner of Lorne Street and Victoria Avenue in downtown Regina, was named a Municipal Heritage Property on April 14, 1986.

ST. JOHN'S ANGLICAN CATHEDRAL
Saskatoon

St. John's Anglican Cathedral has towered over the South Saskatchewan Riverbank in Saskatoon for almost a century.

Saskatoon residents and tourists have been attracted to the architectural features of the Gothic Revival-style structure constructed like a crucifix aligned east-west.

"It's the most attractive church in the city and that's why people photograph it so much," maintains Stan Hodgins, who joined St. John's in 1982.

"I think it's the most beautiful building in Saskatoon. Others might not agree whole-heartedly with me, but it must be near the top of everyone's list."

Many who attend St. John's Anglican Cathedral believe only the Delta Bessborough Hotel, a castle-like structure nearby, has more photographs taken of it each year. St. John's is considered among the top 10 most beautiful churches in western Canada.

Its spire soars 145 feet above the ground and the building was constructed of materials from across

the west: a base of Saskatchewan granite, exterior of Redcliffe brick made in Alberta, interior of Manitoba buff brick, and Tyndal stone stairs; and the timber came from British Columbia.

Decorative material around the doors and windows is terra cotta purchased from the Royal Doulton in Staffordshire, England. Royal Doulton also supplied the altar, pulpit, lectern, and font. All are made of Carrara Ware, a simulated white marble.

A rood screen, with its Gothic openings, separating the chancel area from the nave was also added. The rood screen is adorned with angel statues standing above it.

The steeple is in the southeast corner above the transepts and includes the tubular chimes, which were brought from the first church built by the congregation in 1907.

Throughout the years, gifts from friends of the church and from parishioners have added to the character of the interior, especially the 50 stained-glass windows that are the largest collection of stained glass in the city.

"This church is important to me because I have been attending it for 39 years," said Nancy Baltzan. "Both of my daughters have been confirmed here and one granddaughter recently was baptized here by the bishop."

Baltzan has been an active member of the church, holding various positions over the years on its vestry, or board. "This church is important as an historical landmark for Saskatoon and adds to the beauty of the riverbank. It is the Mother Church for our diocese," said Baltzan.

A highlight of her involvement came on October 18, 1987, when she escorted Queen Elizabeth during part of her visit to St. John's.

"Nancy and I together, carrying our wardens' wands, escorted the Royal party from their cars into the cathedral and to their pews, and out again at the end of the service," recalls Hodgins. "I only spoke with the Queen very briefly, because there was a line of people being presented to her, but I'll remember that moment forever."

For Barry McLennan, his fondest memory of St. John's was spiritual, not regal. He was a student at the University of Saskatchewan in the early 1960s when he attended confirmation classes conducted by Dean Pat Patterson at St. John's Cathedral.

"It was a most interesting confirmation class because it wasn't just for Anglicans," said McLennan. "There were Presbyterians, United Church members, members of the Jewish community, and some of no particular religious conviction in attendance. Dean Patterson wanted the class to be very meaningful for us, and it didn't matter what religious background you had. He made us all feel welcome and we learned a lot about Christianity and the Anglican faith."

As a result of that experience, McLennan opted to begin worshiping at St. John's when he moved his family to Saskatoon and where he began his career as a professor of biochemistry at the University of Saskatchewan in 1969.

Both Margaret and Barry McLennan have served as wardens and on the vestry at St John's. All three of their children were baptized and confirmed there and their daughter Marla was married at St. John's.

St. John's Anglican Cathedral is one of the three most important downtown churches in Saskatoon, built during city's "boom" period from 1910 to 1912. The other two are St. Paul's Roman Catholic Cathedral and Knox United.

All three churches are landmarks in the city and symbols of that period of great prosperity in Saskatoon, as well as the importance that religion held for the city in its formative years.

The church was home to a variety of musical activities in the early days, including the first light operatic performance in Saskatoon: *HMS Pinafore.*

In May 1903, when 1,500 Barr Colonists arrived in Saskatoon from England, the rector of St. John's, Reverend W. E. Edmunds, conducted

The spire of the church towers almost half a football field above the city's streets.

church services in one of their large tents. In 1910, the first Boy Scout Troop was formed in the city in the church.

In 1902, a small group of Saskatoon Anglicans, organized by a local North-West Mounted Police officer, met to discuss establishing a Church of England parish. The list of parishioners totaled just eight persons.

The new parish was named St. John the Evangelist, after the cathedral in Winnipeg. Volunteers built a small church in the fall of 1902 and the building was dedicated in January 1903.

About seven years later, the parish's original property on Third Avenue was sold and a new site on Spadina Crescent with a magnificent view of the river was purchased. Growth in the parish had paralleled the city. From a population of 200 in 1902, Saskatoon had grown to 16,000 by 1912, and the parish needed a much larger building.

Thompson, Daniel and Colthurst, a Saskatoon firm of English-trained architects, designed St. John's. The cornerstone was laid in September 1912 by the governor general of Canada, the Duke of Connaught, who was the third son of Queen Victoria.

Because of financial problems resulting from the fact that 257 members of the parish had enlisted during the First World War, St. John's was officially opened in 1917, at a pared-down cost of $103,000, without furnishings. Cathedral status was granted in 1924

Over the years, contributions to its interior and careful restoration work have increased its beauty. St. John's Anglican Cathedral won a civic heritage award in 1987.

In 1997, the cathedral underwent more renovations. The purpose of the new foyer and excavation was so that a columbarium could be accommodated in the enlarged basement. It includes a large entry area and chapel, with glass doors leading to the niches for storage of cremated remains, all beautifully appointed in oak. There is a very large area for further expansion of the columbarium in future years.

Renovations required the cathedral to be supported on jacks while the crawl space below was excavated to form a complete basement. The addition received two Saskatchewan Architectural Heritage Society Awards of Excellence.

The cathedral continues to have an active congregation, which is closely involved in outreach activities into the community. As part of the centennial celebrations of the Parish of St. John's in 2002, a four-faced clock was designed, with Westminster chimes, and installed in the bell tower.

St. John's Anglican Cathedral is located at 816 Spadina Crescent East in Saskatoon.

THIRD AVENUE UNITED CHURCH
Saskatoon

The Third Avenue United Church, a Gothic style, solid stone building in the heart of Saskatoon, has been the home of music concerts, convocation exercises, political rallies, and religious celebrations since it opened in 1913.

The church was built as a place for worship by Methodists but its uses expanded over the years.

In January 1911, the church engaged the architect M. J. Semmens of Winnipeg, and then work began on the basement in the fall under the direction of the general contractors, Smith Brothers and Wilson of Saskatoon.

The cornerstone was laid on May 13, 1912, and when the Third Avenue Methodist Church officially opened on June 27, 1913, the cost of construction had surpassed $200,000.

"Our building is a source of pride to the congregation as well as a remarkable resource for the community," said Kathleen James-Cavan, a University of Saskatchewan professor and vice-chair of the Unified Board of the Third Avenue United Church.

In 1925, after the union of Methodists, Presbyterians, and Congregationalists, the name was changed to Third Avenue United Church.

The church's architectural design and materials are found in many buildings on the University of Saskatchewan Campus, but are rare elsewhere in the City of Saskatoon.

The stonework on the main body of the church is buff Tyndal stone from Manitoba, with trimmings of the same in pale grey-blue.

The tallest of the two towers that face 24th Street is 100 feet high. The interior, which seats 1,600 on the main floor and balcony, is dominated by a series of hammer-beam oak rafters criss-crossing the ceiling from steel girder trusses as well as three enormous stained-glass windows on the west, south, and east sides.

At the time of its construction, an auditorium without the presence of pillars obstructing the view was considered an engineering feat, Jacqueline Bliss, heritage officer for the City of Saskatoon wrote in a 1988 report.

There are seats for 1,600 in the Gothic-style, solid stone church.
PHOTO COURTESY THIRD AVENUE UNITED CHURCH

Convocations, music concerts and political rallies as well as religious celebrations have been held in the church.
PHOTO COURTESY THIRD AVENUE UNITED CHURCH

Important economic and political events also have taken place in the Third Avenue United Church. For example, on November 24, 1921, T. A. Crerar, leader of the national Progressive Party spoke to a crowd of 3,000 supporters. The Progressive Party merged less than a decade later to form the Progressive Conservative Party.

The founding of the Saskatchewan Wheat Pool, which became the country's largest cooperative at one time with sales of almost $2 billion, can be traced to the Third Avenue United Church.

Aaron Sapiro, an expert on cooperatives from the United States, spoke to a crowd of 2,000 people at the church on August 7, 1923, about the values of farmers "pooling" together.

His speech apparently inspired the Saskatchewan Grain Growers' Association (SGGA) and the Farmers' Union to collaborate in signing up farmers for the pool. Three years later, in the summer of 1926, the SGGA held a convention at Third Avenue while the Farmers' Union met at Knox United Church only blocks away. When both groups voted to form a single organization, the Farmers' Union members joined the SGGA at Third Avenue where the first meeting of the new organization took place.

Educational events were frequently held at the church. Convocation exercises for the University of Saskatchewan were held there from 1931 to 1949. For many years, teachers from the Normal School and graduates of City Hospital's nursing program also held their convocations at Third Avenue.

In 2002, the church hosted the first shared convocation of the Saskatoon Theological Union.

Allister Taylor, who has been associated with the church for more than 70 years, has fond boyhood memories of the facility. "I remember playing tennis on the tennis court next to the church as well as attending the Boys Club that met every Tuesday night in the church basement," said the retired businessman. "The Young Peoples' group met every Sunday night after evening worship which gave us something to look forward to."

Taylor is credited with arranging to have Fernando Germani, who was the organist at the Vatican, give a recital at the Third Avenue United Church.

The three stained-glass windows, 27 feet wide at the base and 22 feet at the apex, depict, in rich colours, life-sized figures from scripture. The south window represents the Last Supper, the east illustrates the Nativity, and the west has the Sermon on the Mount. In addition, other exterior windows, patterned in floral designs, replicate the shape of the larger windows.

On the north wall stands the large Casavant organ having 3 manuals, 39 stops, 2,468 pipes plus, 20 bells. The dark reddish-brown pews of oak and elm with carved end panels complement the church's spiritual appeal.

Third Avenue United Church is significant to Saskatoon for more than its architectural heritage. It functioned as an auditorium in the early days of the city and still is a popular venue for concerts.

Edna Start, a homemaker and retired salesperson, has attended Third Avenue for 40 years. She recalled a fowl supper she helped arrange with Elmer Baker, another member of the church, in the 1960s when her three sons were members of the local Boy Scout Troop that met at the church.

"Elmer obtained the venison from sources unknown, soaked the meat in his own bathtub in a vinegar solution overnight, then took it to a local bakery to be cooked in the ovens " Edna said. "It was delivered to the auditorium on schedule, superbly cooked and ready for consumption. No one ever knew how or where Elmer procured the delicacy, but it was the highlight of the year and an outstanding success."

The Third Avenue United Church continues to be a venue for more than religious celebrations.

"Today, it is the home of the award-winning Saskatoon Children's Choir and the city's Brass Band," explained James-Cavan. "CBC Radio has taped numerous concerts and events in its sanctuary."

The church is located on the corner of 24th Street and 3rd Avenue at 304–3rd Avenue North in Saskatoon.

HOLY TRINITY ANGLICAN CHURCH
Stanley Mission

Holy Trinity Anglican Church at Stanley Mission is the oldest standing building in Saskatchewan and the oldest church west of the Red River.

The Anglican mission was established by James Settee, one of the first native clergymen of the diocese. He was joined by the Reverend Robert Hunt and his wife Georgianna in 1850.

Holy Trinity Church was constructed under the supervision of Hunt, using timbers from Lac la Ronge and hardware, stained-glass windows, hinges, latches, locks, and other interior wood features that he had brought with him from England.

Construction of the church began in 1854 and was completed in 1860.

Its large proportions and towering steeple were in sharp contrast to the traditional one-room log churches constructed throughout western Canada in the latter part of the 19th century.

The church measured 25 metres (67 feet) in length by 10.5 metres (35 feet) in width with an inside height of 15 metres (42 feet). The steeple and spire are 27 metres (76 feet) high.

The church combines English church architecture and regional Aboriginal culture featuring 37 Gothic-arched windows with more than 1,000 pieces of stained glass used in the windows.

A major restoration was done in the 1980s. The steeple was reattached to the church by helicopter after being detached for more than a decade. The church is always open, but access is by water only.

Corporal Gary Ritchie, a member of the Royal Canadian Mounted Police (RCMP) for 28 years, has worked in Stanley Mission twice.

"It was an awe-inspiring sight the first time I saw the church from the settlement across the Churchill River," Ritchie recalled. "My first thought was: What was this beautiful church doing, basically, in the middle of nowhere?"

His opinion grew even more when he entered the Anglican church. "This church is a reflection of the past and the hard work required to construct it more than 150 years ago by some very skilled European tradesmen," the RCMP corporal said. "When you look at the beams across the roof and all of the detail within the church, I can't image how they did it, but the result is amazing."

Rev. Elias Ballantyne, the Anglican minister in charge of Stanley Mission, vividly remembers the first wedding he performed in his newly assigned church.

"It was small wedding party," said Elias of the 1995 event. "There was bride and groom, their bush pilot who had flown them to Stanley Mission, our church warden, and me."

People from across Canada book weddings at Stanley Mission, sometimes a year or more in advance, and sometimes at the bequest of loved ones.

"One bride told me that her father, who had been from Saskatoon, had asked her as his last request, that if she ever got married that she should get married here," Ballantyne said. "With snow falling on September 30 (in 2003), she did get married here."

He, like others before him, has found the craftsmanship to be impeccable. "When I first got there I walked around the church and couldn't believe my eyes," said Ballantyne, whose family has been involved in the Anglican Church in northern Saskatchewan for three generations. "All of the work was done by hand. There were no skillsaws or electric tools back then, yet they built an incredible church."

Ballantyne was a lay reader at his home community of Pelican Narrows for a decade before entering the ministry. His dad had been a lay reader in the same community for 30 to 40 years, a tradition that his father had inherited from Elias' grandfather, a lay reader in the 1930s.

Ballantyne, who is also responsible for ministering at three other communities, has welcomed members of the Anglican Church from England and around the world.

"There was an archbishop who came here to see our church from India," he recalled. "He arrived only wearing his red robes. This was February. So we had to run around and find him a snowmobile suit, boots, and gloves so he wouldn't freeze."

A fishing trip to the Churchill River by John Charlton was a more pleasant experience.

Holy Trinity Anglican Church, located across the Churchill River from Stanley Mission, is the oldest standing building in the province.
Photo courtesy Saskatchewan Heritage Foundation

"Conditions that day couldn't have been better—warm, calm, no bugs, and experienced fishermen to show me what to do and even where to find the fish," said Charlton, a provincial government employee.

"Fishing was great. A wholly unanticipated aspect of that day lingers with me now. It's the unforgettable sight of the Holy Trinity Anglican Church over the Churchill River."

The Stanley Mission settlement is on the south side of the Churchill River while the Holy Trinity Church is on the north side where the former settlement site.

"From where you launch your boat, the church looms large. Surprisingly, as you move farther away on the river, the church becomes no less impressive—in some ways more so."

Returning to dock the boat at Stanley Mission, his group faced a stunning view. "The church sits on a high point of land so it dominates the landscape," Charlton recalled. "That day, rays of sunlight were streaming through clouds bathing the Holy Trinity Church in a heavenly glow."

The Holy Trinity Anglican Church, located across the Churchill River from Stanley Mission about 90 kilometers northeast of La Ronge, was designated a Provincial Heritage Property on August 26, 1981.

KNOX PRESBYTERIAN
Weyburn

The Knox Presbyterian Church in Weyburn has provided people with a glimpse of Scotland in southeastern Saskatchewan since 1906.

Rev. John Ferrier, the congregation's minister since 1979, said the building design was influenced by some of the older churches in Scotland. "It's very square and solid looking," he said. "The church has a very worshipful atmosphere. There is a serenity and calmness about it that fits into my idea of worship."

The architectural style of the church is Gothic Revival, and it is built of formed concrete stones resting on a fieldstone foundation. The only major change to the interior of the church took place in 1928 when what had been the choir loft had to be used to accommodate all the ducts and bellows for the new pipe organ.

"Apart from that change, anyone returning from the era of the Great War and entering the sanctuary would feel right at home beneath the high vaulted ceiling, reading the same words written in an arch above the pulpit that W. O. Mitchell remembered in his novel *Who Has Seen the Wind,* 'This is the house of God and the very gate of heaven.'"

Those words hardly seem an exaggeration, he said, when the sun streams through the stained-glass windows.

"The visitor's eyes might turn first to the east window, where, as W. O. Mitchell described it: 'A blue-and-ruby Christ carried a lamb in His arms, His head turned tenderly down upon it,'" Ferrier said.

Beneath that stained-glass window is a passage from the Gospel of St. John: "The good shepherd giveth his life for the sheep."

The west window portrays Christ standing patiently at a door, with the inscription from the Revelation to John: "Behold, I stand at the door and knock."

The north window is simply a richly coloured and intricate pattern in stained glass.

"Although the windows are beautiful at any time of the day from the inside, the morning sun's perfect highlight of the colours and pictures in the east window are very striking," Ferrier said. "None of the windows ever have been broken since the day they were installed almost 100 years ago."

Colours used in the elaborate designs are still brilliant. "The windows were all releaded in the 1960s at a cost of $5,000," he explained.

Pete McFadden began attending Sunday school at the Knox Presbyterian Church in 1923. "My mother was there when the church was being built," McFadden said. "I think it's a rather unique church. It has some of the nicest stained-glass windows anywhere in Canada."

McFadden has served as a member of the Knox Church Session, the governing board of the local church, for more than 30 years. "This church was well designed for people to worship," he said.

Christina Douglas, who was married in the church in 1940, has been the long-time historian for the Knox Presbyterian Women, a group whose activities include raising money for the upkeep of the church.

"It would be a big loss if the church closed because it has meant so much to the people of Weyburn and our faith over these years," she said. "We haven't heard it will close, but things are changing and all churches are feeling the same pressure."

Douglas said one of the most important events in the history of the church came in 1928 when people raised money to buy a pipe organ from Casavant Freres of St. Hyacinthe, Quebec for $6,000. The original pump organ was moved to Estevan and then eventually was sent to a church in Froude before making its way back to the Weyburn church in 1979, where it may be found downstairs today, in excellent condition and good working order.

"A fire in 1937 caused some minor damage to the church and new bells were added in 1957," she said.

An extension, called Knox Fellowship House, was built in 1960.

Throughout the years, three men and four women from the congregation have entered into full-time service in the Presbyterian Church in Canada as ordained ministers, missionaries, and deaconesses, serving in Montreal, Toronto, and Vancouver, as well as overseas in China, Ethiopia, India, and Japan.

"Lt. Gov. George Porteous, the Queen's official representative in the province, addressed the Saskatchewan synod of the church in 1978," said Douglas. "That was a very exciting and proud moment for all of us."

Her husband, Albert, was elected a member of Parliament for the Liberals in 1968, but died in 1971.

"Today, almost 100 years after it was built, Knox Church stands as testimony to the hopes, faith and optimism of the first Presbyterians to settle in the Weyburn area," Ferrier said.

The Knox Presbyterian Church, located at 136–2nd Street in Weyburn, was named a Municipal Heritage Site on September 22, 2003.

St. Mary's Anglican Church
Whitewood

St. Mary's, with its field-stone exterior walls, has been a cornerstone of Whitewood's community spirit since 1902.
Photo courtesy Janet Blackstock

People have been worshipping at St. Mary, The Virgin, Anglican Church in Whitewood for more than 100 years.

"This stone church was built by our forefathers and was consecrated in 1902. That's before Saskatchewan became a province," explained Ted Pearson, who has served the church as a warden working with the clergy for many years. "We feel because of their hard work and dedication it is most important that we carry on the mission of the church now and in the future."

The building represents more than a place for people to attend church services, say local people.

"St. Mary's has been the cornerstone of Whitewood since the beginning," said Doreen Westcott, who has been attending Sunday services since she was a very young girl. "We hope St. Mary's will be here for future generations."

In addition to being a key part of Whitewood's past, the church also has 500-year-old link to England.

St. Mary's Lych Gate, which is located in front of the Anglican Church, was built in 1924. Designed as a roofed gate under which a coffin is set down to await the clergy, the gate in Whitewood is a replica of one constructed in 1450 at St. Leonard's Church in Heston, England.

It was built by Jack, Francis, and Charles Bachelor, who were said to have been former members' of the St. Leonard's parish in England. For many years this was the only such structure in Saskatchewan.

In earlier years, the lych gate included two wooden gates that have since been removed. In 2001, Whitewood's lych gate was highlighted during a celebration in England, where their lych gate was restored to its original design.

The St. Mary's church is Romanesque in style with grey fieldstone exterior walls, attached buttresses, arched windows, a rounded eastern apse that houses the altar and choir stalls, a steeply pitched roof, and a two-storey bell tower.

"The upper section of the bell tower is shingled and either stained or painted a dark mahogany colour," said Janet Blackstock, an artist, designer, and architecture buff who now works for the Town of Whitewood. "The tower roof is a blunt pyramid with a Medieval or Celtic cross at the apex."

St. Mary's is about 30 feet by 80 feet, she estimated. The interior walls have been renovated with plywood paneling, likely to incorporate insulation. "However, the original dark varnished roof and beams are intact as are the choir stalls and altar," she said, adding that the roof, in recent years, was reshingled in cedar.

"My favourite view of the church is from the back alley at the rear which shows the central stained glass window with two smaller flanking windows on the tall stone end wall."

The western centre stained-glass window was donated by Mrs. Charles Marshallsay in memory of her husband, a lay minister and the first member of the Legislative Assembly for the area. The window came from England. Freight and customs charges cost $7 and posed quite a challenge for the congregation to raise the money at that time.

A history book to celebrate the community's centennial in 1992 indicates that construction of the fieldstone church began in 1900 and was completed two years later. It replaced an earlier wooden church built in 1885 that was approximately 10 feet by 14 feet and cost $80 to build.

St. Mary's is one of Whitewood's most beautiful buildings and is one of only two remaining stone structures in the community 200 kilometres east of Regina along the Trans-Canada Highway.

St. Mary's The Virgin Anglican Church is located at 730 Lalonde Street in Whitewood. Street numbers are rarely visible in Whitewood, so look for the third building north of the intersection of Lalonde Street and Fourth Avenue, directly south of the main business district.

The lych gate is a replica of one constructed in 1450 at St. Leonard's Church in Heston, England.
Photo courtesy Janet Blackstock

St. Mary's Ukrainian Catholic Church
Yorkton

Pope Benedict XV blessed the Icon of May in 1916 that is in the church.
Photo courtesy Saskatchewan Heritage Foundation

St. Mary's, also known as Our Mother of Perpetual Help, was the first Ukrainian Catholic Church in western Canada made of brick. The parish was founded in 1910 and the church was built in 1914.

Artist Stephan Meush, utilizing a dome 55 feet above the floor of the Yorkton church as his canvas, depicts the Coronation of the Virgin Mary in heaven.

The icon of Our Mother of Perpetual Help, which originally hung behind the altar in church, was a certified copy of the original icon in Rome and was hand-painted on wood. It was blessed by Pope Benedict XV in 1916. The icon is on display in the church sacristy.

When the east wing of the church was built in 1955, special care had to be given to the pillars, which supported the dome. That resulted in a narrow and long expansion.

Father Bryan Bayda, pastor of the church since 2002, finds the artwork spiritually uplifting. "After celebrating the Divine Liturgy at the altar, I often enter the north wing of the church so as not to be noticed by the women who have remained to pray the Rosary," he said.

"I join them in prayer. I lay on the floor, positioning myself close enough to view the entire interior of the dome. The impressive and endearing painting lifts my heart and mind to lofty mysteries."

The priest is grateful for the view, enhanced by an avalanche of light streaming through the stained-glass windows along the walls of the church.

"Having some appreciation for the spiritual and theological aspect of architecture, the Eastern tradition has specific guidelines for building churches," Bayda said. "This church in Yorkton is faithful to a visual theology if you will."

St. Mary's, when constructed, was magnificent and breathtaking, soaring higher than the church was long. "It had the potential of being not only a visual jewel as one passed by the impressive structure, but a catechetical experience for the eye of the soul," he said.

The artwork on the dome is as stunningly beautiful today as it was when Meush completed his masterpiece in 1941, after two years of a labour of love.

"The painting of the Coronation of the Mother of God in Heaven as Queen of Heaven and Earth, remains profound to even the untrained eye, never mind when praying the Rosary," Bayda said.

"Stephan Meush gazed upward at a blank dome in 1939 for some time before he borrowed the natural light to peer into heaven. Applying his brush he shared what he saw with generations of faithful Christians. Do you want to get a glimpse of heaven? You should see what I have seen," added Father Bayda.

Meush was trained in Ukraine, studied for three years in Italy, and then spent a year in Poland before coming to Canada in 1932. He was 36 when he began working on the St. Mary's Church project in Yorkton.

Like most artists, Meush worked only when he was inspired. There were days when he sat idly by with his thoughts and then again he would work day and night without stopping to eat.

The top of the dome is 55 feet above the floor and curves 62 feet across. The curvature required that the central figures and the surrounding 157 angels and cherubs be painted in a distorted man-ner so that from floor level they would appear to be on a flat plain.

It was first necessary for Meush to visualize a central point on the diameter of the base of the curve and, working from this point and a corresponding one on the floor, apply a series of geometric angles and logarithms to make his charcoal sketches.

He spent two months making the projected drawings. The main colours—orange, indigo, and dull red—were selected by Meush because he saw them in Saskatchewan sunsets

Meush, who mixed his own inks and paints for the project, applied many coats of varnish to protect the dome painting.

The painting is a Meush original and represents his view of the Coronation of the Virgin Mary in Heaven. The image depicts God blessing Mary. Jesus is holding a crown over Mary's head, and the Holy Spirit is portrayed in the shape of a flying dove. Surrounding the throne are 157 angels and cherubs of different sizes.

Below the feet of Mary, there's a sky blue streamer with a yellow inscription bearing the words: Hail, Virgin, Full of Grace, Queen of Heaven, Holy, Holy, Holy, Alleluia.

Below the streamer, there is an open book that reads: Mary, Advocate, Protectress, and Perpetual

Because of the pillars which supported the dome, an extension in 1955 resulted in a narrow and long expansion.

Help of Christians. Around the dome are eight life-sized angels, painted with a spray gun.

St. Mary's, for many years, has been the destination of an annual pilgrimage. Church records indicate that more than 4,000 persons attended the 1941 pilgrimage when the population of Yorkton was 4,931.

Other works of Meush, who died of a heart attack on June 21, 1951, can be seen in Ukrainian churches of St. Basil's in Regina, as well as the smaller communities of Alvena, Arran and Smuts in east Saskatchewan.

St. Mary's Ukrainian Catholic Church is located at 155 Catherine Street in Yorkton.

GOVERNMENT

"The legislative building . . . was [designed] to be a symbol of the confidence and vision that the early pioneers had for their new province—a monument to democracy."

–Gordon Barnhart, Clerk of the Legislature from 1969 to 1989

Government buildings across the province were often designed and constructed to serve the people of a particular community, region or entire province for many, many years.

Serious and solid, stable and secure, these structures reflected the faith politicians, policymakers and their supporters had in the future.

Sometimes a government building was designed to send a visible message to the taxpayers—and visitors—that projected confidence in Saskatchewan's future. A classic example is the Legislative Building. Walter Scott, the province's first premier, had a vision for Saskatchewan that was as big as the Prairie sky. He used his moral suasion and his political savvy to ensure the Legislative Building was constructed of bricks and mortar and of limestone and marble in a part of the capital city that was quite literally off the beaten path.

In fact, construction of the Saskatchewan Legislative Building was such an usually large project for a government whose term of office was measured in months and not years that it even required a special railway line to be constructed in 1911 to bring supplies to the site.

Scott's stubbornness was not an uncommon characteristic of the community leaders throughout Saskatchewan's history.

Other equally determined civic leaders in Moose Jaw rallied to raise funds to build their public library after their financial request for money from a major United States philanthropist was turned down. Interior design of the Moose Jaw Public Library was said to be matched against the grand plans of the Saskatchewan Legislative Building.

The most common, and often longest lasting, government buildings erected were land titles offices. Built mainly with local brick, the buildings followed virtually the same architectural designs and blueprints in every community where there was a regional need to have land ownership registered. That's why the former land titles buildings in Arcola, Battleford, Regina and Saskatoon are still standing, in some cases more than 80 years after construction was completed.

From time to time, innovation becomes a necessary tool for government when the vision exceeds the physical boundaries of a location. In 1963, architects had to design the SaskPower head office building in the shape of the letter Y to ensure that the number of square feet required could be accomodated on the size of the lot that had been acquired. Premier T. C. (Tommy) Douglas was so proud of the results he described the building as a Poem in Stone.

Government buildings throughout Saskatchewan continue to reflect the vision and values, strength and stability of community leaders.

LAND TITLES BUILDING
Arcola

The Arcola Land Titles Building, completed between 1911 and 1912, now is the home of an art gallery, historic photo museum, genealogical research centre, and tourist information centre.

"This building is an ideal for us to share a glimpse of the life and times of the pioneers who helped develop this part of Saskatchewan," said Adrian Paton, a retired farmer who is the chair of the Arcola Heritage Society. "Many of the photographs are in excellent condition so you get an accurate image of what people did back then and how they looked."

Paton began collecting photographs of activities in the Arcola district as a hobby, but then, after word circulated in the community, people began giving him photographs and negatives from their own family archives.

Today, the South Saskatchewan Photo Museum collection contains the efforts from more than 40 photographers.

"There are some truly remarkable photographs, including one that was taken somewhere between 1886 and 1889," Paton said. "We're not sure of the date but it was a photograph of about dozen people who had gathered at a place we call Picnic Hill near here. Local records say about 100 people came from as far away as Alameda, which was more than 50 kilometres, for the community picnic."

Local history books report that a baseball game and races took place at the picnic, he said, adding this may have been one of the first-ever recorded community Sports Days, now very common throughout Saskatchewan each summer.

The foundation of the collection are the works of Thomas Carlyle Yeward, who took photographs in the area on glass negatives before 1900, Earnest Dalquist, who took photographs from 1900 to 1904, and Donald M. Buchan, who recorded history on photographs from 1904 to 1961.

The Arcola Land Titles Building was constructed soon after Saskatchewan became a province.

To deal with the rush to settle prairie lands in the early 1900s and to more prominently display the presence of the new provincial government, nine new land titles buildings were constructed throughout Saskatchewan between 1907 and 1916.

In some communities, these building replaced the Land Registry offices administered by the federal government between 1870 and 1905, during the era of territorial rule.

Standardized plans—many produced by the prolific Regina architectural firm of Storey and Van Egmond—produced dignified one-storey red brick buildings in several different sizes and degrees of opulence.

Land Title Buildings were constructed at Yorkton (1907–08), Battleford (1908), Saskatoon (1909–1910), and then, finally in Arcola (1911–12).

Designed to be as fireproof as possible, the provincial land titles buildings all maintain some of the same features such as copper doors and copper-clad window frames and door frames, stone sills and decorative details, and marble entranceways. Even the furniture was made of metal or metal-clad whenever possible.

Inside the building, the original copper doors and detailing remain, as well as the small foyer that was decorated with huge slabs of pink and grey marble, and floored with a terrazzo flooring of black and white.

The cairn erected when the Arcola Land Titles Office was created still stands to the south of the building. It marks the exact location and elevation above sea level. This was used to help the early surveyors find plots of land in the area.

In 1961, the provincial government moved the land titles work for the area to Regina from Arcola, which was an economic blow to the community because all of the jobs that disappeared.

A newly formed service club, the Moose Mountain Elks, rented the building from the town, which had acquired it from the province, until 1968. At that time, the building was sold to the Arcola School Unit for use as district headquarters. But a 1999 merger with the Oxbow School Unit to create the Souris Moose Mountain School Division left the building vacant. Two years later, the Arcola Heritage Society bought the building for $1.

People can conduct genealogical record searches in the 100 local history books.
PHOTO COURTESY OF ADRIAN PATON

When the society took it over, the building underwent much restoration. With the help of a professional engineer and other volunteers, the furnace and steam heating system was given a thorough cleaning. The entire firebox had new bricks installed, and the burner was relined. Paint was removed from most of the copper doors. Removing the school division sign revealed the original stone land titles signage.

Paton said the building now is home for the local archives to help people research their genealogical records in 100 local history books, municipal maps, and other records.

To defray costs, the Arcola Heritage Society operates an art gallery and craft area.

The Land Titles Office, located at 301 Main Street in Arcola, was declared a Municipal Heritage Site in 2001.

LAND REGISTRY OFFICE
Battleford

A building that once contained all of the land registration records for two-thirds of the area of Canada now is recognized as Saskatchewan's oldest brick building.

The building was the first Land Registry Office in the North-West Territories, when the territorial area included what now are parts of the provinces of Alberta, Saskatchewan, Manitoba, Ontario, and Quebec.

Constructed of bricks made locally, it was used as a Land Registry Office for about 30 years, closing in 1908 when the new Land Titles Office opened, closer to the downtown of Battleford. It was a private residence until 1990 and was acquired by the Battle River Settlement Foundation Inc. in 1998.

"The Land Registry Office is one of the most important buildings in the history of Battleford and of the province of Saskatchewan," said Julian Sadlowski, a founding member of the Battle River Settlement Foundation Inc. "It's worth investing our time, our effort, and our money to preserve this for future generations."

Sadlowski, a retired school principal who was elected mayor of the Town of Battleford in 2003, has played an active role in helping to educate people about the Land Registry Office.

He has written and illustrated three pictorial colouring books depicting the history of the Battlefords and the area known locally as Government Ridge. Government Ridge is an escarpment overlooking the Battle and North Saskatchewan rivers that included not only the Land Registry Office but other key government buildings including Territorial House, which was consumed by a fire in the summer of 2003.

Sadlowski also researches and illustrates brochures that tell stories of historic sites and places in the Battlefords area in much more detail than regular brochures do. "Teachers are picking up these brochures as either resource material, or they use them as 'units' when teaching early Saskatchewan history," he said.

Battle River Settlement Foundation Inc., while trying to obtain ownership of Territorial House, purchased the Land Registry Office and several lots on Government Ridge. The foundation raised money and bought the property for $36,000. The ownership was turned over to the Town of Battleford in a land and building trust.

Federal government contractors built the Land Registry Office from 1877 to 1878 from local brick. The Land Registry Office is located at the crest of the hill to the west of where Territorial House once stood, on Highway 648 south of Battleford.

It is a low brick single-storey structure divided into three rooms, two for storage of deeds and patents with a vaulted, brick-domed ceiling, and one room for an office with a fireplace. The building measures 22 feet by 38 feet.

The Land Registry Office was the first brick building in Saskatchewan made from locally manufactured brick. The roof was covered in tin shingles and the outside wall was one-and-a-half feet thick and bricked, complete with an earthen cellar.

In 1907, the premise was sold to Henry Felix Smart, son of Frank Smart, who was killed while on patrol during the North-West Rebellion. The Smarts made their home in the Land Registry Building until 1916, when it was sold.

It was then used as a maternity hospital well into the late 1940s. The Land Registry Office was eventually sold to Donald McBain, who used it as a private residence.

He, in turn, sold the property to Clint and Catherine Greenwood in 1955. The Greenwoods constructed a frame addition to the east side of the building in 1956 and subsequently added several sheds, a barn, and a garage to the site.

The property was then purchased by Dr. and Mrs. R. Runge, who expressed an interest in constructing a residence nearby, which would re-create the exterior of the original registrar's residence.

In 1998, Battle River Settlement Inc. purchased the building and seven lots and donated them all to the Town of Battleford to preserve its heritage for future generations.

The Land Registry Office, located on Government Ridge south of the Town of Battleford, was declared a Provincial Heritage Property in May 9, 1983.

It took two years to find a match for the original sheet metal shingles during the building's restoration that resulted in a Lt-Gov. of Saskatchewan Heritage Architecture Excellence Award in 2003.
Photo courtesy Saskatchewan Heritage Foundation

WATER TOWER
Humboldt

A dedicated group of people in Humboldt are trying to restore the community's water tower, "The Little Lighthouse on the Prairie."

"The struggle to obtain an adequate water supply on the prairies is a story of epic proportions," said Norman Duerr, President of the Humboldt-Carlton Trail Heritage Society. "Ultimately, it is the struggle for survival—the struggle for life. Humboldt's Water Tower is part of that story. As a result, it is a significant part of our history as a community."

The Humboldt Water Tower, technically a standpipe water reservoir, was constructed between 1914 and 1915 under the direction of consulting engineers Chipman and Power, who had built similar structures from Halifax to Victoria.

It consists of an inner steel tank, about 20 feet in diameter by 80 feet high with a conical-shaped cedar shingle roof. It was constructed with half-inch steel plates riveted together and anchored to a concrete base by eight 2.5-inch steel rods. The tank capacity was 156,000 gallons, or 670,000 litres, of water.

The design of the tower is striking for its resemblance to a coastal lighthouse and is distinguished by a wooden shell pierced by four slender windows spiraling to the top, giving the visual impression of an interior spiral staircase.

Controversy has surrounded the Humboldt Water Tower for almost a century.

The Humboldt Town Council disregarded the advice from civil engineer F. McArthur in 1914 that the town well would furnish all the water required. The quality of the water was also satisfactory, he told the council.

Instead, the council contracted consulting engineers Chipman and Power of Toronto. The consultants recommended a pumping distribution system, a pipeline to town, a pressure tower, the necessary water distribution system, and a sewage disposal plant and ejector system. The estimated cost was $300,000.

"Stoney Lake, at that time, was to be the source of the water supply," Duerr said. "No one could foresee that a lake literally 22 feet deep would in the future completely disappear."

Humboldt used the water tower until 1977, when a new water treatment system was brought on line. The tower sat idle and neglected for years. The structure was designated a heritage property in 1985, but by 1996 the designation was repealed due to the overwhelming cost of repairs.

As a result, Duerr and others began to rally support in the community to preserve and protect the property. The first major step came in 1999 when three volunteers rolled up their sleeves and donned disposable white coveralls to begin the difficult but necessary task of removing the pigeon droppings from within the former water tower. A hatch on the roof had been left open and the pigeons had made themselves at home.

Duerr joked at the time about being part of the Pigeon Popper Scooper Detail. "The Humboldt Water Tower had been the victim of neglect, summer sun and winter wind, rain, hail, and—pigeons!"

The three-phase restoration project has progressed methodically. "The first phase in 2003 included stabilizing the tiered concrete foundation with a reinforced concrete ring. The entire roof structure was reinforced. A main wooden beam was replaced with a steel beam, while a number of beams that were radiating from the tank top centre as supports for the roof. The catwalk had to replaced," he said.

Phase Two included restoring the exterior walls of the Humboldt Water Tower. "This involves stripping the existing cedar siding, salvaging and replacing what is reusable, and adding new siding where needed," Duerr said. "At the same time, an interior stairway will be constructed, spiraling the inside of the tank to access the upper catwalk."

Improvements to the structure in the final phase of restoration are designed to make the facility a tourist attraction. "We plan to build an interpretative centre within the former water tower detailing Humboldt's long struggle for an adequate water supply," he said. "There will also be an exhibition of equipment and artifacts associated with the

tower, and pictures and diagrams explaining how the former system worked."

The final part of the plan calls for tourists to be able to access a tunnel to see the underground pipes and valves leading beneath the tank. "In the future, we'd like to create a park area around the tower with a planted maze and walking trail linking the area to the city's new Ecological Park," Duerr said.

The Humboldt Heritage Water Tower, located and 407 Third Avenue, was rededicated a Municipal Heritage Property on March 26, 2002.

Humboldt's water tower was constructed by the same consulting firm who had built similar structures from Victoria to Halifax.
Photo courtesy SAHS

PUBLIC LIBRARY
Moose Jaw

The Moose Jaw Public Library, which opened in 1913, is a symbol of the optimism the community had in its own future after being snubbed by a wealthy American philanthropist.

Undaunted by the curt refusal of the Andrew Carnegie Foundation to grant Moose Jaw $50,000 to build a library, the city proceeded to finance the construction and furnishing the building for $100,000.

Moose Jaw did not settle for a simple structure. The Moose Jaw Public Library was the most impressive library ever seen in the province. In addition, the interior had the most marble of any building of its type, second only to the Saskatchewan Legislative Assembly in Regina.

Local architects Reid and McAlpine incorporated traditional designs with state-of-the-art features of the era into the public library, including stylish electric lighting and glass floors that allowed light to flood all areas of the building.

The imposing exterior is constructed of cream-coloured Dickinson pressed brick from North Dakota, with Bedford, Indiana limestone trim on windows, doorways, and steps.

The library boasted one of the finest interiors in the city. It features a magnificent two-storey rotunda surrounded by eight marble Doric columns supporting a balcony, over which are superimposed eight Ionic columns supporting the roof, all surmounted by a beautiful stained-glass dome.

J. W. Sifton, Superintendent of Public Schools and Chairman of the Library Board, reminded residents during the grand opening ceremonies in 1913 that "the library was their own," a reference to the refusal by the Carnegie Foundation not to help the community.

Sifton described the event as a "red-letter day for Moose Jaw," adding that the building would give "accommodation for the readers of a city of 75,000 to 100,000 population so the cost should not be considered for a moment." His enthusiastic speech reflected the optimism in Moose Jaw, a western boom town.

The city had grown from a population of 2,500 in 1903, the year Moose Jaw was incorporated, to 14,000 in 1913. Moose Jaw had been established as a divisional point for the Canadian Pacific Railway in 1882. Unfortunately, the city never achieved the predicted growth, with the population hitting a plateau of 35,000.

Moose Jaw was originally settled as a fur traders' camp. A narrow crossing of the Moose Jaw River, with plenty of water and game for food, made this an ideal place for settlement.

It was a winter encampment for both Cree and Assiniboine nations, and there is said to be burial grounds in the vicinity. The natural protection of the Coteau Range provided the valley with many a "warm breeze." The Cree word *Moosegaw* with a "g," meaning *Warm Breezes,* is translated to the city's name of Moose Jaw.

The opening of the public library in Moose Jaw received media attention in Winnipeg, almost 1,000 kilometres to the east.

"A more ideal situation could hardly be imagined than is occupied by this fine public library," said an article in the August 16, 1913, edition of *The Winnipeg Free Press* newspaper. "The beautiful rotunda is all in marble with a stained glass cupola. . . . The building is thoroughly fire proof and there are already over 6,000 books. The location of the library is only two minutes off Main Street, but it is in Moose Jaw's prettiest park, surrounded by flower beds."

More than half a century later, Leith Knight also found the location of the public library to be an attractive feature. "I think it was really neat to go to work in a park setting," said Knight, who worked at the Moose Jaw Public Library from 1962 to 1983. "This was a jewel for our city and the province. It was a remarkable feeling of peace and tranquility and made you want to go to work and, I believe, made people want to come to the library."

Knight said retired Moose Public Library staff still keeps in touch. "We were a close-knit staff," she said. "Even today, after 20 years being away from the Moose Jaw library, we get together every now and again for lunch."

Knight pinpointed the pioneering, customer service approach of her former boss as a key reason for the closeness of the former employees. "Chief Librarian, Ida Cooke, employed a service-to-the-public approach," Knight said. "Regardless of what you were doing, you dropped everything to wait on that customer. She [Cooke] set an example for all of us. I think that's why we still enjoy getting together today."

In 1992, an expansion at the rear of the library building was completed. The expansion connected the existing library and Art Museum buildings, providing much needed additional space for both operations.

For the library, the expansion allowed one of the original reading rooms and both of the meeting rooms to be returned to their intended use. The collection and much of the study area is housed in the expansion. De Lint & Taylor were the architects for the expansion.

In order to build the expansion, the rear wing, that housed the glass floor and part of the stack area, had to be removed. A portion of the glass floor was incorporated into the expansion.

Although controversial at the time, the final product of the expansion to the two buildings is a pleasing blend of the old and the new that is much more practical and efficient to use. The library was closed for two weeks to allow the staff to move the 75,000 catalogued books, paperbacks, videocassettes, and furnishings.

"After two years of construction and nearly 10 years of controversy, the $6.9 million facility is now being looked upon as a source of civic pride," the *Moose Jaw Times Herald* concluded in a March 29, 1993, article.

The Moose Jaw Public Library and Art Museum Complex, located at 461 Langdon Crescent, was designated a Municipal Heritage Property on July 12, 1982.

SASKATCHEWAN LEGISLATIVE BUILDING
Regina

It took three years to complete the construction of the Saskatchewan Legislative building, but Premier Walter Scott showed he had a great vision for the future of the province.

Built from 1909 to 1912, the legislature cost $1.5 million to finish, including the custom-made furniture. The Legislative Assembly Chamber was built to accommodate 125 elected Members at a time when there were just 25 Members.

Even the choice of where the seat of government was to be located showed that Scott, the first premier of the province, believed in the future of Saskatchewan.

Instead of building on one of the more popular choices of the day such as near Government House along Dewdney Avenue West or in the heart of the business district in Victoria Park, a decision was made by Scott's government to have the Legislative building located on the south side of Wascana Creek.

This was one of many controversial, yet forward-thinking, decisions Scott made. Having the

Saskatchewan Legislative Building constructed on 162 acres of land in a then-remote area of the capital baffled many people.

In hindsight, the decision looks almost brilliant.

The city and provincial governments have worked together to improve the area, and thousands of tourists flock to the 2,300-acre Wascana Centre to enjoy the manicured lawns, beautiful flower gardens, summer concerts, and carefully planted trees and shrubs. By comparison, Central Park in New York City is 834 acres.

During the Great Depression, Wascana Creek was the focus of a massive, man-made dredging operation that resulted in the creation of a lake and islands. In the winter of 2003–2004, another multi-million-dollar, tri-government project enhanced the depth of the lake even more, and created a water fall.

"The legislative building was not designed to be just any ordinary structure," says Gordon Barnhart, who was clerk of the Legislative

Assembly from 1969 to 1989. "Rather it was to be a symbol of the confidence and vision that the early pioneers had for their new province—a monument to democracy."

Barnhart, now a professional affiliate with the Political Studies Department University of Saskatchewan faculty, wrote a biography about Scott in which he details the vision and courage of the Premier. "Premier Scott envisaged a building which would be large enough to meet not only the province's needs at the time but for future requirements as well," he said. "Just imagine how this massive building would look under construction from 1909 to 1912. There was virtually nothing else around here except for this huge building."

Edward and W. S. Maxwell, two architects from Montreal, were at the height of their careers when they were awarded the contract to design and supervise construction of the Saskatchewan Legislative Building.

Key factors the Maxwells had to consider included the British parliamentary system of governments in Canada, Premier Scott's request to include a dome so the building could be seen for miles around, and the local weather featuring bone-chilling winters and hot, dry summers. In addition, the architects were told to design a building that was visually pleasing.

Their result combines English Baroque details, such as the square-drummed tower, with a Beaux-Arts façade and massing. The building is faced with Tyndal limestone and has a total floor space of more than 200,000 square feet (18,600 square metres). More than 34 different types of marble are used throughout the building.

"To enter the building fills one with a sense of the past, knowing that many of the most important debates and decisions in Saskatchewan's history took place in either the Legislative Chamber or the Executive Suite," Barnhart wrote in his 2002 book about the legislature. "One can imagine the many people who walked the corridors or climbed the stairs, carrying with them the heavy burden of office."

The building originally was the home of all 25 elected Members of the legislature, the premier, and his cabinet, as well as the then-entire provincial civil service. Today, the 58 elected Members and support staff along with the cabinet and premier occupy the building with some support staff.

Many important events in the history of Saskatchewan have taken place inside and outside of the Legislative Building. Visits to the province by the royal families and heads of foreign countries almost always begin with a ceremony at the legislature.

Placard-carrying demonstrators have marched outside the building to protest the creation of Medicare, privatization, and labour disputes involving public and private-sector unions.

The building is 56 metres, or 183 feet high. End-to-end, the building is 167 metres, or 542 feet long, and from the north to the south wings the building is 94 metres, or 308 feet, wide. About 40 percent of the building's 3,151 foundation piles are under the dome. There are 300 rooms.

Even after thousands upon thousands of red bricks had arrived at the construction site to be added to the exterior of the building, Premier Scott

Several different types of marble, granite and limestone create an impressive rotunda area.
PHOTO COURTESY SASKATCHEWAN PROPERTY MANAGEMENT CORPORATION

The distance from one end of the building to the other is more than the length of one and half football fields.
PHOTO COURTESY SASKATCHEWAN PROPERTY MANAGEMENT CORPORATION

Visitors can view the rotunda from an impressive third-floor balcony.

the governing and opposition political parties literally have to cross paths in the rotunda each day they take their seats in the Legislative Assembly.

The Chamber or Legislative Assembly is where the elected members debate budgets and bills to formulate laws and strategies that shape the future of the Saskatchewan

History is made not only by the politicians in the Legislative Building but exists there in different forms, as well. For example, the red carpet of the Legislative Chamber is an anomaly within the British Parliamentary system of government.

Traditionally, only the Senate has a red carpet, but for some unexplained reason, a red carpet was initially laid when the building opened in 1912 and has been maintained by successive governments. One thought is that Premier Scott did not want to have a green carpet in the Legislative Chambers, because green was the predominant colour of his political party, the Liberals, at that time.

Another item debated by academics and historians is a table now located in the Legislative Library. It is said to have been used at the 1864 Confederation Constitutional Conference held in Quebec City, where the leaders of Upper and Lower Canada (now the provinces Ontario and Quebec) met with their counterparts from the Maritimes to discuss creating the country of Canada.

Premier Scott also started a tradition in the very early years of the legislature's opening. He commissioned Edmund Morris to create a series of portraits of Plains Indian leaders to be displayed in the hallways as special galleries for public viewing.

Over the years, that collection has grown. When galleries featuring portraits of former premiers and all of the lieutenant governors who served as the Queen's representative in Saskatchewan are included, the collection totals more than 200 works of art.

Free public tours of the Legislative Building are conducted daily.

The Saskatchewan Legislative Building, located at 2405 Legislative Drive in Regina, was declared a Provincial Heritage Site on April 20, 1978.

changed his mind. He opted to use fossilized limestone, sometimes referred to as tapestry stone from Manitoba. That decision added to the cost of construction, in part, because special roads and rail lines had to be built to move the Tyndal stone to Regina from the quarries near Winnipeg.

The exterior of the building is elaborately decorated with intricate carvings of gargoyles, lions, and even chains of interwoven grains and fruit. Because the building was completed during the reign of King George V, many of the carvings also bear the inscription of GR for *Georgius Rex,* Latin for King George.

Inside, the rotunda on the second floor is one of the most spectacular features of the building. Designed with an arched ceiling under a false dome to create a sense of beauty and grandeur, the rotunda forms the crossroads for elected politicians. Because of the room assignments, members from

SASKPOWER BUILDING
Regina

The SaskPower headquarters in downtown Regina was described by Premier Tommy Douglas as a "Poem in Stone" when it opened in 1963 and continues to attract words of praise and pride today.

"The SaskPower Building still stands out as a special experience, even after 500 additional projects have been designed and completed," said Joseph Pettick, the architect who designed and supervised construction of the head office building. "At the time, it was the largest architectural commission in the province and Regina's tallest structure."

Built for $6.4 million over a two-year period, Pettick estimated replacement costs today would be in the $21 million range.

"We still receive complimentary letters from people who visit Regina and we would not have changed the design solution if we were to address the project as a current assignment," he said, adding the only deviation from the original plan might be the use of more prefabricated construction units.

"Flexibility of internal components was a major design strategy, and SaskPower has taken advantage of that element during the life span of the building to keep astride of current office methods and procedures."

Originally, the building was planned to be a 26-storey structure, but the provincial cabinet thought it would be too ostentatious for Regina and cut the proposal to half the height. Design challenges of accommodating the required amount of office space on a downtown property without increasing the height of the building resulted in a flowing, curved Y design.

"Its significance to the city and province relates to the departure from the rigid form of the conventional box style of building," Pettick said. "It is a signature building identified with the strength and dynamics of a 'Power' utility."

The SaskPower head office building has 13 storeys and is 180 feet high to the cooling towers placed on top of the building to save space. The building is 270 feet long by 44 feet wide.

The official opening of the SaskPower building in 1963 was deferred due to the death of U.S. President John Kennedy.
PHOTO COURTESY OF SASKPOWER CORPORATION

The Y curve of the building results in a façade longer than the lot on which it sits. It contains 2,300 tons of structural steel and more than 650,000 Saskatchewan bricks. The original windows on the 11 office floors could be turned in for cleaning, but those have been replaced.

For 1963, there were two very modern features: a drive-in to allow customers to pay bills without getting out of their vehicles, as well as pre-cast cellular flooring that accommodates easy movement of electrical and computer or communications wiring.

"I don't think any designer is ever totally satisfied, but the building has turned out to be a very functional unit and an economical building to construct," Pettick said in a promotional film made in 1963 by the power utility to record the opening of the new head office.

The SaskPower Building is set back from the intersection of Victoria Avenue and Scarth Street to prevent a walling effect. The head of the Y faces east while the tail curves toward the southwest. This design solved the traffic flow problem by providing an on-site unloading strip entrance from Scarth Street and traffic movement east across the front area through the building and out to Hamilton Street. In this way, traffic does not emerge onto Victoria Avenue, one of the city's busiest thoroughfares.

"It's an outgrowth of the problems of the site, the circulation of the one-way street system of traffic at ground level, and the efficient area for office space. The clear span steel dictated the width of the building. The main part of the building faces diagonally towards Victoria Park to take advantage of the view."

The grand opening for the building was delayed one day because of the assassination of United States President John F. Kennedy in Dallas, Texas.

The Regina building was an international architectural and design effort. Structural and mechanical engineering was co-ordinated by Mendel Glickman, an American engineer and architect, who was the prime engineering consultant for the major works of the famous American architect Frank Lloyd Wright on projects from 1934 to 1959.

Glickman taught classes at the University of Oklahoma and was Pettick's mentor while he was a student at the university in Norman, Oklahoma, from 1956 to 1959.

The SaskPower project won top prize and international recognition in 1962 from the Illumination Engineering Society for breaking new ground in the field of lighting for office buildings throughout North America.

"Over twenty tradesmen were brought to Regina as tile setters from Italy to work on the SaskPower Building by Antonini and Sons to install glass and mosaic ceramic tile throughout the project," Pettick said. "Most became Canadian citizens."

Two new industries were established in Regina as a result of design decisions: a pre-cast concrete plant for Conforce Products and the Dominion Bridge Steel Fabrication plant.

"We carried out extensive research on new office buildings in Canada, the United States, Mexico, England, France, Venezuela, Brazil, Argentina, and Chile to research major trends on a global basis," Pettick said. "Despite the 'flowing Y' floor plan, building costs were competitive with those for a standard square box design, due to adoption of repetitive modular systems and careful attention to detail."

The Saskatchewan Power Commission (SPC) was created by the province in 1929, when Saskatchewan's population was about 900,000 people.

By 1960, SPC staff in Regina occupied 25 floors in 10 buildings scattered through the capital city. These included the two original head office buildings at 1739 and 1753 Cornwall Street. Projected growth patterns showed there would be 835 head office employees by 1963 and at least 950 by 1968. Options included renting more space, leasing, or construction of a new head office.

A chance meeting by David Cass-Beggs, general manager of SaskPower, with Pettick at a reception led to the decision to commission him as the architect of the new head office resulting in the unique building.

The SaskPower head office is located at 2025 Victoria Avenue in Regina.

GOVERNMENT HOUSE
Regina

A core group of Regina people who began work on a project to celebrate Canada's centennial in 1967 turned their collective efforts over the subsequent decade towards the renovation and reopening of Government House, home of the Queen's representative since 1891.

"There were many, many people in this city and in the provincial government who thought we wouldn't be successful," recalled Glen Stinson, a small business owner and key member of the volunteer group. "It was a challenge. But we did it."

The 1967 project the Regina Chamber of Commerce had launched was the Trial of Louis Riel, the re-enactment of the trial of the Métis leader based on the transcript of the 1885 court proceedings.

Although the Trial of Louis Riel was moved from Government House a few years ago, it continues to be one of the most popular summertime attractions in the city because people from the

audience are selected during each performance to become members of the jury.

Over the years, Stinson and his friends remained focused on their goal, working towards their objective with provincial government officials and both Liberal and New Democratic Party administrations.

"The building was a mess, but we thought it was an important part of our history that we should continue to work towards reopening the house," Stinson said.

The group's name changed throughout the years, he said, beginning as the Saskatchewan House Committee in 1969 and then being renamed the Society for the Preservation of Saskatchewan House in 1971. After the facility reopened, the group became known as the Government House Historical Society.

"It was a great moment to see the house restored and officially opened to the public as Government House in 1980," said Les Donnelly who succeeded Stinson as president of the Society for the

The Government House Museum and Heritage Property is currently undergoing a major expansion to add a gallery, coach house, admin centre and gift shop.
PHOTO COURTESY SAHS

Preservation of Saskatchewan House in 1976. He served as president of the preservation society and then historical society until 1987.

"The house represents the foresight of our early government leaders to establish this building as a symbol of their faith in our province and in its people as well as their future. In this respect, I think it ranks in importance with our Legislative Building."

Government House was built between 1889 and 1891 in the late Victorian style by Thomas Fuller, Dominion Architect of Canada.

Government House is typical of many late 19th-century structures and is one of a only few surviving territorial buildings. For many years, it was the hub of social life in Regina. The south wing, containing a ballroom, was added in 1928.

Government House was the home of the lieutenant-governors of the North-West Territories between 1891 and 1905 and the Province of Saskatchewan between 1905 and 1945. It was closed by the Co-operative Commonwealth Federation (CCF) government of Premier Tommy Douglas.

As a result, between 1946 and 1984, the Queen's representatives had offices in the Hotel Saskatchewan in downtown Regina.

During that period, there were other uses for Government House. The Department of Veterans Affairs operated a rehabilitation centre there from 1946 to 1957, then adult education classes were conducted from 1958 to 1978.

The Hotels Association of Saskatchewan held food-server training courses in the building. The Saskatchewan Safety Council, where Donnelly worked in the 1970s, conducted a number of safety training courses there.

"Through these activities, as well as with my involvement with the Trial of Louis Riel, I was quite familiar with the condition and state of the building," said Donnelly, who was the area manager with A&W Food Services Canada in the late 1960s.

"After our success with the Trial of Louis Riel in 1967—it had 34 performances—we decided to continue to stage the play at Saskatchewan House, as it was called back then. However, many people expressed concern about the state and decline of the building."

The late Ruth Hunt, representing the Regina Council of Women, and Glen Stinson, representing the Regina Chamber of Commerce, co-chaired the first meeting of the Saskatchewan House Committee.

A construction contractor told the group the building was structurally sound, noting the foundation and walls were in good condition.

The catalyst to focus their work was a rumour that then-Premier Ross Thatcher was considering demolishing the building and utilizing the property for an expansion to Pioneer Village, an adjacent government property.

"This got the group motivated, and they organized the Saskatchewan House committee," Donnelly said, noting that eventually the group realized a long-term project would require a more formal organization, that resulted in the 1971 creation of the Society for the Preservation of Saskatchewan House.

Regina residents and visitors continue to enjoy the fruits of the group's work today. The restored portion of the residence is open for tours. Government House is open Tuesday to Sunday 10:00 A.M. to 4:00 P.M. year round. Public tours are available every half hour from guides dressed in period costumes.

Government House is one of Saskatchewan's grand and glorious heritage sites because of the blend of history with a "living museum" atmosphere. Guests walk through 14 rooms lavishly decorated with period furnishings. There are almost 10,000 artifacts that represent life from the late 1880s to 1900s.

"We wanted this to be a living museum," Donnelly said. "We're overjoyed with what it has become."

The ballroom and attached greenhouse are often used on special occasion for public events. The offices of Lt.-Gov. Lynda Haverstock are in the north wing of the building, but are segregated from the public area by security doors.

Government House, located at 4607 Dewdney Avenue in Regina, was declared a Provincial Heritage Property on August 26, 1981.

Exterior restoration of the historical property resulted in a 1999 Saskatchewan Architectural Heritage Society Vintage Building Award.
PHOTO COURTESY SAHS

A ghost—who flushes toilets, moves a mirror and can be heard walking on hardwood floors—is said to inhabit the house since 1938 when a cook died in the house.
PHOTO COURTESY GOVERNMENT HOUSE

ALBERT MEMORIAL BRIDGE
Albert Street, Regina

The Albert Memorial Bridge spans 120 feet of water with about 1,200 feet of reinforced concrete.

The construction of the Albert Memorial Bridge in 1930 and its restoration in 1988 was laced with controversy, political intrigue, and urban mythology.

The bridge, located between 19th Avenue and Regina Avenue along Albert Street, the main north-south corridor in the capitol city, spans 120 feet of water with 1,200 feet of reinforced concrete.

"Many stories about its design, construction and its restoration have become part of the local Regina folklore," explained Bill Henderson, who was the founding chairman of the Saskatchewan Heritage Foundation and now specializes in restoration of heritage buildings for Prairie Restoration Ltd.

The Albert Street Memorial Bridge was designed by the architectural and engineering firm of Puntin, O'Leary and Coxall, and built by Parsons Construction Company in 1930. The bridge's distinctive Art Deco design features Egyptian-style terra cotta balusters and lamp standards cast in a multi-coloured lotus flower design.

Egyptian-style concrete obelisks give a sense of grandeur to the bridge entranceways. The bridge is also adorned with many colourful terra cotta plaques of Queen Victoria and buffalos.

Since the conclusion of the First World War, three attempts have been made to complete a Saskatchewan commemorative memorial for those from the province who perished in the Great War.

The first effort was initiated in 1919 and ended in failure in 1924 with the cancellation of plans to construct a provincial war memorial museum in Wascana Park. The Albert Memorial Bridge was the second attempt.

The construction of the Albert Memorial Bridge in 1930 began as one of several labour relief projects undertaken in Regina in the first years of the Great Depression.

Construction of the bridge over Wascana Creek occurred in the electoral riding of Saskatchewan Minister of Public Works James F. Bryant, whose residence was located on Albert Street, just five city blocks south of the site. The minister announced that the bridge would be dedicated as a provincial war memorial to the Saskatchewan servicemen who perished in the First World War.

However, spending $230,000 of public money to span a narrow creek basin with a long ornate bridge resulted in the project being nicknamed "Bryant's Folly."

The public furor over James Bryant's motive for proceeding with the project was heightened when the provincial government called upon the City of Regina to raise $262,000 to pay for labour relief public works projects already completed in Regina, including "Bryant's Folly."

"The question of the completion of the bridge as a suitable provincial war memorial was brought into focus when the bridge was formally dedicated on November 10, 1930," said Henderson, a past president of the Saskatchewan Architectural Heritage Society.

"The promised bronze plaques listing the war casualties from Saskatchewan in the First World War mysteriously were not cast for the unveiling. Two bronze commemorative plaques that were provided for the occasion carried a dedication description that failed to signify the bridge was even a provincial war memorial."

Henderson explained that the bridge's designer, Colonel O'Leary, objected and ordered the commemorative plaques removed. The provincial government then countermanded his order and had the plaques reinstalled.

"In typical Canadian tradition, the argument over the wording of the plaques and the need to list the names of the war dead was referred to a special committee," he said. The committee failed to reach a conclusion and was disbanded in 1931.

"Given that approximately 5,500 Saskatchewan servicemen died in World War I, it was obvious that the existing design of the bridge was not suitable to fulfill the task of displaying the required number of bronze plaques," Henderson said.

The matter was left unresolved for 60 years.

The whole memorial fiasco and the affectionate amusement of Regina citizens for this ornate Egyptian-style bridge only fueled the controversy and folklore surrounding its construction.

The bridge has a distinctive Art Deco design.

"For many years the Albert Memorial Bridge was reputed to have been listed in the Guinness Book of Records as the longest bridge over the shortest body of water," he said.

"Unfortunately, the Guinness Book of Records confirmed in 1984 that the bridge has never been listed in any edition. Many Regina citizens still stubbornly refuse to believe this."

The Albert Memorial Bridge was neglected during the 1970s and early 1980s. Many of its colourful balusters were damaged and the bridge fell into poor repair.

"Still, zealous citizens like solicitor Dr. Morris Shumiatcher and architect Willem de Lint showed Regina's true appreciation for the bridge by organizing annual volunteer spring-cleaning bees," Henderson said. "Every year these dedicated volunteers appeared on the bridge to wash it down with mops, brushes, and copious pails of soap and water."

One year after its municipal heritage designation in 1984, controversy and intrigue again swirled around on the Albert Memorial Bridge.

The City of Regina Public Works and Engineering Department, headed by Director David Schnell, proposed several design options to widen Albert Street by removing the gracious old elm trees along Albert Street and replacing the Albert Memorial Bridge with a wider six-lane modern bridge.

The public outcry was immediate.

About 100 residents along Albert Street organized a coalition of community groups and professional

The bridge features a color-ful terra cotta plaques of Queen Victoria.
PHOTO COURTESY SAHS

Department, the "Albert Street Vigilantes" and their community coalition convinced city council to defeat the engineering proposal and to instead restore the Albert Memorial Bridge.

In 1988, the city council, with provincial funding assistance, proceeded with a $1.3-million restoration to bring "Bryant's Folly" back to its former glory and enhance the historic elm-lined boulevards of Albert Street.

Another controversy erupted after the restoration was completed. The city council decided to have its names listed on a new plaque placed on the bridge along in commemoration of the restoration work. This sparked more controversy over why the names of Saskatchewan's First World War casualties were again ignored.

This finally triggered a successful provincewide campaign to construct a proper provincial First World War Memorial on the nearby legislative assembly grounds in 1993. That war memorial records all of the names the Saskatchewan war dead of the First World War as originally promised in 1919.

The Albert Memorial Bridge, located between 19th Avenue and Regina Avenue on Albert Street in Regina, was designated a Municipal Heritage Site on October 1, 1984.

associations to oppose the city engineering plans and save the Albert Memorial Bridge. Led by a small band of six heritage activists, jokingly referred to as the "Albert Street Vigilantes," this community coalition developed their own design concept to restore Albert Memorial Bridge and save and enhance the historic elm-lined boulevards of Albert Street.

Ironically, one of the community leaders, Ann Phillips, lived in Minister James Bryant's former home on Albert Street, and hosted community strategy meetings in Bryant's former residence to save his beloved Albert Memorial Bridge.

After eight months of skirmishing with the City of Regina Public Works and Engineering

COURT HOUSE
Weyburn

The Weyburn Court House, built in 1928, has a distinctive, red-brick Colonial style and beautifully manicured grounds that make it a popular location for anniversary, family, high school graduation, and wedding photographs.

Charles Eddy and Kelly Neville, daughter of Provincial Court Judge Raymond J. Neville, are among the hundreds of people whose wedding pictures include the Weyburn Court House.

"As a young girl, I would pretend the Court House was my 'Victorian Home' and loved the beauty and grandeur of the building and grounds," Kelly would recall years later. "I often would wander throughout the empty building in the evening after begging my dad to take me along the Weyburn Court House while he caught up on some paperwork."

Raymond Neville presided over court for 27 years until 1992.

"So fond are my memories of the building that I asked dad if I could have my wedding pictures taken inside the Court House," she said. "As a result, our wedding pictures were taken on October 15, 1983, in the court room, on the 'Judges Bench,' down the grand staircase, and outside among the beautiful evergreen trees as well as in a tree!"

She said her memories of her childhood wanderings in the court house and the uniqueness of having her wedding pictures taken inside the court house will always be very special to her

Designed by Provincial Architect Maurice Sharon, the elegance of the Weyburn Court House building reflected the confident aspirations of Saskatchewan communities in the last good harvest year before the onslaught of the Great Depression.

The architectural design was inspired by 17th- and 18th-century structures and the Colonial Revival style popular in the early 20th-century southern United States.

Construction of court houses in this style in Prince Albert, Weyburn, and Estevan in the late 1920s symbolized the growing influence of the

The Weyburn Court House was inspired by Colonial Revival style popular in the early 20th century in the southern United States.
Photo courtesy Saskatchewan Heritage Foundation

United States on the cultural and economic life of Saskatchewan.

Lloyd Carr recalls some of the first decisions he made soon after he was hired in 1949 as the caretaker and the groundskeeper at the Weyburn Court House.

"I had been working in the hardware department of the local co-op store when the job came open," said Carr, who retired in 1982. "One of the first things we did was remove most of the hedge work because it hadn't been kept up very well. Then, we decided to start planting some trees around the property."

There are about 48,000 square feet of grounds around the building that required the care and attention of Carr each year. As impeccable as the outside of the building was, the interior of the Weyburn Court was just as impressive.

For Carr, the Weyburn Court House wasn't just a place he went to work. It was a place he called home with his wife, Nellie, and their four children—two boys and two girls.

Donna Hastings, now a City of Weyburn employee, grew up a half a block from the court house. "As a child, what I remember about it was that the caretaker and his family lived in a suite in the basement," Hastings said, noting some of their children were about her age so she spent some time there in the court house.

"There were a couple of holding cells, used by police, so that was always intriguing to see if there was someone in them." The only time the children were allowed upstairs was to deliver a message to Carr.

"To a child this building was huge," Hastings said. "The ceilings were very high, the floors gleamed and it smelled of wax, cleaners, and polish for the woodwork. The grounds provided a wonderful place for children to play hide-and-seek, as there were large numbers of trees and bushes that provided great hiding places!" Children were allowed to play only at the back of the property where no one could see them from the street.

"Today, the building hasn't changed a great deal," Hastings said. "This brick building is very impressive and is a wonderful part of Weyburn's history."

Carr, meanwhile, never dreamt he would spend most of his life living and working in a court house. "After the Second World War, I was looking for something and this was a wonderful opportunity," said Carr who saw duty as a tank commander in North Africa, Italy, France, Belgium, and Holland.

The first sitting at the Weyburn Court House was on January 22, 1929. Court continues to be held there five days a week.

The exterior of the building is a dark red brick with white mortar joints. The interior is highlighted by the use of quarter-cut oak. The building was constructed by Wilson and Wilson of Regina at a cost of $81,274.

Wooden shutters grace the second-storey windows. There are also ornate dormer windows and a cedar-shingled roof. All door handles bear the emblem of the province.

The Weyburn Court House, located at 301 Prairie Avenue NE, was designated a Provincial Heritage Site on February 15, 1988.

COURT HOUSE
Wolseley

The Wolseley Court House is the oldest existing court building in Saskatchewan and the only one remaining that was built during the era of North-West Territorial government.

Designed under the direction of Thomas Fuller, chief architect for Canada, it was built in 1894–95 to serve the judicial district of Eastern Assiniboia. The general contractors were E. A. Banbury, the founder of the Beaver Lumber stores, and R. A. Magee, a prominent Wolseley businessman, whose brick plant probably supplied the brick used in the court house.

Until the creation of the provinces of Saskatchewan and Alberta in 1905, the Assiniboia district ran from the Manitoba border to just west of what now is Medicine Hat, Alberta, and extended south to the United States border. The northern boundary of the district was an imaginary line just south of Saskatoon.

The only other remaining territorial court house is in Fort Macleod in what was the Alberta district

of the North West Territories before becoming the province of Alberta.

After the Wolseley Court House was closed in 1909, the building was used as a jail and as a boys' detention home until 1921, when it became an annex to the newly constructed nursing home.

Annie Edwards, a resident of Wolseley since 1913, has a clear recollection of the building as it was then used. Edwards' mother began work at the nursing home almost as soon as it opened.

As a young girl, Annie would often stop by the nursing home after school so she and her mother could walk home to the south side of town by way of the historic "Swinging Bridge."

"As part of the nursing home, the Wolseley Court House was initially used as a nurse's residence and superintendents office for a short time," Edwards recalls. "It then became a patients' dormitory on the main floor with the main laundry and a power plant in the basement."

It took two years to build the Wolseley Court House, ending in 1895.
PHOTO COURTESY SASKATCHEWAN HERITAGE FOUNDATION

flagpole still in place in front of the main entrance. The north end of the replication of the historic swinging bridge that crosses Fairy Lake now rests on the south lawn of and immediately in front of the territorial court house.

The Wolseley Court House, located on the corner of Richmond and Ouimet Streets, was declared a Provincial Heritage Site in 1982.

"In the basement, the four detention cells, barred doors and all, were used as well," Edwards remembers. "One cell was used for storage; one was locked so they could keep the drugs and medicinal alcohol safely, and two cells were used as private rooms for patients."

The nursing home was torn down in stages and the new Lakeside Nursing Home was erected in its place.

The Wolseley Court House, now owned by the Saskatchewan Property Management Corp., is used only for storage. Among other odds and ends stored there are several long mahogany waiting-room benches from the CPR station in Regina.

Located at 303 Richmond Street, the building remains in excellent physical condition with some alteration to the interior on the main floor.

It is a one-storey brick structure on a fieldstone sub-basement to which there is an outside entrance on the west face. The basement contains detention cells in their original condition—steel bars and locking doors.

The main entrance to the court house is a half flight of stairs centred on the south side, which overlooks Fairy Lake. The Canadian Pacific Railway created the lake by damming Wolf Creek to ensure a water supply for steam locomotives running along the railway's mainline across Saskatchewan.

The hipped roof is metal and is topped with a copper wind vane. The court house has mature trees and lawn surrounding it with the original

HOMES

"There's a black and white photograph of our home taken from the west wing of the Legislative Building several years after both were completed. All you can see is our house . . . and a few farms."

–Frederick W. Hill, on the Hill family home built in 1911

Homes in Saskatchewan, like virtually everywhere else in the world, reflect the personality of the owners, their financial background and even the pattern of settlement. Material used to construct those Saskatchewan homes matched the cunning, ingenuity and affluence of people across the province over the years.

In the early years of settlement, immigrants found little to use on the bald Prairie except the tents they brought with them and the soil beneath their feet. As a result, sod houses popped up faster across the region than weeds in a vegetable garden.

Problems, however, often arose because of the engineering prowess of the settlers. The roof over their heads quite often became the roof on their heads as the walls crumbled under the weight of the sod.

Farmers, being naturally inquisitive people, weren't shy about asking their friends and neighbors about solutions to the sod house problems. Learning from each others' mistakes helped solidify sod house design and make one sod house near Kindersley inhabitable to this very day.

A benefit of living in a home with walls more than metre thick is that the sod, now covered with exterior siding and reinforced with wooden supports inside, provides natural insulation, keeping the home cool in the summer and warm in the winter.

At the other end of the spectrum are Saskatchewan homes that prove that some homes are literally castles. Key Hole Castle in Prince Albert got its nickname from the unique shape of windows on the third floor of the house that took two years to build, ending in 1913.

Other homes have become famous not because of the design employed or material used in construction but because of the people who once lived there. For example, the house of John Diefenbaker, who was Prime Minister of Canada from 1957 to 1963, now is a museum.

The 1911 home built by Regina entrepreneur Walter Hill is considered the first show home in the province's first subdivision because it was featured prominently in newspaper advertisements to attract settlers to Saskatchewan. The house is a private residence.

Whatever their location and whatever their method of construction, Saskatchewan residents continue to erect homes as diverse as the people who call the province home.

ADDISON SOD HOUSE
Kindersley

Edith Gardiner continues to live in the two-storey sod house her father and uncle built northeast of Kindersley almost 95 years ago.

The Addison Sod House, which measures 40 feet by 16 feet, is considered the oldest continuously inhabited sod house in western Canada by the Saskatchewan Heritage Foundation.

"We were used to living in this sod house," said Gardiner, who was born in 1909 and was almost two years old when her family moved from Saskatoon into their sod house home. "Some people came here and thought they'd see sod on the inside walls with roots sticking out. That wasn't the case."

She explained that the interior walls were like a regular house and were covered in wallpaper. It is impossible to tell from the exterior that her home is built from sod because of siding and a gabled roof.

A key difference, however, is the fact the walls are four-feet thick. "One time, a fellow came to put vents into the walls because we were using propane to heat our house," Edith said. "He came back a few weeks later and was surprised with how little we had used and told us he'd go broke if all of his customers used as little propane as we did."

She taught in a variety of country schools throughout Saskatchewan, including Trossachs near Weyburn and in nearby Kindersley, before retiring in 1963 and returning home.

Her parents, James and Edith Addison, sister, and brother arrived from Liverpool, England, in 1907 and lived in Saskatoon for the first two years. Edith was born in Saskatoon.

James Addison was a skilled carpenter and worked at his trade in the city while looking for his own place to call home. In 1909, he travelled alone by oxcart to his newly acquired homestead site near Kindersley, studying farm buildings along the way. Lumber was scare. Brick was expensive.

Many of the buildings were built of sod at the time, but many also collapsed after a few months or years of service.

As a result, James Addison resolved to build a sod structure that would last and began construction almost immediately upon his arrival at their homestead.

Addison later returned to Saskatoon and resumed his carpentry for the winter of 1909–1910. The following spring, James, joined by his brother Charles, obtained a settler's railway car to take their belongings to the farmstead—four oxen, a cow and calf, farm implements and furniture.

The entire Addison family then travelled on the newly completed railline to Kindersley to begin their new life. After months of frantic activity, the Addisons moved into a lean-to building because the sod house wasn't finished.

The lean-to had an earthen floor and a cowhide over the door opening.

In 1911, the Addison brothers worked to finish the sod house, adding the three attic bedrooms, and completed the interior. Both contributed to the establishment of Charles' farmstead, near James'.

A few years later, two more children, Walter and Jane completed the family. The Addisons settled down to survive the uncertainties of farm life.

James Addison carefully chose the flattest site for his home. A dry slough bottom was the source of his materials. He made sure the cut sod would contain enough plant roots to keep the blocks intact.

Addison next began the arduous task of assembling the house walls. He carefully laid each course of sods, interlocking them to a double thickness. Addison hollowed out the centre of each layer and narrowed the walls as he built upwards. This allowed the walls to slump downward rather than fall in or collapsing outward.

The second storey was a traditional wooden-gable design divided into three rooms. The floor was reinforced because the sod walls were to be replaced eventually with a wood frame. That part of Addison's plan was never completed, and the sod remains inside the walls to this day.

The exterior was covered by vines, planted by Jane Addison, acted as weatherproofing, protecting the walls from wind and rain.

In the 1940s, the vines were replaced by wood siding and then covered by asphalt siding in the 1960s.

Jane Addison died in 1929 followed by her husband in 1963.

The Addison Sod House, located 10 miles north of Kindersley on Highway 21 and 6.5 miles east, was designated a Provincial Heritage Property on November 23, 1992.

To arrange a tour, phone Edith Gardiner at (306) 463-3364.

KEY HOLE CASTLE
Prince Albert

Alan Logue and his family have become used to seeing thousands of people each year walk or drive by his Prince Albert home, known as Key Hole Castle.

"Key Hole Castle represents to me the optimism and vision of limitless future prospects that many of the earlier citizens of Prince Albert and northern Saskatchewan brought with them from their many and diverse homes and backgrounds," said Logue, a lawyer, who has lived in the home since 1982.

"While there may be larger homes built in Prince Albert at about the same time, none compare with the workmanship and materials that were incorporated into Key Hole Castle."

The house was constructed between 1911 and 1913 for Samuel McLeod, the most prominent businessman in the Prince Albert area at the turn of the century. Logue believes an architect from Chicago moved to Prince Albert to personally supervise construction of the home, named after the unique keyhole-shaped windows on the third floor.

Key Hole Castle had all of the modern amenities when it was completed. "At the time of its construction the house was equipped with central hot water heat provided by a coal-fired boiler, a central vacuum system, and an intercom system with a station on each of four floors in the home," he said.

The 4,000-square-foot home is made of brick and has three bedrooms, three-and-half baths, and several other miscellaneous rooms, including a ballroom, library, maid's room, and even a sunroom.

"It draws upon many types and styles of architecture, although Queen Anne Revival is the most commonly applied general term," Logue explained. "Its exterior has extensive scroll work, gabling work, unique keyhole-shaped windows, clay tile roof, and many other embellishments that set it apart from most of the homes constructed in that era in Prince Albert."

The original McLeod home site encompassed one-third of an entire city block, and spanned from 20th to 19th Streets. The grounds, at one time, accommodated a gardener's residence as a separate detached house.

Interior appointments included quarter-cut oak, Honduran mahogany, hand-tinted Italian tile work, and extensive Italian stained glass work. Gold leaf finishes were applied in the dining room, and bevelled glass abounds throughout the house. All of the interior doors are inlaid with exotic woods and the hardware on the windows and doors were custom cast in matching brass or copper motifs.

The living room fireplace was specified to be constructed of matched marble blocks on the architect's blueprints. However, the material was recently identified as matched blocks of onyx, most likely from Nicaragua.

The upper floor of Key Hole Castle is occupied by a large domed room known locally as "The Ballroom" but identified as "The Billiards Room" on the original blueprints.

Daniel Finbar Dunn, a noted local artist, recently completed a year-long mural project in the domed ceiling. His work was consistent with traditional mural methods and landscape subjects at the turn of the century and complemented the Italian gold-leaf chandelier hanging in the centre of the dome.

Sam McLeod, the original owner who lived in the home until 1939, cast a huge shadow on the economic, political, and social landscape of Prince Albert. He owned and operated the Prince Albert Lumber Company, which employed more than 2,000 men, working 24-hour shifts, at its peak. The lumber company occupied a large part of what now is called the East Flat residential area of the city along the shores of the North Saskatchewan River.

"McLeod served as mayor for a time, and one of the things he is remembered for most is that he personally guaranteed the debts of the Prince Albert School Board," Logue said. "This was at a time just before 1920 when the City of Prince Albert itself was on the verge of bankruptcy because of a failed power project at La Colle Falls."

After McLeod's death, there were a succession of homeowners, mostly businessmen and professionals who had relocated to Prince Albert and were impressed by the magnificent structure.

The home was the focal point for many lavish social gatherings for more than 75 years. "Lucy Maud Montgomery, author of *Anne of Green Gables,* spent a couple of years of her childhood living in a house on the next block to Key Hole Castle," Logue said. "She recounted in her memoirs attending lavish parties in Key Hole Castle while residing in Prince Albert."

Logue bought Key Hole Castle in 1982 and his family has become the longest residents of the home since the McLeod family.

"Its unique architecture, extraordinary quality of construction and finishing are a lasting testament to the optimism and resolve of early settlement in Prince Albert and northern Saskatchewan," said Logue, a partner in the law firm of Harradance Logue Holash.

Key Hole Castle, at 1925–1st Avenue East in Prince Albert, was recognized as a National Historic Site in 1985.

It took two years to build the 4,000-square-foot home for Prince Albert's most prominent businessman, Samuel McLeod
PHOTO COURTESY SASKATCHEWAN HERITAGE FOUNDATION

DIEFENBAKER RESIDENCE
Prince Albert

The Prince Albert home of John Diefenbaker, who was prime minister of Canada from 1957 to 1963, now is a museum.

Diefenbaker was born in Neustadt, Ontario, and educated in one-room schools in the region then known as the North-West Territories before it became the Province of Saskatchewan.

He was elected to the House of Commons for the area in 13 consecutive federal elections from 1940 to 1979. Yet, political success did not come easy for Diefenbaker.

He practiced law for three years in Wakaw, about 60 kilometres southeast of Prince Albert, before moving into the city in 1922.

Voters turned their backs on Diefenbaker for many, many years. He was defeated in the federal general elections of 1925 and 1926. He lost when he ran for a seat in the Saskatchewan Legislature in 1929 and then in 1938, when he was the provincial Progressive Conservative Party leader. Between provincial campaigns, he

also lost in his bid to become mayor of Prince Albert.

Diefenbaker earned his place in Parliament in 1940, but was defeated in his first bid two years later to become the national Conservative leader. Re-elected to the House of Commons in 1945, he was defeated in his second attempt to become Conservative leader in 1948. Again returned from Lake Centre in 1949, redistribution eliminated his constituency.

It was at this point in his life, following the death of his first wife, Edna, in 1951, that he nearly abandoned politics. He thought about devoting his full energies to the practice of law, where his continuous success before the courts had earned him a very considerable reputation.

Diefenbaker married Olive Freeman Palmer two years later, and they retained his Prince Albert home.

Had his supporters in Prince Albert not rallied to his cause, assuring his victory in the 1953 election, it is doubtful that the Conservative Party would have elected Diefenbaker their leader in 1956. The slogan of the Prince Albert supporters had been: Not a partisan cry, but a national need.

In 1957, the Conservative Party, under Diefenbaker scored an electoral upset, ending 22 years of Liberal rule and formed a minority government. The following year, Diefenbaker's party took 205 seats in the Commons, recording the largest majority in Canadian political history.

Then, riding the crest of his enormous majority, Diefenbaker was able to pass legislation that reflected his populist philosophy. As an experienced criminal lawyer sensitive to the legal position of citizens, he was particularly proud of the Canadian Bill of Rights.

The Diefenbaker government gave Native people the right to vote in federal elections. He restructured social programs to provide more aid to the needy. His "northern vision" inspired some economic development of the far north.

Internationally, Diefenbaker played a key role in forcing the apartheid government of South Africa out of the British Commonwealth.

"I got to know Diefenbaker very well before and after he was elected prince minister," recalled longtime friend Max Carment. "We spent many, many hours plotting strategy and talking politics in his home."

Carment said John and Olive Diefenbaker relished the time they were able to spend in Prince Albert. "Travel wasn't as easy as it is today, but they did come home when the Commons wasn't in session and they loved seeing old friends," Carment said.

After the 1974 general election, he said Diefenbaker began getting his affairs in order.

"It was Diefenbaker who came up with the idea of donating the house to the City of Prince Albert. It wasn't the other way around," explained Carment. "I know he wanted the City to have it. Maybe he thought it might motivate someone to get involved in politics like he was." Sadly, Diefenbaker's second wife, Olive, died a few weeks after arrangements had been finalized for their Prince Albert home to be turned into a museum.

In Saskatoon, about 150 kilometres southwest of Prince Albert, a statute depicts youthful Diefenbaker selling newspapers on a street corner.

Local oral history tells of an encounter between Diefenbaker selling newspapers and then-Prime Minister Wilfred Laurier that is said to have motivated the youth to enter politics.

Gord Dobrowolsky became active in what he called the Diefenbaker Organization after his family moved to Prince Albert from the small Town of Gronlid. "We never referred to it as the federal Progressive Conservative party," he said.

Dobrowolsky, who rose within the Diefenbaker Organization from his early days as a youth worker, putting up lawn signs and making coffee, to be vice-president, vividly recalled a conversation with Diefenbaker one election night in the early 1970s.

"Dief had won in a walk and we were sitting together on the chesterfield. There were campaign workers all around celebrating his latest victory and there we were, just the two of us—my hero and I—sitting together talking like old school chums for probably 20 minutes: the former Prime Minister and I—Wow!"

The conversation shifted from the recent campaign to Diefenbaker's popularity. "I mentioned to him that it must be tremendous for him, being a former PM, to be recognized anywhere he went, known internationally, and having friends everywhere," recalled Dobrowolsky. "To which Dief quickly replied: 'You know young man, it's not as great as you might think. It is because almost all my friends have passed on, and because of that I have some very lonely moments.'"

Diefenbaker then went on to talk about how much Max Carment's friendship meant to him, the Prince Albert businessman said.

"That statement has had a lasting impact on me," Dobrowolsky said. "Here was a former Prime Minister admitting to me he was lonely because most of his friends had already died and he was left virtually alone."

Diefenbaker died on August 16, 1979. His state funeral was held in Ottawa three days later and, following a two-day trip on a funeral train, he was buried outside the Diefenbaker Centre on the banks of the South Saskatchewan River in Saskatoon according the detailed instructions he left in his will.

The Diefenbaker Home is located at 246–19th Avenue West in Prince Albert.

THE WALTER HILL RESIDENCE
Regina

Frederick W. Hill fondly remembers growing up at 2990 Albert Street, a house built in 1911 by his father, Walter Hill, one of Saskatchewan's first and most successful land developers and a partner in the McCallum-Hill Company.

"There's a black-and-white photograph of our home taken from the west wing of the Legislative Building several years after both were completed. All that you can see is our house, the nearby McCallum home, and a few farms," said Hill, now the patriarch of Saskatchewan's most successful business family.

"Because the photograph was taken from a high angle, perhaps from one of the top floors or the roof of the legislature, I think my dad wanted to show people what was possible in the area he called Lakeview."

The Hill residence, in effect, became the province's first show home in Regina's first residential subdivision.

Since then, four generations of the Hill family have helped grow Regina and the provincial economy. The core business for the Hill family remains in residential and commercial real estate, but they have diversified their interests in Canada and the United States, with holdings in oil and gas operations as well as radio stations.

Walter Hill's home was based on an English house he admired and had the Regina architectural firm of Clemesha and Coltman copy, but reduced by one-quarter.

The home, built at a cost of $30,000, featured elaborate chimneys, a steeply pitched roof, stone parapets, and strings of double-hung windows with stone mullions.

Materials and craftsmanship were of the highest quality. Exterior walls, for example, are of two layers of brick. The floors of all three storeys are pegged quarter-cut oak.

The design of the first floor was planned around a reception hall and a simple staircase carved with a leafed-branch design. The living room, which opened through French doors to the screened veranda, was panelled with oak to a height of six feet, and the coved ceiling was crosshatched with oak beams.

Originally, the dining room was panelled above the oak wainscoting with tapestry custom-made in Paris. The ceiling was stencilled with a border that matched the staircase cutouts. The adjustable chandelier had an elaborate brass ring of shields with a skirt and matching wall sconces. Light figures throughout the remainder of the house were of a more graceful Art Nouveau design.

The master suite with its green-tiled fireplace, the sewing room, and the children's bedrooms were on the second floor. All connected to the central vacuum system and the in-house telephone to the kitchen.

The third floor contained the maids' bedroom at the top of the stairs and a huge room that had a billiard table around which the house was built.

"The upper floor had the area we called the Billiard Room," Fred said. "That's where all the young people gathered. We recreated there with our friends and neighbours playing pool all the time."

Tucked away in one corner of the room was an area where Fred's brother Jim tinkered with a new invention—wireless radio. "My brother Jim, who was 14 years older than me, had a work area in one corner of the room where he was constantly working on his short-wave radio equipment trying new things," he said.

Hill said that his brother Jim, while an undergraduate student at the University of Toronto, conducted some significant research that brought him notoriety. "I remember seeing clippings from the *New York Times* about an experiment Jim had conducted when he moved to Toronto in which he was able to send a radio signal around the world," Fred recalled. "We were quite proud of Jim, but most of the time we didn't really understand what he was doing."

Jim Hill, after obtaining his degree in electrical engineering, joined the Saskatchewan Power Commission in 1929. However, his budding career was short lived because the following year he died when the plane he was flying crashed near Winnipeg.

The Hill family home was a social magnet. "There was a lot of social activity in our house,"

Fred said. "Whether it was our parents entertaining or the kids having friends over, there were lots of very fun times. We had a huge living room, and we'd often clear the furniture aside for dances."

The Hills entertained lavishly, routinely holding dinners for 24 people and often entertaining their guests with a string quartet. They travelled extensively, annually visiting New York to shop, conduct business, and learn the latest dance steps—the Castle Walk, the Hesitation Drag, and the Sensation Stroll—which they taught to their friends on their return home to Regina.

Walter Hill was born near Guelph, Ontario, and arrived in Saskatchewan in 1899. He met his future wife, Grace O'Connor, who was from Halifax, while attending Regina's Normal School, or Teacher's College. They married in 1905.

He taught at Edenwold, a small community about 50 kilometres northeast of Regina, where he spent his weekends writing insurance policies for the local homesteaders. That moonlighting led him to a full-time position as an insurance agent based in Regina.

When Walter Hill was organizing his territory, he realized there was more money to be made in land development than in selling insurance. So, in 1903 he joined E. A. McCallum to form the McCallum-Hill Company. A year later, the company purchased 11,000 acres north of Swift Current and brought in a homesteader for each section.

The company soon became the premier real estate company in Regina as well, with the homes of the two partners setting the tone for the development of what is now called Old Lakeview.

By the time Walter Hill died in 1971, the McCallum-Hill Company had also formed Saskatchewan Guarantee and Fidelity, Western Surety, Canadian Devonian Petroleum, Regina Cartage and Storage, and a stock and grain business later sold to James Richardson.

In the 1960s, the company developed the 600-acre subdivision of Hillsdale, south of the Legislative Building, which had been land obtained from an area farmer in the original transaction that created the Lakeview subdivision.

"My dad bought around 1,000 to 1,200 acres from Robert Sinton, an early pioneering farmer,"

Fred recalled. "What made it interesting was that my dad always carried around this satchel of money. Legal tender then was $1 and $2 bills. He had about $20,000 with him, so, when Sinton finally made up his mind to sell, he could buy the land!"

Grace Hill died in 1959 and Walter passed away at the age of 93 in 1971. Soon after, the Hill family home was sold.

The Hill residence, at 2990 Albert Street in Regina, was declared a Municipal Heritage Property on August 3, 1982.

THE MARR RESIDENCE
Saskatoon

The Marr Residence, a home requisitioned by the government of Canada as a field hospital during the 1885 North-West Resistance, is the oldest building in Saskatoon on its original site.

Built in 1884 for stonemason Alexander Marr and his family, the house was constructed with lumber from a bargeload of building material sent down the South Saskatchewan River for the new Temperance Colony.

Transported west by the Canadian Pacific Railway, the lumber came from sawmills on Lake of the Woods, Ontario. At Medicine Hat, the lumber was made into rafts that were assembled and disassembled each time they ran aground in the river's shallows. The Marr Residence was once known as one of the finest and largest homes in the heart of the early Nutana district. Its simple, wood-frame structure of one-and-a-half storeys has a Mansard-style roof typical of the Second Empire style introduced during the rebuilding of Paris in the 1850s.

The popularity of the Mansard style was declining as the North-West Territories were settled, leaving the Marr Residence as one of the few remaining domestic examples of the Mansard style of architecture in western Canada today.

The home originally measured just 18 feet by 24 feet, but featured a scenic view of the riverbank through its dormer windows. Later additions made to the house include a bathroom and pantry (1903-1911), front porch (1929), and a hand-dug basement (1931). The only portion of the house completed in the fall of 1884 when the Marr family moved in was the double room at the front of the residence.

The City of Saskatoon bought the Marr Residence in 1979 to ensure its place in history and within the community. The house now is maintained by a management board and a group of dedicated volunteers who organize heritage-related programmes throughout the year.

"When we, as volunteers, work in the Marr, it feels like we are there in the house 100 years ago,"

The Marr Residence is one of the few remaining examples of a Mansard style architecture in Western Canada today.
PHOTO COURTESY SASKATCHEWAN HERITAGE FOUNDATION

says Sue Barrett, chair of the Marr Residence Management Board. "Because it still sits on the same site, and the part that existed in 1885 is intact and has been restored, it allows us to get a sense of returning to another time, and gaining an appreciation for what life must have been like for the early pioneers."

She explained that the management board has reports from the deputy surgeon general crediting the recovery of soldiers wounded in skirmishes with Métis leader Louis Riel's forces at Batoche and Fish Creek to the Marr Residence. "I am convinced that much of the success which followed the treatment of the sick and wounded billeted here was due to the remarkably healthy condition of the place (Marr Residence)," wrote Deputy Surgeon General Thomas Roddick.

Alexander Marr was responsible for building Saskatoon's first centre of learning, The Little Stone School in 1887. Today, the school is appropriately located on the University of Saskatchewan campus. This proved to be a very important building in the early Temperance Colony. It was a place not only for education but for a variety of community activities.

"The Marr Residence carries on that tradition of educating and sharing in the community through programs which explore the many layers of meaning found within the site—familial, political, military, medical, architectural, archeological and individual," explained Linda Stark, another member of the Marr Residence Management Board.

The strong sense of community felt by early residents of Saskatoon was called upon in the spring of 1885, when the North-West Resistance began at Batoche.

As one of three largest homes in the settlement of just 70 colonists, the Marr family residence was requisitioned by the government for use as a field hospital between May and July.

These partially furnished homes were situated close to the river landing and so provided easy access to fresh water and the wounded carried from the steamship, the *Northcote*. More than 60 wounded from Batoche and Fish Creek received treatment in Saskatoon. Field hospitals at these sites and at the Marr Residence share the distinction of flying the Red Cross flag for the first time in Canada. Years after the Marr family left Saskatoon, the house was home to a variety of families and individuals who enjoyed its unique history and riverbank setting. It was owned by William Henry Sinclair who was a cattle buyer, partner in the area's first creamery, promoter of the *Saskatoon Phoenix*, policeman, and member of the territorial legislature.

"The house is a museum, but it still feels like a home," explained Barrett. "It has an ambience and warmth that attracts people and makes them feel comfortable."

School tours of the Marr house introduce young persons to one of the many heritage sites within the city while encouraging them to explore the history of their own neighbourhood. "Children relate to the Marr very well," Barrett said. "That's because they can put themselves into history and feel what it would have been like to live in a house on the riverbank at that time in Saskatoon's history."

In addition to the summer programs and workshops, the Twelve Days of Christmas are celebrated at the Marr Residence each December with a mixture of song, crafts, caroling, and other community events. The practice of storytelling and reviving traditional ways is vital to the longevity of the Marr Residence. As when it was first built, the Marr Residence will continue to be a key gathering place in the community for many years to come.

The Marr Residence, located at 326–11th Street East in Saskatoon, was designated a Municipal Heritage Site on January 11, 1982.

STEBNER / ALEXANDER HOME
Saskatoon

A fieldstone house with wood shingles feels like a lodge in a northern forest rather than a residence on Spadina Crescent overlooking the South Saskatchewan River as it meanders through Saskatoon.

Constructed in 1912, the heritage home displays some of the simplicity of the popular early 20th-century Arts and Crafts movement in North America.

The house has a rustic appearance and features a prominent fieldstone front veranda with an associated single-storey turret and stone chimney. The rest of the building and the roof are sided with wood shingles. The stonework is carried on into the interior, including a substantial fireplace. Leaded windows and fine woodwork accentuate the interior view.

"We are only custodians of this property, and our research has been a rewarding process that has taught us so much about the beginnings of Saskatoon," explained Annette Stebner, whose family bought the 3,200-square-foot home in 2000. "The lives of so many people have been touched by this house. It is rewarding to know that we have been a part of its 90 years of existence and that our restoration will continue to make it a valuable part of the neighbourhood and a sound monument to our forefathers who built the beautiful City of Saskatoon."

The house, built during the city's massive construction boom in 1912, was often featured in local newspapers as an example of the community's lifestyle.

It remains a focal point of interest for tourists and visitors to this day. "People who walk or drive down the street sometimes stop to acknowledge its rustic beauty," Stebner said. "Some even have asked to use it in class projects or have stopped in to tell stories about visiting or babysitting in the house many years ago."

Henry A. Bruce took out an $8,000 mortgage to build the house, which his family lived in until he sold it to Dr. H. E. Alexander in 1916.

The 3,200-square-foot fieldstone home in downtown Saskatoon was built in 1912.
PHOTO COURTESY ANNETTE STEBNER

Dr. Alexander was head of surgery at St. Paul's Hospital in Saskatoon and also had surgical duties in North Battleford and Davidson. He was highly respected in medical and agricultural circles. Dr. Alexander owned Riverview Farm and was well known for his Belgian draft horses and purebred shorthorn cattle.

The Alexanders raised four children—Margaret, Robert, Doris and William—when they lived in the home from 1916 to 1946.

Margaret became the first female doctor in the Canadian navy and married Roy Gentles who became president and chief executive officer of Alcan, the Aluminum Company of Canada.

The Gentles' son dropped by the home unexpectedly one day. "The most significant visitor to sign our guestbook is the grandson of Dr. H. E. Alexander and his own family," Stebner said.

"Brian Gentles had never seen the inside of the home and casually stopped by on a flight layover returning back to his home in Ontario. He introduced himself with his name and a handshake. No further explanation was necessary, which was all it took for him and his family to receive an enthusiastic welcome."

The Stebner's rolled out the proverbial red carpet for Gentles. "We gave him an extensive tour and showed him pictures of his family's past generations," she recalled. "I believe it must have been somewhat unnerving to hear us, complete strangers, speak with such enthusiasm and detail about his family. It was an amazing visit which helped us keep a positive outlook on a somewhat overwhelming vow we've made to restore and maintain this house."

Doris Alexander, meanwhile, married Russel "Rusty" Macdonald, a prominent Saskatoon resident who was editor of *The Western Producer* weekly newspaper. A branch of the Saskatoon Public Library has been named in his honour.

The Arts and Crafts style construction of the house is highlighted by the use of natural materials and hand craftsmanship. The front of the house is an expansive wraparound porch built of local fieldstone. On the side of the house is a large stone chimney.

"Upon entering the front of the house, you enter into the living room," Stebner explained. "This room is very typical of Arts and Crafts homes. At one end is a massive fieldstone fireplace."

The ceiling is a box-beamed ceiling made of oak. Off of the living room is a small den that also has a fireplace, this one made of brick. All of the wide, extensive woodwork is oak. Around the living room walls, which are made of sand-finished plaster, benches are built to create a cozy atmosphere.

Off the other end of the living room is the dining room, complete with oak wainscoting that runs up to a plate rail. The ceiling again features oak beams.

Hardwood floors run through the entire house. All windows on the main floor are leaded glass, casement windows. The third floor was originally home to the maid. Remnants of the original maid call system remain in the house.

There are four fireplaces in the home—one in the living room, in the main floor den, in the second floor family room, and one in the master bedroom.

The woodwork on the second floor was all removed by previous owners, but the Stebner's are replicating it to match the main floor.

During the 2001 renovation, craftsmen spent six weeks replacing the two layers of rotting shingles with authentically installed cedar shingles.

The yard's landscape still holds rock paths, rock gardens, a pond, and many lilacs from the Alexander years. Although having been rented out during a time, the house has always been a single-family dwelling.

The Stebner/Alexander Residence, located at 1020 Spadina Crescent East in Saskatoon, was designated a Municipal Heritage Property on November 5, 2001.

PIKE FARM HOUSE
Waseca

The house Everard Pike bought from the T. Eaton Company mail order catalogue in 1918 and then built near Waseca in northwestern Saskatchewan has outlasted the Canadian retail institution.

"There are four Eaton's houses in a row here, so to speak: Blyth's, Pike's, Foster's and Wesson's," explained Christine Pike, youngest child of Everard and Winifred Pike. "This building, here on the Strathdene Farm, had an influence on the lives of the hundreds of families in this area."

She said that despite a lack of money at times, the gardens and landscaping around the home were maintained over decades as a result of sheer hard work. "The house and grounds were a gathering place in summer and winter," Pike explained.

"In the summer, it would be tennis or cricket or soccer practice, or people coming just to see the grounds or to buy fruit and honey, or to swim in the dam. An ice house supplied ice for homemade ice cream."

In the winter, the local men would organize billiard tournaments on the big table in the basement.

"The original cedar shingles have been replaced by metal shingles, covered with resin and, oddly enough, this does not look out of place," she said.

Piece by piece, the material to construct the 40 foot by 28 foot house was hauled to the farm from Waseca by a horse-drawn team and sleigh during the winter of 1917 and 1918. Everard Pike froze his face more than once.

In the spring, he used his team of horses to dig the basement. Gravel for the concrete was hauled from five miles away. It took 100 loads.

The Pike family still has the original blueprints for the home, the list of materials, and the letter from a contractor in Edam agreeing to build the house. Material for the mail-order home cost $1,000, while labour to construct the house was another $1,000.

Thousands of families across western Canada turned to the T. Eaton Co. Catalogue for their

Settlers sometimes opted to buy blueprints and supplies for their homes from the T. Eaton Co. catalogue.
Photo courtesy Christine Pike

Located near Waseca in northwestern Saskatchewan, the Pike farm house has become a tourist attraction.

families pored over the catalogue and soon begin to write in for orders.

Timothy Eaton had unwittingly stumbled upon a new business enterprise. At the time, Canada was a sparsely settled country where most people lived miles from the nearest town. In just more than a decade, the size of the Eaton's catalogue grew to 400 pages.

By the early 1900s, the Eaton's mail-order catalogue had become a Canadian institution. Often called the "Homesteaders Bible" in the west, the catalogue offered rural Canadians all the merchandise available in a big city and more. Beside clothing, furniture, and appliances, Canadians could purchase farm equipment, seeds, and even live chickens. The Eaton's Christmas catalogue was first published in 1897.

Complete house packages appeared only in the Winnipeg edition of the catalogue. The first mention of houses was in the 1910 *Spring & Summer* catalogue, with the first pictures of houses appearing the subsequent catalogue for *Fall & Winter* of 1910–11.

The first house was the T. Eaton Co. Limited Design No. 101, described as an attractive eight-room house of simple, two storey gable-end design with a full verandah and a back porch. The dining room and parlour (living room) arrangement of Design 101 was repeated in many of the dozens of Eaton's designs to appear over the next 22 years.

The complete lumber package, including windows, doors and frames was $945 delivered to the nearest rail station. Eaton's dealt only in carload lots, and so, if an order was too small to fill a rail car, customers had to join with neighbours to fill the railcar. Because took it 19,000 square feet to fill a railcar, it may explain why there are four Eaton's homes near the Pike homestead in the Waseca area.

The lumber was shipped directly from lumber mills in British Columbia, thus saving the customer, as the catalogue said, "All middleman's profits and all storage, trackage, insurance and handling."

Eaton's would supply complete blueprint plans and details for $2.50. When a house was ordered, they would refund the $2.50.

Eaton's homes, contrary to popular belief, were not prefabricated. In fact, an Eaton's home was not

barns, buildings and homes between the two World Wars.

Few, however, have weathered the test of time.

In 1869, Timothy Eaton started his first store in Toronto with five employees. He revolutionized the retail industry in Canada. The T. Eaton Co. grew into a chain from coast to coast, but succumbed to the winds of changing economic fortunes, with the last store closing on Feb. 26, 2002.

The mail-order business began almost by accident for the company in 1884, when Eaton's gave away a 32-page, pink-covered catalogue at a farmers' exhibition in Toronto. Back on the farms,

even pre-cut. The company supplied all of the necessary lumber, millwork, hardwood, and the blueprints, but the buyer had to engage a competent contractor to build the house.

As a result, it's quite common to find an Eaton's house that does not match perfectly to any of the 39 houses in the 6 plan books the company eventually published.

Over time, a customer could choose designs that included 4, one-storey, 21 one-and-a-half-storey, 8 two-storey and 6 two-and-a-half-storey (with the attic that was sometime called a third storey) homes. In addition, Eaton's business evolved to include custom design work through which buyers would send their own ideas and plans into the company, and Eaton's would fill their order right down to the type of nails and doorknobs to be used.

Everard Pike used his Eaton's home as the focal point of his business and family activity. Soon after completing the home, he began an aggressive landscaping strategy, including more than 1,000 plum trees, dozens of apple and crabapple trees, and small fruits. He became a registered beekeeper in 1923, a business that flourished for 32 years until the bees were wiped out by the foul brood disease.

Today, the Eaton's house that Pike built and the loving care he and his family provided to the adjacent garden and grounds continues to draw interest from friends, neighbours, and visitors.

"Our home must be one of the most photographed houses in the province," Christine Pike said.

The Eaton's house on the Strathdene Farm is located on the southeast section of 9–49–24 W3, six miles north and one mile east of the Village of Waseca, which is on Highway 16 between Lloydminster and The Battlefords.

POWELL RESIDENCE
Weyburn

Sarah Powell grew up in Weyburn, was educated at the University of Chicago, and later became the wife of the prime minister of Iraq.

Sarah was the youngest of the six children of Harold and Elizabeth Powell, who had moved to Canada from South Dakota. Harold was the first manager of the Weyburn Security Bank, the only bank to operate with a Saskatchewan charter.

She grew up in the home that her parents constructed after their arrival in Weyburn. The three-storey, wood-and-brick building had a full basement and foundation of fieldstone.

Hardwood floors, doors, and moldings throughout the Powell residence provided an aura of elegance in the community that, at the time, had many houses built of sod or people living in tents.

The first floor covered about 1,110 square feet and had the kitchen, dining room, two parlours, washroom, and a sunroom off of the kitchen. The second floor was the same size with four bedrooms, a nursery adjacent to the master bedroom, and

another washroom. The third floor was the residences for the Powell's hired help.

The Powell's mark on history goes beyond the boundaries of the City of Weyburn and into the Middle East to this day.

"We knew when we bought the house in 2001 that it was a heritage home and that one of the owners, Harold Powell, was the general manager of the Weyburn Security Bank when it was Chartered. We knew their youngest daughter, Sarah, married an Iraqi diplomat," explained Jeannine Kater. "But it wasn't until we really researched and found the Powell's grandchildren and great-grandchildren that we realized what an amazing and inspiring family they were. They were pioneers in so many ways."

Jeannine and Brian Kater pieced together the Powell family tree and traced their descendants. "The Powells were both lawyers and found it equally important that each of their six children find themselves in a career," Jeannine said. "Although only Sarah was born in Weyburn, all of the children grew up in this home and received their primary education at Weyburn Collegiate before pursuing their own careers."

Harold Powell had helped to start the State Bank of White Rock, South Dakota, in 1896. He was elected justice of the peace from 1897 until 1900. To become more familiar with business law, he and his wife studied law from 1896 to 1899. He passed the bar at Pierre, South Dakota, in 1899 and his wife became the first woman lawyer in South Dakota a year later.

Harold and Elizabeth Powell moved to Weyburn when he became general manager of the Weyburn Security Bank. It was a subsidiary of the Canadian Investment Company, that had bought 50,000 acres of land in the North-West Territories of Canada.

They became pillars of the community. Harold was a member of the Better Farming Commission, which investigated agricultural conditions in Saskatchewan in 1919 following a succession of dry seasons. After the Weyburn Security Bank had been acquired by the Imperial Bank of Canada in 1931, Harold took a job working for the Dominion Agricultural Credit Company as vice president and general manager in Regina.

Elizabeth Powell was very active in the Women's Temperance Union movement and was president of the Knox Auxiliary Women's Foreign Missionary Society in Weyburn for two years beginning in 1909. She also won citations in Canada for her work in the Women's Temperance Union. An avid collector of pressed flowers and plants, she had a collection exceeding 1,000 specimens of pressed plants from much of Canada, New York, Wisconsin, California, and South Dakota.

"The Powell children grew up to have varied careers," explained Kater.

Knox Powell was an engineer and worked for Honeywell in Minneapolis. Oliver Powell was a banker and he served under United States President Harry S. Truman on the Board of Governors of the Federal Reserve System. He resigned that post to become president of the Federal Reserve Bank of Minneapolis.

Lyman Powell worked as a bank examiner for the state of Minnesota, Louis Powell became a civil

engineer, and Lydia Powell became a puppeteer and writer.

Sarah Powell became the most well know of the six children, said Kater.

"Sarah met her future husband at the University of Chicago were they were both attending. She was married in 1933 to Dr. Mohammed Fadhel Jamali, an Iraqi citizen and a Moslem teacher," she said.

"He would become the minister of foreign affairs, twice prime minister of Iraq, and the man who signed the United Nations Charter in San Francisco on behalf of Iraq in 1945."

Sarah accepted a position in Baghdad teaching English and later went on to head the English Department at Queen Alia College in Baghdad.

"One of the things she did to introduce herself to her students was to draw a map of North America and put a mark on it to show Weyburn, Saskatchewan, her birthplace." Jeannine said. "Her life was full of happiness and sorrow, especially as the result of damage to her eldest son Laith's brain following measles and encephalitis at age five. She had helped found the first school for mentally handicapped children in Baghdad, Iraq."

When her husband was exiled to Tunisia for political reasons, she launched a society to start the first school for the mentally handicapped. Now there are more than 70 institutions throughout Tunisia to take care of the special needs of the mentally handicapped of all ages operated by the society the former Sarah Powell of Weyburn founded.

Harold Powell had this home built when he moved to Canada from South Dakota to be general manager of the Weyburn Security Bank.
<small>PHOTO COURTESY SASKATCHEWAN HERITAGE FOUNDATION</small>

After her husband's death, she moved to Jordan to live with one of her three sons, Abbas, where she passed away in 2000.

Mrs. Powell-Jamali had written and published two books while her husband, Dr. Jamali, wrote more than 40 books. He was a member of both houses of the old Iraqi Parliament, foreign minister, and prime minister.

The Revolutionary Military Tribunal of 1958 sentenced him to death, but this was later commuted to ten years imprisonment. He was released in 1961 after serving three years and was appointed the following year Professor of Philosophy of Education at the University of Tunis.

Kater has been able to track down many of Sarah's children and grandchildren, communicating with them through the Internet.

"Your interest in the old Weyburn girl, Sarah Powell Jamali, our mother, keeps alive my dreams of publishing more of mother's projected materials especially *East Marries West* in which Weyburn is mentioned," Dr. Abbas F. Jamali, wrote Kater in an e-mail from Jordan.

The legacy of the Powell home in Weyburn is found half way around the world, yet many Saskatchewanians aren't aware of its significance. "I don't think many people realize there was such history with our home," Kater said. "We were told the City of Weyburn should be proud of the heritage it holds."

The Powell Residence, located at 815 Fourth Street South in Weyburn, was declared a Municipal Heritage Property on August 8, 1989.

MAGEE HOUSE
Wolseley

James Taylor grew up in Assiniboia and practised law in British Columbia before buying a two-story fieldstone-and-brick house built by Robert Magee, the first mayor of Wolseley and a prominent area businessman.

"I purchased the house in May 2000, to restore it, knowing full well that it would be like building a new house," Taylor said.

"The stone structure itself was in good condition. However, the roof had leaked and the interior was seriously damaged. In another year or two, the house would have been beyond saving."

"The architectural style of the home—a stone house with a Mansard roof—is not unique but it is unusual in the North-West Territories at the point in time," Taylor explained.

"The historical significance of the house lies with Robert A. Magee who came to Wolseley in 1883 from Quebec, which might explain the Mansard roof. He was a veteran of the Riel Rebellion of 1885 having served in the Moose Mountain Scouts."

He was Wolseley's first mayor and operated several businesses including a brick plant. Magee served as a member of the Legislative Assembly from 1912 to 1921 and then was the sheriff and local registrar for the judicial district of Moosomin.

The Magee home is a fieldstone house with brick corners, and brick surrounds on the doors and windows. Built in 1896, with dormer windows for the two bedrooms and the bathroom on the second floor.

The house is just 20 feet by 26 feet with an 8 by 4 front bay. The main floor has a large living and dining room coming off the small front foyer, that has an attractive staircase winding up to the second floor. A single-storey brick addition measuring 12 by 22 was finished in 1920 as an extension of the original wood-construction summer kitchen.

The house has one-inch tongue-and-groove fir floors throughout. "These will be sanded and refinished as they were originally," Taylor said. "The brick addition containing the kitchen and

The fieldstone and brick home of Robert Magee, the first mayor of Wolseley, was built in 1896.
PHOTO COURTESY JAMES TAYLOR

utility room is being finished to be compatible with the main structure."

Taylor is doing most of the restoration work himself, with the help of skilled tradesmen when necessary. A new roof and windows have been installed, while the interior was gutted and then fully insulated. Electrical and plumbing have been completely redone.

Several articles were discovered during renovation including newspapers from 1898; lumber stamped R. A. Magee-Wolseley, and a Golden Text Card dated August 15, 1897.

"The interior is being restored with the original casing, bulls-eyes, and doors, including original hardware," he said. "The bathroom now is on the second floor with a 300-pound claw foot tub that we slid in through the window by forklift."

Taylor's restoration work caught the eye of research scientists with the Canada Mortgage and Housing Corp. (CMHC) in Ottawa. "The CMHC installed 20 temperature and moisture probes which are read and reported every two weeks," Taylor said. "There isn't a lot of information available about fieldstone houses, so not only has this become my home, it's become a mini-laboratory as well."

Scientists from the Saskatchewan Research Council and CMHC are preparing a research paper based on the results from the Magee House, he said.

The Magee House, located at 104 Richmond Street in Wolseley, was declared a Municipal Heritage Property in 2000.

HOTELS

"The Senator Hotel has become a passion. It's in my blood now."

–Chris Beavis, whose family is only one of three to have owned
and operated the Senator Hotel since it opened in 1908.

Hotels provide rest for weary business travellers, a hot meal for visitors and townsfolk alike and often a place to congregate for a cold brew after work.

Hotels were also a symbol of a community's growing stature and economic importance. Every little hamlet, village, and town dreamed about becoming a centre of commerce for their particular region of Saskatchewan. That symbol of success was often seen as having a hotel that reflected the prosperity and lifestyle of the community.

The Hotel Saskatchewan in downtown Regina is known locally simply as "The Hotel." It was the 14th hotel built as part of the Canadian Pacific Railway across the country and opened in 1927. Steel and other building material from another hotel abandoned on the edge of Wascana Park several blocks away were used to construct the Hotel Saskatchewan.

Key to its construction was the work ethic of local tradesmen. At the peak of construction, more than 1,000 men worked around the clock to complete in less than one year what would become arguably the finest hotel in the province.

The Hotel Saskatchewan also became an early focal point of the rivalry between the cities of Regina and Saskatoon. Soon after the Hotel Saskatchewan opened, the Canadian National Railway was approached by a group of Saskatoon business leaders to establish a grander hotel in their city.

Economic woes associated with the Great Depression and drought delayed Saskatoon's efforts, but finally in 1935 the Bessborough Hotel, known as the "Castle on the River," opened.

Some communities became known for not only the hospitality of their hotels but for what took place under them as well. One such example was the Brunswick Hotel, which was located in the heart of Moose Jaw's rowdy River Street district during the flamboyant 1920s and 1930s. Local urban folklore abounds with stories about how many hotels and buildings in the city's downtown district were linked with secret tunnels to disguise opium dens and drinking parlors used by some of the community leaders.

Hotels across Saskatchewan had an important role in the growth of each community, and in turn, the province as well.

BRUNSWICK HOTEL
Moose Jaw

Documents to incorporate the City of Moose Jaw were signed in the Brunswick Hotel in 1903.
PHOTO COURTESY SASKATCHEWAN HERITAGE FOUNDATION

The Brunswick Hotel, located in the heart of Moose Jaw's rowdy River Street District during the flamboyant 1920s and 1930s, also played a sober role in the history of the community.

Documents to incorporate the City of Moose Jaw were signed in the hotel on November 20, 1903, soon after it opened.

John Henry Kern commissioned architect S. A. Clark of Regina to design and build the hotel. It took less than a year to construct the late-Victorian style three-storey structure from Wellington White brick made in the area.

Kern, who had owned and operated two other hotels in Moose Jaw before he had the Brunswick Hotel built from scratch, had a seven-room apartment suite added as his family's residence.

He had a unique sense of humour. His Brunswick Hotel, which featured a veranda around the entire second floor, was built literally across the street from another hotel of the same name, The Brunswick Hotel.

"The building is one of the largest and best hotel buildings west of Winnipeg and certainly the largest and best hotel building in Moose Jaw," the *Moose Jaw Times* reported on February 23, 1903.

Walls on the main floor were finished in white plaster with cedar woodwork, and ceilings were oil-stained in natural shades. A large kitchen equipped with the latest appliances adjoined a spacious dining room. Also on the main floor were the office, reading room, sitting room, card room, and a stand-up bar.

A wide staircase lead to the second floor with its 14 guest rooms, a large parlour, and Kern's seven-room suite. On the third floor there were 20 guest rooms as well as a parlour.

As part of the set of hotels along River Street near the city's Main Street and within walking distance of the railway station, the Brunswick Hotel's past is interwoven with the shadowy history of the city.

This includes local folklore that Al Capone, one of the world's best-known gangsters, spent time in

Moose Jaw. In fact, a new tourism initiative builds on the theme.

A tour called Tunnels of Little Chicago spices up the apparent connection between the famous Chicago criminal and the maze of tunnels that have been found linking hotels and other buildings in downtown Moose Jaw.

Drinking establishments and the purchase of liquor for beverage consumption were banned in most parts of Canada, including Saskatchewan, during the early 1920s. But Prohibition in Canada was not nearly as strict as it was in the United States, where it lasted until 1933.

As a major centre for the Canadian Pacific Railway linked to the United States by the Soo Line, Moose Jaw was ideally suited as a bootlegging hub straight to Chicago.

Moose Jaw's River Street had a reputation as the prairie capital for brothels, opium dens, and illegal gambling halls in the 1920s and 1930s. Newspapers from that period of time are filled with accounts of raids by police trying to control prostitution and gambling along the cobblestone roadway.

Although it remains unclear if the tunnels of Moose Jaw were connected to the bootlegging activities of Al Capone and his business associates, The Brunswick Hotel has some unexplained rooms in its basement.

Roger Duncan, office manager at the Brunswick, said in a 2004 interview that access to the basement of the hotel was through the manager's office or by way of the housekeeper's stairs at the rear of the building. "Gentlemen would take a room on the second floor and could be escorted to the basement by way of the maid's private stairwell at the rear of the hotel," Duncan said.

"In the basement, along the west wing, were—and still exist today—four small rooms or cubicles to one side of a board walk. The cubicles are only about eight feet by 10 feet in size to one side of a board walk."

The floors of the rooms are tongue-and-grove four-inch planking set on top of dirt.

"Across the board-walk hallway from the cubicles were a large bathroom with a sink, toilet and oversized tub, and a large common room that's about 14 feet by 25 feet," Duncan said, adding that

this room would have been furnished with stuffed chairs, a chesterfield, tables, and lamps.

"The cubicles were outfitted sparsely—iron bed, side table and chair, large bowl and water pitcher. Just what might have gone on in this portion of the basement is left to the imagination."

The Brunswick Hotel, located at 82 River Street West in Moose Jaw, was declared a Municipal Heritage Property on September 2, 1997.

The Brunswick Hotel is linked to Moose Jaw's colourful history associated with the flamboyant 1920s. Photo courtesy Saskatchewan Heritage Foundation

HOTEL SASKATCHEWAN
Regina

The Hotel Saskatchewan Radisson Plaza, overlooking Victoria Park in downtown Regina, has provided an Old World aura, charm, and service amid the hustle and bustle of the capital city for more than 75 years.

Kings and queens, presidents and prime ministers, Hollywood movie stars and professional football players, wrestlers, business travelers and vacationing families have all enjoyed their stay at the property known locally as the Hotel.

Built for the Canadian Pacific Railway as the 14th hotel in its nationwide chain, the Hotel Saskatchewan opened in May 1927. CPR officials had opted for the Victoria Avenue location in the downtown business district rather than build on the site of the Grand Trunk Pacific Railway's abandoned construction of the Chateau Qu'Appelle in Wascana Park.

Steel and other building material from the Grand Trunk project was absorbed into the new project, while earth removed from the Hotel Saskatchewan site was dumped into the ruined basement of the Chateau Qu'Appelle.

The Hotel Saskatchewan was designed in a Modernist-Classical style by the Montreal architectural firm of Ross and MacDonald.

General Contractor Smith Bros. & Wilson of Regina supervised 25 subcontractors. Built on the site of Mayor E. N. Darke's first home, the Hotel Saskatchewan was completed in 11 months. At peak construction, 1,000 men worked in shifts 24 hours a day to complete the hotel, often working behind flimsy canvas tents that did little to keep the bone-chilling, minus 30 degree temperatures out.

The lower façade features a row of arched windows with stone Corinthian pilasters between them surmounted by a stone balustrade. The three lower storeys were faced in Tyndal stone and the nine floors above in grey brick. Stone courses ran along the terraced roofline.

The elaborate interior features a foyer that runs the entire length of the main floor. The foyer and rotunda had a "Spanish character," with walls treated in an antique plaster effect, decorated wood beams, and a panelled ceiling. Terrazzo floors and marble thresholds were found throughout.

The ceiling in the main dining room (once named the Ranch Room) had remarkable hand-painted designs depicting the agriculture, wildlife, and fauna of Saskatchewan: the bowl of plenty, wheat, the prairie chicken, ducks, Canada goose, wolf, bear, fox, and even the gopher.

The Hotel Saskatchewan was designed as a self-contained unit that could operate even if nothing else in Regina was working. It was like a ship on the ocean, except the ocean was prairies. It even had its own sheet-fed printing press in the basement.

Originally, water was pumped from the hotel's private well in the basement. A refrigeration plant was equipped to manufacture pure—not cloudy—ice and there was a separate steam-driven pump for fire protection purposes. In addition, the hotel had its own steam plant for heating and hot water. Huge boilers in the basement devoured 18 to 29 tonnes of coal a day to produce steam for the power generators that created electricity.

When the hotel converted to gas in the 1950s, a backup diesel motor was installed that is rumoured to have been from a German U-boat. Today, if the hotel's natural gas system stops working for any reason, the diesel—which has enough fuel to run for 36 hours—starts in less than a minute.

Between 1945 and 1984, the Hotel Saskatchewan served as the official residence of the province's lieutenant governors. The reason is because the Co-operative Commonwealth Federation (CCF) government of Tommy Douglas closed Government House in 1945, saying it was inappropriate for the lieutenant governor to be living in such luxury after the people had just undergone years of depression and the Second World War.

Like almost all of the grand Canadian hotels, however, the Hotel Saskatchewan began falling into disrepair during the 1960s and 1970s. Upgrading facilities and competing with the newer hotel chains was expensive.

The hotel changed hands a few times and renovations continued, but bad luck struck in 1982 when a fire gutted the Qu'Appelle Ballroom and

closed the convention floor for months. Noted Regina architect Joseph Pettick was pressed into service to restore the ballroom's lustre. However, lost revenue and costly renovations forced the owners into tax arrears, and in the late 1980s the hotel went into receivership. During this time of financial uncertainty, creditors and others helped themselves to some of the hotel's artifacts and oil paintings.

In 1992, the property was rechristened the Hotel Saskatchewan Radisson Plaza. The new owners undertook interior renovations to restore the hotel's original beauty. The removal of a low false ceiling revealed hidden surprises—original chandeliers on the convention floor and damaged but beautiful plaster mouldings that served as models for the mouldings installed in the current Victoria Tea Room.

Norm Brooks spent almost half a century working at the Hotel Saskatchewan, beginning as a pageboy on August 18, 1952, and retired as the head porter on January 31, 2001.

"I had been working at a garage, where the assistant head bellman had his car serviced," Brooks recalled over a cup of coffee. "They had just bought new uniforms, and I got the job because I was right size. I weighed about 92 pounds."

He still, however, had to provide six references before he began his job that paid him 46 cents an hour. "The CPR ran the place like a ship," Brooks said. "We had everything on staff: upholster,

Overlooking Regina's Victoria Park in the heart of the downtown, the Hotel Saskatchewan Radisson Plaza has seen a wealth of guests from Royalty to wrestlers and ballerinas to rock groups.
PHOTO COURTESY HOTEL SASKATCHEWAN RADISSON PLAZA

carpenters, polishers. We even had a lady whose job it was to clean silver all day, every day."

As the winter snow began to melt and the streets turned to mud and slush, he noticed the hallways were mopped 12 to 14 times a day to keep them clean.

The day Norm's wife Hazel gave birth to their son, he mentioned the event with pride to a guest, Prime Minister John Diefenbaker.

"On the back of a blank, time-stamped registration card, the prime minister wrote my son a note that read: 'Kirk, best wishes on your future endeavours, Dief,'" Brooks said, adding the note has become a cherished family keepsake.

Brooks' first job was to walk around the hotel "paging" people to let them know they had a telephone call. Those were the days before public address systems. Almost six years later, he graduated to become a bellman. "There were eight bellmen per shift, who all sat patiently on a 16-foot bench waiting for guests to arrive by train," he said.

When he first began, guests arrived with five or six suitcases while bellmen unloaded 100 trunks per day for the commercial travellers selling their hardware, dishes, fur coats, or men's and women's shoes.

Roger Currie remembers staying at the Hotel Saskatchewan for the Labour Day weekend in 1962. "I was a strapping lad of 15, poised to enter high school, and this was the first family trip where I was entrusted with the luxury of my very own hotel room," Currie recalls. "I didn't have to share with my older brother or camp out on a rollaway with the parents. The bed was all mine, the bathroom was all mine, and the TV was all mine. Mom and dad were two floors up."

Currie, who would move to Regina more than 15 years later to become the news director of a radio station, recalled that the mystique began long before he and the bellboy reached his room.

"The Hotel Saskatchewan began life as one of Canada's great railway hotels," he said. "All of them have a certain grandeur which was born in a very different era, an era when travelers were a truly privileged class. There was still some of that in 1962. The lobby of such hotels are the great meeting places of the world. Staff in spotless starched uniforms moved to and fro with great efficiency, transporting luggage on a brass-railed dolly, or a cocktail on an elegant silver tray."

Among the guests on this Labour Day weekend were the giants of that era of Canadian football, Bud Grant's Winnipeg Blue Bombers, winners of three of the previous four Grey Cups.

"Like the other guests of that day, the Bomber players and coaches didn't go anywhere without the jacket and tie, even if they were tossing a football back and forth in the lobby," Currie said. "I got to stare up at them in the lobby and the elevators."

On game day, the Bombers ate their pre-game steak as a group in the Oak Room. "Through an open door, I caught a glimpse of powerful linemen Frank Rigney and Cornell Piper. They smiled at me and waved. I had arrived," he said. "In my many visits to the Saskatchewan in the years that followed, I have always checked to make sure that the Oak Room is still there. I have half expected Rigney and Piper to emerge ready to do battle with the Saskatchewan Roughriders. What a wonderful introduction to the world of living in hotels!"

The Hotel Saskatchewan first opened its doors in 1927, offering a unique experience, which, almost instantly, became legendary. The passing of time has simply enhanced the hotel's worldwide reputation for luxury, elegance of decor, and an unsurpassed quality of personal service.

The Hotel Saskatchewan Radisson Plaza, located at 2125 Victoria Avenue in Regina, was designated a Municipal Heritage Site in 1993.

BESSBOROUGH HOTEL
Saskatoon

The Delta Bessborough Hotel, known as the Castle on the River, has been recognized as Saskatoon's most distinguished landmark since opening in 1935.

Situated in the heart of downtown Saskatoon on five acres of private waterfront gardens, the Delta Bessborough is nestled between two riverfront parks on the South Saskatchewan River.

The Bessborough has ridden the economic rollercoaster of success over the years and now is celebrating a renaissance following extensive renovations in 2000.

Gloria Erickson, a hotel employee for the past 35 years, recalls her first visit to the Bessborough when she was just 12 years old. "My parents took me to the Prairie Room for dinner and dancing," said Erickson.

"I remember the big showcases in the lobby, as you entered, and the large mural on one of the walls, which now is located on the mezzanine floor. It all seemed so huge and impressive. I was so enchanted with the Castle, never dreaming I would someday work here."

She began in the Willow Cafeteria, then worked in the accounting, front, and executive offices. Her career at the Bessborough Hotel has spanned 11 general managers and several ownership groups ranging from Canadian National Railway to the Legacy REIT, a real estate income trust that bought the property in 1998.

"I feel very proud to work at such a landmark. Often when I meet people they have either worked here at one time themselves or someone in their family has worked here or helped in the building of the hotel. It seems most people somehow have a connection to the Bessborough," Erickson said.

Erickson's has fond memories from all of her positions, including meeting special guests such as Prime Minster John Diefenbaker, who sent her a photograph of himself and his dog, and entertainment giants such as Bob Hope and Liberace.

The Delta Bessborough Hotel's spacious convention floor foyer leads to painstakingly-restored ballrooms and smaller meeting areas.
PHOTO COURTESY DELTA BESSBOROUGH HOTEL

Renovations in 2000 provided hotel management with an opportunity to recognize and market their property's history. The new lobby lounge was christened Stovin's to honour the first guest to register at the Bessborough Hotel on December 10, 1935.

"Horace N. Stovin was the western Director of the Canadian Radio Commission, which eventually became the Canadian Broadcasting Corporation [CBC]," explained Stefan Deprez, the Bessborough's director of sales and marketing. "Stovin had arrived at the Bessborough to make final arrangements for the opening musical broadcast and to take personal charge of the announcing."

In the process, Stovin inadvertently added Bessborough history to his own personal legacy as a radio broadcasting pioneer, Deprez said. In his capacity as western director he was one of three people responsible for creating all the Canadian Radio Commission programming for the entire country.

In 1940, Horace resigned and quickly established himself as a radio, and later television, representative. "The firm Horace established became one of Canada's most prominent representative companies, with offices in Montreal, Toronto, Winnipeg and Vancouver," Deprez said.

Horace's passion for broadcasting made him a legend in the industry. His son, Bill Stovin, also had a remarkable radio career, including managing Saskatoon radio station CKOM for 20 years. His grandson, Bill Gerald Stovin, became regional

Dominating Saskatoon's skyline, the "Castle on the River" offers tours of the facility during the Summer months.
PHOTO COURTESY DELTA BESSBOROUGH HOTEL

director of radio for CBC, a position similar to what Horace held when he first registered at the Bessborough.

The "Bes" is an early example of the rivalry between civic leaders in Saskatoon and Regina.

When the Canadian Pacific Railway opened the Hotel Saskatchewan in 1927, Saskatoon businessmen canvassed the Canadian National Railways for a hotel in their city. Saskatoon, with a booming population of 40,000, was a rail hub for the CNR's western network.

Sir Henry Thornton, president of the CNR, believed in the future of the city, and the company bought property on 21st Street, near the railway's passenger station.

Built on the site of a former garbage dump along the banks of the South Saskatchewan, the Bessborough Hotel exceeded the hopes and dreams of even those who had petitioned CNR to establish a hotel in Saskatoon. The Bessborough Hotel became the last big chateau-style hotel built in Canada.

Architect J. S. Archibald designed the hotel with a more romantic flare than the traditional French medieval chateaux. Archibald did not live to see the opening of the Bessborough, the last of his grand CNR hotels. After his death, CNR architect John Schofield and his assistant George Drummond supervised completion of the project.

Construction began in 1929 and spanned more than three years because the booming economy had gone bust with the start of the Great Depression. The hotel sat empty for three full years. However, there were special events such as a

Shriners' Charity Ball and two visits by Vere Brabazon, the governor-general of Canada at the time. The hotel was named after Barbazon, who was the ninth Earl of Bessborough.

When the hotel opened in 1935, local newspaper reports marvelled at the modern conveniences, including elevators that "levelled automatically sparing passengers the aggravation of toe stubbing." There was a central vacuum system as well as a pneumatic tube carrier system for dispatching messages, telegrams, and keys. Every room had its own telephone and bath, including hot water that was regulated to "prevent scalding."

Mattresses were nine-inches thick and padded with lamb's wool on one side for the winter and cotton on the other for summer comfort.

The Vice Regal Suite, created for the governor general, had a fireplace, canopied bed, and an unheated room for fur storage.

The hotel's kitchen had six coal-fired ranges, a charcoal broiler that could hold 50 sirloin steaks, a six-foot cast iron vegetable steamer with three separately ventilated sections, and the capacity to make two tons of ice each day.

The 1935 grand opening luncheon attracted 350 business and professional people, while the supper dinner and dance accommodated 1,000 guests. All ran remarkably smoothly considering both were the first functions ever held at the Bessborough, built with primarily Tapestry brick from Claybank, Saskatchewan, and Tyndal stone from Manitoba.

Restoration work began in 1999 and continued until 2004, when all of the public areas, the elegant convention level as well as the 225 guest rooms were upgraded. Stovin's was created, the trademark Samurai Japanese Restaurant was enhanced, and the Pro Fit Athletic Club was launched after the renovations were completed.

"We believe the Delta Bessborough is a hallmark of taste and luxury for the new millennium. Our core value is to celebrate and preserve our history," said Deprez. "It is Saskatoon's landmark place of occasion and grand old lady of hospitality."

The Delta Bessborough is located at 601 Spadina Crescent East in Saskatoon.

Affectionately known as "The Bes," the hotel's majestic garden area is annually transformed into an outdoor jazz festival venue.
PHOTO COURTESY DELTA BESSBOROUGH HOTEL

SENATOR HOTEL
Saskatoon

The Senator Hotel, built from 1907 to 1908 by flamboyant Saskatoon entrepreneur Jimmy Flanagan, has been owned and operated by only three families for almost 100 years.

"I don't know which senator the hotel is named after, but I do know that the name was changed some time in the 1940s from the Flanagan Hotel," explained Chris Beavis, who now owns the downtown landmark with his father and sister.

"I honestly don't know if there's any way of finding out today. We do know that it was named after a senator who frequently stayed in the hotel when visiting Saskatoon."

Jimmy Flanagan bought, built, and sold businesses with a high level of success after arriving in Saskatoon in 1902. Within a year of buying a livery business, he sold it and used the profits to build the Western Hotel, which he sold in 1907 and began construction of his newest venture.

Flanagan was rather modest. He had wanted to name the new property the City Hotel, but residents insisted it be named the Flanagan Hotel, after the owner, because it was a lavish structure that added a degree of high-class hospitality to the boom town.

Upon his death in 1909, Flanagan owned six other pieces of land in the city and two parcels of farmland. Stories abound, even today, about his business acumen, wit, and sometimes lack of common sense.

Travelling salesmen apparently enjoyed doing business with him because he often would sign a long work order and leave it blank except for his signature. Once he ordered $56 worth of crockery only to have over $700 arrive at the hotel.

Yet, other stories tell of his nimble mind. A guest was complaining that the room was too small. So Flanagan solved the problem by ushering the guest to a nice large airy room—the street.

Flanagan often boasted that he never drank alcohol alone. To make sure that this practice did not inconvenience him, Flanagan kept a mirror by the bar.

Flags flew at half mast on all public buildings, and the largest funeral ever seen in Saskatoon occurred when Flanagan died in 1909.

The Senator Hotel was sold to Henry Haskamp in 1910 and remained in his family until 1967, when the father and uncle of Chris Beavis bought the property.

During the Haskamp ownership, many exterior and interior alterations were completed, the most notable was that the landmark cupola was removed in 1944.

In 1964, an aggressive modernization took place on the exterior of the building and much of the façade changed appearance.

Beavis said that although the property was originally bought as a straightforward business deal, the Senator Hotel now is near and dear to his family's hearts.

The emotional attachment to the Senator Hotel spurred the family to reshape the hotel so that its former glory matches today's needs. It is now marketed as "Saskatoon's Boutique Hotel."

The Beavis family has done this by re-creating specialized and beautifully appointed suites combined with specialty dining and drinking. "The Senator Hotel has become a passion," Beavis said after receiving a Municipal Heritage Award for renovations. "It's in my blood now."

Walter LaChance, one of the first architects to locate in Saskatoon, was the hotel's original architect. He went on to design Saskatoon City Hospital, Fire Hall No. 1, and Victoria School.

Construction was contracted to the Shannon Brothers, which was their first major contract in Saskatoon after arriving from Ireland. Shannon Brothers grew to become one of the major construction companies in the city.

The three-storey, L-shaped building was made of solid brick with one 130-foot wing facing Third Avenue and one 115-foot wing along 21st Street. On the northeast corner, there was a turret surmounted by a cupola.

Every modern convenience was installed so that when completed in 1908 the hotel had steam heating, electrical lighting, and telephones. Every room had hot and cold water, and some rooms even had a bathroom.

Lavish use of marble, ornamental scrolls and plaster ceilings, crystal chandeliers, ornate mouldings and friezes, and intricate wrought-iron work on the interior are notable throughout the building.

The Senator Hotel was, for many years, the most elegant hotel in Saskatoon. The location was a prominent one in the early years, and politicians often used its portico to launch campaigns or make important announcements.

"It has been a well-known meeting place for folks of all backgrounds from the very beginning," said Beavis. "Meet You At the Senator needed no explanation then or now because everyone knows where you are."

The Senator Hotel has been transformed by time very little, and it plays the same role today as it did in 1908—hotel, restaurant, and community landmark.

Winston's Pub in the hotel is one of the oldest in Saskatoon and continues to be a meeting place just as it was in the early years.

Today the Senator Hotel has been reshaped into a boutique style European hotel that serves 42 guests. Complementing their stay are Rembrandt's—a discriminating restaurant, and Winston's Bar, with its unique beer list and Old World atmosphere.

The Senator Hotel is located at 243–21st Street on the corner of 21st Street and Third Avenue in downtown Saskatoon.

SHAUNAVON HOTEL
Shaunavon

Vicki Williams is giving the Shaunavon Hotel, built in 1915 and believed to be the largest free-standing wood structure in Saskatchewan, a new lease on life.

"I bought the hotel because I love the building and its history," said Williams, who gave up a 20-year federal government career in 1992 to raise her teenage daughter in Shaunavon, a small town with a population hovering around 1,700 people.

"I had been deeply saddened by the lack of attention the hotel was getting from previous owners. I am dedicated to bringing this building back to its original splendour. It may take me years, but then I never did see myself retiring into a quiet life!'

Williams was the librarian at the public school when she bought the Municipal Heritage Property in 2003.

She has a nifty revitalization plan. "I'm getting the community involved by asking groups and families to "Adopt A Room," she said, noting a

dozen rooms were booked within a few weeks of the community project being unveiled.

"The idea is that a family or group will supply the labour to tear apart rooms. Professionals will then make the electrical and plumbing repairs. The volunteers will return to complete the room, including installing Gyproc, painting, etc."

For the next five years, five percent of the rent of each room will be donated to a charity or organization of the group or family's choice, Williams said.

"The group or family will decorate the room with their own pictures and written history," she said. "Each room will then contain a piece of our town's heritage."

Shaunavon, located 51 kilometres south of the Trans-Canada Highway from Gull Lake, can trace its roots to the development of the west by the railway.

Railroad engineers determined that Shaunavon's water was ideal for the steam locomotives. "In 1939 when King George VI and the Queen went across Canada by railway, and even as late as the 1980s when Prince Charles and Princess Diana used the railroads, water from Shaunavon was brought to the train in water cars by the CPR," Williams said. "This water was utilized for their entire rail trips. Our community uses the term 'Royal Water' now, thanks to the Canadian Pacific Railway decision to use Shaunavon's great water."

Great West Rail now operates the Shaunavon rail link that still connects to the CP Rail system.

Railway employees were key customers of the Shaunavon Hotel after it was opened in 1915.

The Empress Hotel, built in 1913, burnt down on December 17, 1914. Construction of a new hotel began on January 2, 1915, and was completed on March 25, 1915. For superstitious reasons, the owners opted to name the new building the Shaunavon Hotel. It was not named the Empress Hotel because the Empress Hotel in Shaunavon, the ship named the Empress of Ireland, and the Empress Hotel in Moose Jaw all met disastrous fates.

"The Shaunavon Hotel's stature and presence next to the railway is a major part of the story of Shaunavon," Williams said. "Our town is very proud of its past."

An April 1, 1915, article in *The Shaunavon Standard* reported that the "new Shaunavon hotel was constructed in record-breaking time" when it is considered that the building was put up in the coldest season and construction was held up for want of material for the period of two weeks.

"The architect, O. M. Akers, designed and superintended the construction," the newspaper article said. "The rotunda is 32 by 32 with two entrances, one of which is specially designed for the accommodation of ladies. The dining room is large, light and well ventilated with a seating capacity for 50 guests."

The newspaper described the bedrooms on the first floor as "exceptionally well furnished with six private baths and hot and cold water in each room."

It added, "The building contains 54 rooms for guests with a commodious parlour and writing room."

The Shaunavon Hotel had its own private water system with a pressure tank in the basement.

"The electric light system is modern with sufficient capacity to supply the light for the building which will consist of about 600 lamps when entirely connected," the newspaper article noted.

Williams is slowly making progress toward her goal of restoring the Shaunavon Hotel. While restoration work continues, she is open for business on the main floor. The Station Pub is a beverage room that seats 200, Trax is a dining room for 60 people, and a banquet room can accommodate 66.

Williams lives on the second floor, where most of the renovation activity is taking place. "There will be four offices, two suites, an exercise room, and 19 hotel rooms with bathrooms on that floor when completed," she said. "I expect there will be 35 to 40 rooms when we are finished, along with several suites, the exercise room, office, and staff facilities. I plan to add bathrooms so that all rooms will have their own bath."

There are 16 original claw-foot tubs, numerous old sinks and taps, 15 original dressers and bedroom tables, as well as a handful of chairs that are being refurbished for use whenever possible. There are more than 100 windows that will be repaired or replaced as well.

Stair treads on the main stairway entrance remain unusually wide. This stems from the days when cowboys wore spurs on their boots.

"Our intention is to utilize any original fixtures that can be located," Williams said.

Her long-range plan includes converting the third floor, which has not be used for many, many years, into a banquet room that would provide a view of the entire farming community.

The Shaunavon Hotel, located at 189 Centre Street, was designated a Municipal Heritage Property in 1999.

OUR RURAL ROOTS

"I find the fact that a building of this size was built completely by hand remarkable."

–Fred Bjornson, who still uses the hip-roofed barn today that his father built near Elfros in 1917

The wide open and often quite flat spaces of Saskatchewan became the natural marketing tool for the Dominion of Canada more than 100 years ago. Advertisements promoting 160 acres of land for just $10 became the carrot that helped entice thousands of people to uproot their families in Europe, Africa and even the United States to emigrate to the area now called Saskatchewan.

They came from predominantly rural backgrounds, where families supported themselves by growing vegetables and raising livestock such cattle, pigs and chickens on tiny plots of land. So the lure of owning a quarter section of land for just one family was an appealing prospect.

Saskatchewan's history—and perhaps the province's future as well—is linked to the family farm. Farming is forever in Saskatchewan.

The fabric of our rural roots and the unique culture created by diverse ethnic backgrounds is reflected in barns, buildings and homesteads. Form and style used by the settlers were often different, but barns often reflected the immigrants' dedication and desire to ensure the structures would be functional and last for many, many years.

From a hip-roofed barn that has stood on the same foundation near Elfros for almost a century to a U-shaped barn north of Moose Jaw, the icons of the province's rural roots sprouted on the prairies. These barns have survived decades of decay and the harsh weather to continue to provide the farmers with a place to shelter their livestock, store their feed and, in some cases, a venue to kick up their heels when the work is done.

People across Saskatchewan today are rediscovering and redefining their rural roots.

What do 23 people meeting in the Battlefords during a bitter winter snow storm have in common with 100s of persons who meet on a hot August Sunday in Whitewood?

What do 12 folks in Eatonia have in common with a farm family near Southey?

What does the Outlook District Museum and Gallery have in common with the Murals of Moose Jaw?

The common answer is people intent on preserving Saskatchewan's heritage. In January's snow, the Battle River Settlement Foundation convened its annual meeting to elect a new board. A hot Sunday in August brought out hundreds of townsfolk to open a new Heritage Centre, located in the restored Merchant's Bank Building on Main Street.

The Eatonia group hopes to restore an Eaton House (circ. 1920) purchased from the T. Eaton Company catalogue. Its design is similar to one currently occupied by a young family near Southey.

Like so many communities in Saskatchewan, residents of Outlook take pride in their accomplishments, including the huge murals painted on walls of their railway museum. That pride is shared by the townsfolk of Moose Jaw who are equally proud of the murals gracing their town.

Heritage properties not only stand as physical examples of our province's architectural history, but they also reflect the accomplishments, practices, beliefs and aesthetics of rural Saskatchewan pioneers. The homestead of the province's first agriculture minister, barns that have survived decades of decay and weather, and a cultural centre that provides a focus for Francophones in one community, are among icons that symbolize our rural roots.

MOTHERWELL HOMESTEAD
Abernethy

The homestead of William Motherwell, one of Canada's greatest agricultural innovators and pioneers, now is a National Historic Site and has become a life-sized learning lab for school children.

In the spring of 1882, at the age of 22, Motherwell settled on a 160-acre parcel near present-day Abernethy. He called his homestead Lanark Place, after the county in Ontario where he was born. For the next 14 years, he worked his land with oxen and horses while he and his family lived in a log cabin.

He embraced new "dry-land farming" techniques such as summer fallowing, the practice through which some of the farm land each year is taken out of production in order to conserve soil moisture and nutrients, as well as to control weeds.

By 1897, Motherwell had gathered enough stones from the surrounding land to build a stately two-storey home.

Ever practical, he divided the land around the house into quadrants, each with a specific purpose.

The house quadrant includes ornamental trees and a tennis lawn. The barn and garden quadrants are sheltered on all sides by trees, and the quadrant containing the dugout was designed to maximize exposure to the weather in order to collect the winter's snow.

As busy as he was, he always found time for community involvement.

"He was a born leader," recalls Edison Stueck, whose father travelled west with Motherwell and settled near him. "Anytime there was any type of community effort, he was right in the middle of it."

In 1901, Motherwell helped establish the Territorial Grain Growers' Association, a group of western farmers protesting, among other things, federal government tariffs that forced them to sell their grain at below-market value.

When the Province of Saskatchewan was formed in 1905, he was the natural choice to be the first minister of agriculture, a position he held until 1918.

William Motherwell was Saskatchewan's first Minister of Agriculture from 1905 to 1918.
Photo courtesy ParksCanada

As a provincial cabinet minister, Motherwell constantly expounded the benefits of scientific agriculture. As part of that effort, he created "Better Farming Trains," that travelled the rails sharing the latest in agricultural techniques and advancements with the widely dispersed farming communities of Saskatchewan.

"His most important contribution was that he recognized the need for education in the new settlers who came here," says Tim McCashin, site coordinator for the Motherwell Homestead. "Farming was a different ball of wax here on the prairies, and the settlers had to relearn many techniques in order to make agriculture viable here."

When the University of Saskatchewan was founded in 1908, Motherwell successfully lobbied for the inclusion of a College of Agriculture. "I took a vow to myself that if I ever got in a position to do it, I would try to reverse the idea that farming is a subservient occupation," he once said.

It was a mandate he continued to pursue as federal minister of agriculture under Prime Minister Mackenzie King, from 1921 to 1930. Motherwell also established the Dominion Rust Research Laboratory in Winnipeg, a facility whose purpose was to develop heartier varieties of wheat.

Motherwell helped eradicate tuberculosis in cattle by establishing a new policy of quarantine and destruction that compensated owners for their losses.

"Motherwell had a huge influence on the improvement of farming practices in Saskatchewan," says retired crop and soil specialist Earl Johnson. "In many cases, he'd proven things work for himself."

Motherwell retired from politics in 1939 and died in 1943. But his legacy as the "Grand Old Man of Canadian Agriculture" is preserved at the Motherwell Homestead.

Staff in period costume carry out day-to-day chores just as they were undertaken in Motherwell's day. Visitors can explore the property and tour the home.

Authentically costumed interpreters run the farm in-character, performing chores such as baking bread, caring for the animals and even acting out vignettes. More than 10,000 people annually visit the site, which is open from late May to early September.

"We really try to make the place come alive for the people who visit," says Tara Walker, an eight-season veteran of the site. "It's fun to do some of the old-fashioned things and let people take part in them."

The Motherwell Homestead was acquired by the Canadian Parks Service in 1966 and later restored to the 1910–1914 period. The Motherwell Homestead is three kilometres south of Abernethy on Highway 22. Abernethy is 100 km east of Regina on Highway 10.

HIP-ROOFED BARN
Elfros

Fred Bjornson, like all Saskatchewan farmers, is proud of his rural roots, his family farm and, in his case, a unique hip-roofed barn that has been a landmark in the east-central part of the province near Elfros since 1917.

"I find the fact that a building of this size was built completely by hand remarkable," said Bjornson, whose father homesteaded in 1903 when he was 21.

"Over time the use has been converted from the raising of livestock to at present being used as a granary, garage, and farm supply storage. To have lasted this long and still be straight, the concrete walls and floor only suffering from minor cracks and the lumber still solid, is a testament to good planning, good materials, and workmanship of the pioneer workers."

The hip roofed barn is 60 feet long by 54 feet wide by 40 feet high. It has concrete walls that are 10 feet high by 10 inches thick as well as a concrete floor. The stalls, loft floor and walls, and roof were built using fir lumber. The original shingles were cedar. All the concrete was mixed by hand. Forms for the walls were made from planks that were later used in the construction of the barn. Many loads of field rock were used to extend the concrete.

The stalls in the main part were designed for horses. There are two rows of stalls separated by a wide alley, with a large door at both ends. The 13 open stalls and 2 box stalls could accommodate 30 horses.

A third row of stanchions, which would hold 20 head of cattle, was facing the second row of horse stalls. A narrow alley separated them. Hay and straw were carried to the mangers down this alley.

Hay, straw, and grain were stored in the loft. Loose hay was hauled to the barn on a hayrack and pulled into the loft using slings and a rope and pulley, and track system powered by a team of horses and, in later years, a tractor. Straw could also be put up in the same way, but usually straw was blown in from the threshing machine as the bundles of grain were being threshed.

A hip-roofed barn that was 60 feet long, 54 feet wide and 40 feet high was built near Elfros in 1917.
PHOTO COURTESY FRED BJORNSON

Unique to the Bjornson barn are three rows of stalls with the loft over the entire floor area.
<small>Photo courtesy Fred Bjornson</small>

Chop made from crushed grain was also stored in a bin in the loft. An elevator from an old threshing machine mounted on the barn wall and driven by the belt pulley of a tractor was used to fill this bin. A chute brought this grain to the ground floor, where it was measured out in gallon pails and fed to the livestock.

The original cedar shingles, which lasted 50 years, were replaced by asphalt shingles, which were on for 35 years. Roofing now is metal.

"Dad ran a mixed farm, raising grain, cattle, horses, pigs, sheep, and poultry," Bjornson recalls. "He also did custom threshing with a steam outfit from 1908 to 1934. Over the years, he hired many men for his farming and threshing crews. He turned the crop land to me in 1954, but continued to raise cattle until the early 1960s.

Fred Bjornson seeded his first crop when he was 16 in 1955. "I have been farming it ever since, but due to health problems the past few years I consider myself semi-retired because I've had to rent part of the land and hire out work done," he said.

In the early years, Bjornson said his father held barn dances in the loft. "There is a wide stairway inside the barn, which made it easy to enter the loft and bring in musical instruments. Brackets were nailed to the rafters and planks were laid across them for seating," he said. "Lighting was provided by lanterns or by electric lights powered by a 32-volt electrical generator."

A country school, called Prairie Grove #187, is only about 500 feet from the barn. In 1944, the Argyle School was closed for that year and the children were transported to the Prairie Grove School in a closed-in cutter pulled by horses. The driver kept his horses in the barn during the school day, so he only had to make one trip a day.

In the winter, when the loft was filled with hay, some of the teachers occasionally allowed the students to play in the barn loft during the noon break.

"Climbing a ladder on the east wall to a platform and jumping down to the top of the haystack, swinging on the sling rope, and sliding down the stack were great fun," Bjornson recalled.

When there was a Christmas concert, dance, or annual school meeting at the school, many of the people attending kept their horses in our barn during the event.

"The unique thing about the barn is that it has three rows of stalls with the loft over the entire floor area," he said. "Most barns have two rows or their third row is in a lean-to attached to the side of the main building."

The loft is large enough that feed for the livestock for an entire winter can be stored in it.

"The barn is almost 90 years old and has stood the test of time," Bjornson said proudly. "It is still straight, solid and in good repair."

The barn is located on the NW Sec32–T32–R13 W2nd that is seven kilometres north of Elfros on Highway 35 and one kilometre west.

BELL BARN
Indian Head

Saskatchewan's oldest agricultural building is a round fieldstone barn built by Major William Bell in 1882 just north of Indian Head.

It is all that remains from Bell's effort to establish a corporate farm in the Canadian west before the railway had even reached the area. However, the 64-foot-diametre barn is in jeopardy of disappearing from the prairie landscape like so many other agricultural structures from the province's past.

"I always took a liking to barns," explains David Aldous, a retired schoolteacher who has been trying to save the Bell Barn for almost a decade. "I've seen so many other beautiful barns across Saskatchewan deteriorate and disappear from the landscape that I thought this one was worth saving."

Aldous, who was born in 1917 and grew up in Whitewood, can't remember the first time he saw the Bell barn, but figures it was during one of his many trips into the capital of Regina as a youth.

"I think this barn is not only worth saving but worth restoring so future generations can, perhaps, have a sense of what Bell and others thought about the possibilities for this part of Canada."

Aldous launched a letter-writing campaign to politicians and policymakers trying to not only get the Bell barn declared a National Heritage Site but also to obtain funding to restore the fieldstone building.

"We haven't been successful yet, but I'm not willing to give up," said Aldous, who retired to Saskatoon after a 37-year teaching career that began in a one-room school house in Bengough and ended as a principal in Coronach.

The Bell Barn is part of a 10-acre farmstead that Dan Walker bought in 1985. Walker appreciates the passion and determination Aldous has shown towards the barn.

"People in the community are interested in the barn but they are either unable or unwilling to contribute financially to restore it," Walker said.

Appearing rather dilapidated on a farm near Indian Head, a movement is afoot to raise funds to make repairs to the Bell Barn.
Photo courtesy SAHS

The wood and stone structure is one of the few round barns remaining in North America.
PHOTO COURTESY SAHS

land for just $10, that created unbridled optimism about the future of the area.

William Bell, born in 1845 in what is now Brockville, Ontario, was among those early pioneers who saw great opportunity in the west and acted on his vision. Bell likely developed his flair for business from his father, who was a large-scale lumberman.

Bell returned to what was then called Upper Canada to defend the area as part of the British army during the Fenian Raids. Discharged with the rank of major, he headed west again and set out literally on foot from Brandon, Manitoba, the end of the new Canadian railway, in 1881 to explore the land where the railway would soon pass.

"He was taken with an area south of the Qu'Appelle Valley," explained Aldous. "It was marked with an Indian skull on a post, which is how the community became named Indian Head."

Bell was so impressed with what he saw that he convinced friends in Ontario and Minnesota to finance a huge project, the Qu'Appelle Farming Company. About $600,000 in capital was raised from 24 investors.

The proposed farm was a block of 10 square miles, extending 7 miles north and 3 miles south of what now is the Town of Indian Head. The even-numbered sections, owned by the Canadian government, were bought for $1.25 per acre in 1882.

"In return, Bell agreed that by the fall of 1888, place 128 families per township on the land, have 20,000 acres under crop and spend $60,000 on improving the farm," Aldous said.

During the first summer, a 2-storey, 16-room house was built as well as the fieldstone barn that could store 4,000 bushels of oats, 100 tons of hay, and had an office.

"The barn had no windows, only evenly spaced gun ports around the circumference," he said. "The central silo also doubled as a lookout tower. Rumours of a rebellion apparently persuaded Bell to build a barn that could also be used as a fort if the need arose."

An ice house, a cattle barn, chicken coup, stable, and several cottages, 25 by 30 feet for labourers, were also erected in the first summer.

"Because it's located a few metres away from our home, I think that some people are uncomfortable with the idea of raising money for something that is on private property."

Aldous and Walker are uncertain why efforts to have the Bell Barn declared a National Historic Site and federal funds made available for restoration through Parks Canada have failed. "I can't see why we can't get the same level of support as, say, the Motherwell Homestead has at Abernethy," said Walker, who is a tree-research technician at Agriculture and Agri-Food Canada's PFRA Shelterbelt Belt Centre near Indian Head. "To me, the Bell Barn played a significant role in the history of Canada and of this province."

Both vow to continue their fight, but Walker is worried that the harsh prairie winters and wind will eventually turn the fieldstone barn into a pile of rubble.

The Bell Barn is a window into a period of time when the Government of Canada was luring immigrants into the west by offering quarter sections of

When Bell met with shareholders later in the year he reported that the fields were fenced, 1,000 trees had been planted for windbreaks, an artesian well had been drilled at the main house, and a road had been built to the brand-new Indian Head Railroad Station.

By 1883, there were 160 horses and oxen at work at the Bell farm, which now employed 82 people. More than 4,000 acres of land had been broken, half had been sown to Red Fife wheat, and the balance to oats, potatoes, and other root crops.

The company bought the Town Site of Indian Head, except for railway property, from the Canadian government at $8 per acre so that deeds could be given to merchants and other business they hoped to attract.

However, by 1884, things began to go downhill at the first corporate farm in the North-West Territories. Crops were hit by an early frost, and the 130,000 bushels of damp grain that were threshed were fit only to feed the 300 pigs on the farm. To make matters worse, 22 of the farm horses were stolen, squatters had begun to pop up across the Bell farm, and the CPR demanded another $15,000 payment for the Indian Head town site.

Then, the North-West Rebellion of 1885 erupted.

The government commandeered 30 teams, men, and wagons from the Bell farm for military service. Work at the Bell farm slowed, with only 1,000 of the 8,000 acres of land that had been broken being seeded.

This, accidentally, is said to be how the practice of summer fallow began.

"When the 1885 Rebellion was over it was too late to seed the crops so the land was worked under to kill the weeds and left until the following spring to seed," Aldous explained. "The crop was so much better on this land the next year that the practice of summer fallow was started."

Bell, himself, was asked to be the officer of transport for the government expeditionary force.

The 1885 rebellion was the last straw for the Bell farm. In 1886, a new company was formed, the Bell Farm Company, to refinance the operation. Yet, there were too many debts and that company was liquidated in 1889.

"As a farming adventure, the Bell farm was a financial failure, but the international attention it had attracted brought many people to the area," Aldous said. "Some of the men who came to work at the farm stayed to become successful farmers."

Bell's wife died in 1895, and he returned to England the following year and remarried. He formed a company in Dublin to make briquettes from peat moss. In 1900, he sold the company and returned to Canada, buying a coal mine in Alberta and a seat on the Winnipeg Grain Exchange. He lived comfortably with his second wife and four children until his death in 1913.

The Bell Barn is located on the west side of Highway 56 about a half a kilometre north of Indian Head.

Ravaged by the some of the enemies of built heritage— harsh weather and neglect—survival for the barn depends on people's passion to preserve such buildings.
PHOTO COURTESY SAHS

SCHMITZ BARN
Moose Jaw

Andy and Mike Schmitz opened their hearts and wallets in 1986, then rolled up their sleeves to save a massive 21,000-square-foot, U-shaped barn.

Built in the late 1920s by William W. Jones for the original owner, Percy Lasby, the black-and-white barn is about one kilometre northeast of the Main Street exit from the Trans-Canada Highway into Moose Jaw.

When the barn was being built people would actually drive, some on their honeymoons, great distances by horse and buggy to watch the gargantuan rafters being erected. Today, pictures of the barn in its various stages of construction are displayed in the loft.

The Schmitz brothers, who grew up west of Moose Jaw, saw the barn begin to deteriorate in the late 1970s and early 1980s.

"We could not bear to see this magnificent structure go by the wayside, as has been the fate of many other barns in Saskatchewan and other parts of Canada," explained Andy. So Andy and his brother Mike bought the barn and adjacent land.

"With the aid of our wives and our combined workforce of 12 children, we have restored, re-nailed, and re-painted the building," Andy explained, noting that the workforce has applied about 3,000 litres of paint to the barn and has replaced more than 1,000 panes of glass.

"Of course, we also have enjoyed the comradery of others that ensued after each work day, which has included our family, friends and many Moose Jaw locals."

The Schmitz families have beef cattle and grain farms located in the Moose Jaw, Centre Butte, and Chaplin areas. Mike lives on the Chaplin farm where their cattle operation is based.

Andy, who returns each summer to help with the family farm business, is currently a Professor of Agricultural Economics at the University of Florida, Gainesville. He also holds faculty positions at the University of California at Berkeley and the University of Saskatchewan, Saskatoon.

"This is one of the largest barns still standing in North America," Andy concludes.

The barn required 156,000 shingles, 173,000 feet of clear-heart fir that was imported from Ontario, 800 yards of stone, 2,350 bags of cement, and 6,076 man-hours of carpentry to build.

Hardware for the building came from Thatcher Hardware in Moose Jaw and the more than 100 French-paned windows that give light to the inside of the barn came from Cushing Millwork in Moose Jaw.

The barn housed 150 head of cattle and numerous horses. The dairy and horse stalls remain intact. The hayloft is about 40 feet high in which both hay and grain were stored.

The barn roof structure is that of the new-style truss framing for a Gambrel roof. The Schmitz Barn has three of these that resemble the inverted hulls of massive ships set firmly atop the Saskatchewan plains.

The floor that supports this colossal roofing system is made up of mainly clear-heart fir 2 by 12s, each one foot apart.

The Schmitz barn is not open to the public as a tourist attraction, but people visiting Canada from various parts of the United States, including New York City, as well as Ireland, Mexico, Turkey, the United Kingdom, and Ukraine have pulled into the farm yard to take a peak at the massive barn. Several antiques have been added to the loft, including horse buggies and cream separators.

For entertaining friends and family, the Schmitzes added a regulation-size stage to the northwest part of the loft and a restaurant seating area. This comes in handy when the barn is used for celebrations such as anniversaries, BBQs, weddings, or agriculture-related conferences and tours.

The 10th anniversary of the Farming for . . . *Profit?* Conference was held in the Schmitz barn in 2003. And in 1999, the Nuffield Scholar Tour, a select group of outstanding farmers from around the world, stopped at the Schmitz Barn as well.

The barn has many unique features. The north side was backfilled with dirt to allow hay wagons to drive into and out of the loft through two large sliding doors. Hay wagons equipped with hay slings were unloaded using hay tracks and pulleys that ran along the top of the loft.

Three large concrete milk sheds are located under the backfilled area. Milk was transferred in milk cans to these sheds from the cows milked at the lower level of the barn through doors built into the lower concrete foundation. The milk was then elevated from these storage sheds on the outside of the barn's north side through a trap-door enclosure, transferred to waiting wagons, and taken to market.

The barn's south side is U-shaped and houses huge concrete cisterns that collect rainfall from the massive eave-trough structure of the expansive roof.

The Schmitz Barn has a miniature train-track system built into the ceiling of the lower level that moves grain from the loft to individual feeding areas for the livestock. On this track are feeding buckets that were loaded from grain chutes in the loft and moved along the track to various locations throughout the barn. Handles on these buckets allow the buckets to be tilted sideways to dump the grain. These are still in operation today.

In the early years of the barn, dances were held in the hayloft. Amazingly, the barn never caught on fire, even though straw, hay, and grain were stored in the loft. Horse auctions were held on the property and the Lasby's, the original owners, offered tours of the barn.

For years, the barn, like many others in Saskatchewan, was home to thousands of pigeons. Fortunately, for the new owners, pigeons no longer roost in the barn's rafters since the many windows have been screened.

"This is one modern addition that has been truly welcomed by our many visitors, friends, and family who annually fly from various parts of the United States to help us maintain the barn," Andy said. "However, one son, now a doctor living in California, questions why he spent years studying medicine only to shovel behind the pigeons!"

The Schmitzes have long-term plans for the barn. "We plan to keep this barn in A-1 condition for many, many years to come," Andy said.

The Schmitz Barn, located about one kilometre northeast of the junction of the Trans-Canada Highway and Main Street in Moose Jaw, is not a heritage property.

LABRECQUE BUILDING
Rosetown

In 1939, engineers told Eugene Labrecque his plan to build a 100-foot, two-storey arched wooden building wouldn't work.
PHOTO COURTESY LUCILLE NAWROCKI

Lucille Nawrocki vividly recalls stories about the day in 1939 when engineers from the University of Saskatchewan told her dad, Eugene Labrecque, that his plan to build a 100-foot, two-storey, arched building made of wood wouldn't work.

"His dream house machinery and seed cleaners on the main floor and grain on the second floor," she said. "However, the university professor, Dr. Harding, said it was an impossible task because a 'free-standing' structure could not withstand the weight of the grain."

Eugene, like many Saskatchewan farmers, couldn't walk away from his idea without trying to make it work first. "This arched structure would be the first of its kind ever built," recalled Lucille.

Labrecque ordered lumber from British Columbia, demolished his existing seed cleaning building, and broke up the foundation for use in the foundation of the new structure. Nothing would be wasted.

Construction began in the spring of 1940 and was completed before the first snow fell. Concrete footings were three feet wide at the top, tapering to two feet at the bottom, and are two feet above ground.

Arch rafters were made by laminated and nailing four 1-inch by 4-inch boards together on a special jig to make 4 by 4s, she said.

"The university professors thought there should be more boards, one on top of the other, for more strength to hold up under the weight of the grain," Lucille said.

"The jig had two posts four feet deep into the ground and four feet above ground and four inches apart, in the shape of a semi circle. At the two-foot level were crosspieces to hold the boards in place and level. The boards were 1-inch by 6-inches thick on edge."

The arch rafters are set at two-foot spacing.

"Once the rafters were up, they found the top of the roof or the peak was too flat, requiring dad and his helpers to construct a point with lumber," Lucille said. "A wedge, made with 2 by 6s on edge, increased the height by one and a half feet."

The entire structure was covered with 1-inch by 6-inch fir boards, starting at a 45 degree angle at the bottom and ending up crossways to the arch rafters at the peak. Cedar shake shingles with no knots were over the boards.

"Dad had a plan in his head but did not know how to do it," she said. "How to make the walls strong enough to hold grain was the hardest part to visualize as a finished project. The university professors did not believe 5,000 to 6,000 bushels of grain could be successfully stored upstairs in separate bins."

Labrecque, who had built his family farm home and barn with second-hand lumber, had hired a carpenter from Meadow Lake to work on his newest project. They solved construction problems together.

"To provide the required strength for an upper floor, two walls, two feet apart were to be built," Lucille said.

"The outside arch rafters sat on the outside edge of the footing, while a frame of 2-inch by 6-inch studs two feet apart, built straight up to meet the curve of the roof, was placed on the inside edge of the footing. This was to be the strength to hold up the grain bins."

This created an eight-foot-high arch that is seen as a triangle. The weight of the floor for the grain bins above is distributed to the outside and inside of the footings by this triangle.

The upper floor, originally, was made of 2-inch by 6-inch fir tongue-and-groove on 2-inch by 6-inch joists at two-foot spacing on three beams of 2-inch by 8-inch laminated three layers thick.

Lucille said that many years later four more beams were added to strengthen the upstairs floor.

"There are very few posts in this free-standing building," she said. "Only two partition walls exist: one to make a heated workshop at one end and the opposite end is for the combine storage. Between these two areas, in the middle room, there are posts, eight feet apart along the width for trucks and the seed cleaning equipment."

The top floor has a dozen windows (20-inch by 3-feet) along the length on each side and at each end. Windows along the length of the building allow access of the auger spout to put grain into the top bins. Windows at each end are for lighting. The floor of each compartment has a sliding trap door to let out the grain into the truck below. On the second floor, several adjustable compartments were made to separate different grains for crops and seed.

"The grain trap doors on the floor became very helpful in the first winter after the shop was completed," Lucille said.

A Canadian Wheat Board quota for grain came through while her parents were away, so her oldest sister, Rose, took charge, ordering three girls to work.

"They [the older sisters] shoveled and hauled a whole train boxcar of grain to the Thrasher elevator about three miles from home," Lucille said. "They were 15, 18 and 20 years old. This illustrates the convenience of the trap door for the grain above where the trucks are parked. I think, jokingly, that today girls go to the gym to work out and have nothing to show for it!"

The main floor is all dirt except for the shop area, which is concrete. Everyone in the family shingled the building. The original roof paint was a mix of used crankcase oil and soot. This gave the roof a black colour.

"For two years after the shop was finished, the University of Saskatoon professors came out several times to see the shop and made blueprints of the building," Lucille said.

"Can you imagine how astounded they would be if they came today to see the building which is fully functional more than 65 years later!"

Lucille's brother Leo owns the farm, while his son, Raymond and wife Rosemarie Labrecque now live on the family farmstead today which is located about 15 kilometres south of Rosetown on the east side of Highway 4.

UNIVERSITY OF SASKATCHEWAN BARN
Saskatoon

A stone barn has been a landmark on the University of Saskatchewan Campus for more than 90 years.
PHOTO COURTESY SASKATCHEWAN HERITAGE FOUNDATION

A stone barn, with a distinctive French-Canadian or "down east" architectural character, has been a landmark on the University of Saskatchewan campus for more than 90 years.

Built at a cost of $150,000, the barn opened in 1912 and was designed by architects Brown and Vallance of Montreal. The architects also designed 14 of the major original University of Saskatchewan buildings as well as several buildings in the City of Saskatoon.

The stone barn, home for primary livestock research for almost half a century, now holds the replacement animals for the dairy research unit.

"The story of the University Barn begins with the first Dean of Agriculture, William Rutherford," says C. M. "Red" Williams, who has been a professor in the Department of Animal Husbandry, now called the Department of Animal and Poultry Science, at the university for 50 years. "He created a College of Agriculture that not only served the students but also the people of the province. His

asset as a great teacher, special friend to farmers, and proficient director resulted in a college critical to the development of rural Saskatchewan."

Dean Rutherford embraced the radical concept of University President Walter Murray that a college of agriculture should be included along with the colleges of arts and sciences on site of the University of Saskatchewan, "That was not university practice at the time and some people had serious concerns with this proposition." Nevertheless, agriculture became the second college at the new university.

The site for the entire University of Saskatchewan was related to available farm land and, of course, the scenic view of the South Saskatchewan River. About 300 acres were set aside for the campus buildings and 1,000 acres were for cropping.

"The major objectives of the Department of Animal Husbandry were to acquire and propagate superior horses, cattle, sheep, and swine for use in teaching students and for demonstrations to farmers," Williams said. "That role fit the barn—or vice versa—for well over half a century."

The west wing of the barn housed the internationally renowned Clydesdale horses. Purchases from Ontario, Scotland, and Massachusetts led to horses that won ribbons in Regina, Brandon, and Chicago exhibitions. Of course, initially all farm work was horse-powered.

The east wing held highly esteemed dairy herds of Ayrshire, Jersey, and, most notably, Holstein-Friesians. In 1950, one heifer set a world record of 20,823 pounds of milk in 365 days.

For many years, the lofts were full of hay and grain, which could be dropped via chutes to the animals below. Access was by two ramps that allowed wagons into the loft. The barn couldn't match the changes in animal science practices, however, and from the 1960s newer buildings and research facilities were built on campus. The stone barn now serves as a minor research area and houses yearling dairy animals.

At one time, there were more than 100 workers and researchers directly linked to the university farm. A whole culture was very evident as many workers and their families lived on campus. Often the children of farm workers became students.

The Barn Raisers Committee, part of the Saskatchewan Agricultural Graduates Association that has been conducting a feasibility study on retrofitting the University barn.

Williams said the barn's special character and its continuity with the university's founding departments constitute it as the perfect icon for the campus, and alumni find the idea of retrofitting appealing.

"There are a number of hurdles to jump," he said. "The $15-million price tag for conversion to people-use, plus the embedded smell in the concrete, are just a few of the issues to adaptive reuse."

The west wing of the barn is a huge facility originally 48 feet by 176 feet long, and with an expansion of the east wing added another 160 foot by 48 foot area.

The roof line is 44 feet high and rises above 50 feet with the ventilator cupolas on the Gambrel-type roof. The foundation walls are concrete, clad

with granite fieldstones. The exterior cladding of both walls is cedar shingles, and the roof is asphalt shingles.

A low stone wall of granite encircles an outside pen giving a French-Canadian or European feel to the area. The two, 120-ton concrete silos that flank the north ramp are believed to be the first built in Saskatchewan.

The interior of the building has changed little since completion and the 8 BY 10 timber beams are still sound and impressive, as is the original loft floor. A couple of original horse stalls have been saved in the west wing.

The University Barn is located on Farm Lane of the University of Saskatchewan Campus, north of College Drive and west of Preston Avenue.

Two, 120-ton concrete silos that flank the barn are believed to be the first silos built in Saskatchewan.
PHOTO COURTESY SASKATCHEWAN HERITAGE FOUNDATION

CONVENT OF THE SACRED HEART
Willow Bunch

The boarding school and Convent of the Sacred Heart in Willow Bunch has been a pillar of strength for the community for more than 90 years.

"The convent is a symbol of the faith and pioneering spirit which make Willow Bunch the oldest Francophone community in southern Saskatchewan," says Mayor Jordan Dosch.

Construction of the building began in the spring of 1914 but was interrupted by the First World War when skilled workers returned to France to fight for their country. The third floor wasn't completed until 1921.

The building, which measures 83 feet by 44 feet, is comprised of a central tower housing a small bell and ordained with a niche where a statue of the Sacred Heart stands.

"The convent served as a public boarding school where the Sisters of the Cross taught the Catholic faith and offered a French education that was unparalleled in the surrounding country school until 1983," said Dosch.

Two years later, the Town of Willow Bunch purchased the building for $1 to house the ever-expanding museum. It was declared a Municipal Heritage Site in 1986, the same year the building was sold to the local Francophone association, also for $1.

"The building now is owned by the Francophones de Talle de Saules who operate a French cultural centre in the lower floor and who continue the tradition of the convent as an historic landmark and symbol of the Francophone presence in rural Saskatchewan," said Dosch.

Edouard Beaupre is a local hero who is featured prominently in the Willow Bunch museum. Born in 1881, he became known as the Willow Bunch Giant when he grew to be eight-feet-three-inches tall because of a problem with his pituitary gland. He toured North America with the Barnum & Bailey Circus, displaying his size and strength.

"Today, his "footprints" are painted on the sidewalk leading to our museum," Dosch explained.

"We have a life-size statue of Edouard in the museum as well as his actual coat, shirt, ring, and bed."

Considerable renovations have been done to the convent, located at 8 Fifth Street East in Willow Bunch. The top storey was closed and new bathrooms, heating, and sprinkler systems were installed. The foundation was shored up, and new stairs were added. The Francophone Community Centre is in the basement, and the top two floors house the museum.

Many people in the community, located on Highway 36 about 150 kilometres south of Moose Jaw just a few minutes from the Montana-Saskatchewan border, still have fond memories of the boarding school and convent.

"The devotion of the Sisters of the Cross really touched me," recalled Delvina Martin, who boarded at the convent during the 1940s. "They were dedicated to their work whether it was for teaching, cleaning or cooking. They always greeted us with a smile." Mass was celebrated every day at 7:00 A.M., she said.

Louise Boisvert vividly remembers the laundry system. "In the wintertime, I remember the Sisters used to hang the sheets and linens from the dormitory to dry on the banisters of the stairwells in the convent," she said.

As an eight-year-old, Viviane Boisvert-Jewell found the routine of life at the boarding school quite strict. "You were awakened early, attended prayers in the chapel and then were served breakfast," she said. "You attended school until 3:30 when you got one hour of free time, then you had a study period for half an hour before supper. Then, it was clean up, another study break, a bit of personal time, and then you got ready for bed at 9:00 P.M."

A few days after moving to the school, she and a friend snuck downstairs during the middle of the night from the dormitory to the large dining hall, where they strapped on roller skates.

"Oblivious to all else we enjoyed ourselves for what seemed like hours but it was more like 20 or so minutes before we saw Sister Juliette Marie standing the doorway," Boisvert-Jewell said. "I remember the panic that ran through me when she asked what we were doing."

She told the nun that they were having some fun and invited her to join them. "She simply smiled her beautiful smile, chatted with us for a bit, and, to our amusement, then strapped on a pair of roller skates and skated with us, enjoying the moment."

After a few rounds, the trio put their roller skates away and the sister tucked the two young students into bed.

Architect Maurice Soulodre said the former Willow Bunch convent is similar to other buildings at Prud'homme, St. Brieux, and Zenon Park, because most of the religious orders who established the convents all originated in eastern Canada where there was a lengthy tradition of wood-frame construction.

Records about the architect and construction of the building are unavailable, but Soulodre said the Willow Bunch convent likely is a wood frame building with a reinforced concrete foundation.

"It's not uncommon for these buildings to have massive reinforced concrete footings approximately four feet below the ground and to have reinforced concrete walls which extend to the underside of the main floor," he said. "This allowed for the basement to have large window and thus become valuable living space."

The exterior finish is cement stucco on metal lath. Interior walls were generally 2 by 4 construction with wood lath-and-plaster finish. Windows were wood "double-hung" style that allowed storm windows to be added to the exterior in the cold winter months.

The Convent of the Sisters of the Cross was named a Municipal Heritage Site in 1986.

PIONEERING SPIRIT

"This is a wonderful place where they're bringing history back to life."

–Laura Parsonage, who has lived 3 kilometres from Fort Walsh for the past 55 years.

Saskatchewan's pioneering spirit can be seen and experienced today at several sites across the province.

Saskatchewan people clearly don't want to forget those whose blood, sweat and incredible desire to build a new life in a new world forged the province into a unique cultural mosaic.

That pioneering spirit is visible today in National Historic Sites as well as Municipal Heritage Properties ranging from forts and farms to former opera houses and train stations.

Dedicated volunteers, organizations and agencies continue to carry the architectural heritage torches passed on from generations past. And such built heritage provides a focal point for great pride in being able to convey the past to future generations.

The most visible examples of Saskatchewan's pioneering spirit can be seen at a series of national historic sites that commemorate an era before the region was part of the wild, wild West. It was a time in the history of armed conflict and open rebellion by a group of Métis.

Today, people can stroll along the banks of the Saskatchewan River near the settlement of Batoche, where the final conflict between the British expeditionary force lead by the General Middleton overwhelmed and then captured Métis leader Louis Riel.

For some, 1885 conflict is known as the North West Rebellion, for others it was the North West Resistance.

Visitors to Fort Walsh, amid the scenic Cypress Hills of southwestern Saskatchewan, and to Fort Battleford, in the northwest, view a snapshot of history as though they were walking into a large-time capsule. In addition, people of all ages, shapes and sizes are encouraged to dress up in the period costumes the settlers or of the North West Mounted Police (NWMP), the forerunners of the Royal Canadian Mounted Police (RCMP).

A common thread that weaves amongst all of the heritage or historic sites—municipal, provincial and federal—is the fact local people volunteer their time, effort and skills to work alongside a small, professional support staff that operate each location.

These local volunteer groups work in relative isolation.

As a result, members of these local groups welcome activities by such province-wide organizations as the Saskatchewan Heritage Foundation, SaskCulture and provincial cultural organizations, and the Saskatchewan Architectural Heritage Society in lessening the risk of cultural isolation, promoting awareness of buildings and activities in other locales.

Development of province-wide cultural initiatives by bringing these disparate groups together through educational and communications programs, meetings and workshops ensures the legacy of heritage pioneers lives on.

BATOCHE
National Historic Site

Batoche, the Métis village where the final battle of the North-West Rebellion of 1885 was fought, is a National Historic Site operated by Parks Canada that still touches the hearts and minds of Saskatchewan residents and visitors to this day.

The site displays the remains of the Village of Batoche that had been selected by Louis Riel as the headquarters for his Provisional Government of Saskatchewan.

Several buildings have been restored at the site along the shores of the South Saskatchewan River. The National Historic Site depicts the lifestyles of the Métis of Batoche between 1860 and 1900, including the trails they walked, their homes, their renovated church, and the Battle of Batoche that lasted from May 9 to May 12, 1885.

Originally declared a National Historic Site in 1923, the initial focus was to commemorate the armed conflict between the Canadian government and the Métis provisional government. However,

Batoche now also commemorates the history of the Métis community of Batoche, home of Métis culture and heritage

Ray Fidler, who was born in Batoche in 1958, has worked for Parks Canada since 1982. "My grandparents were born in the Batoche area, and my dad lived here 'til 1999. I have a vested interest in carrying on the past history and the living history of Batoche," said Fidler, who is the grounds supervisor.

"I work at Batoche National Historic Site and enjoy preserving the cultural perspective of the site for future generations. My roots will always be here."

Fidler said Batoche may have more significance to people from across the country than across the province.

"My thought is that Batoche is more important to the people of Canada than the local community," he said. "When visitors come to Batoche they can feel a part of their history, either white or

Aboriginal. It preserves a time in history that is important to the whole of Canada."

During the late 18th Century, French Canadian *voyageurs* carried the fur trade into the western Canada. Children born of the relationships the *voyageurs* had with Aboriginals they encountered, including Cree and Saulteaux women, became known as Métis.

Between 1783 and 1821, the Métis worked for the North West Company and the Hudson's Bay Company hunting, fishing, guiding, and paddling the canoes of the two rivals across Rupert's Land, as most of the west was known then.

However, many Métis became unemployed when the two great competitors merged in 1821. Settling along Red River Valley in Manitoba, the Métis turned to buffalo hunting, the York boat brigades, and hauling freight to provide for their families.

By 1850, the Métis were successfully challenging the Hudson's Bay Company monopoly. Many were trading independently with the First Nations peoples in the west.

The inability of Riel's Provisional Government to obtain guarantees for the Métis in Manitoba in 1869, as well as the dwindling herds of buffalo, convinced many that they must adopt some of the agricultural ways of the whites or be swallowed up by eastern settlement.

The Métis looked westward to Saskatchewan as a place to make a fresh start. Their fathers and grandfathers had wintered there in the past, and in 1872, a decision was made to establish settlements along the South Saskatchewan River. It would stretch from St-Louis-de-Langevin in the north to Fish Creek in the south, spanning the Carlton Trail, the main trade route between Fort Garry, now part of Winnipeg, and Fort Edmonton.

In 1873, Xavier Letendre dit Batoche built a ferry where the Carlton Trail crossed the South Saskatchewan River. A little village sprouted and grew to about 500 people by 1885.

The Métis laid their farms out in long river-lot fashion, cultivating a small portion of them, but living principally by freighting, trading and raising cattle. They were a sociable people holding parties and dances in their homes to celebrate weddings,

New Year's and other special occasions, or just to make the long winters pass more quickly.

In 1878, the federal government had surveyed some of the traditional river-lot farms of the Métis already at Batoche, but many who arrived later had to settle on lands surveyed in the eastern Canadian square-township system.

There were also difficulties with acquiring legal land titles, obtaining script (a certificate that could be exchanged for a land grant or money), resurveying the rest of the settlement and acquiring greater representation in territorial and federal politics.

First Nations Peoples were demanding food, equipment, and farming assistance promised in treaties. Settlers across the northwest were upset with Prime Minister John A. Macdonald's national policy of railway development and protective tariffs.

Farmers couldn't get their crops to market and had to pay higher prices for eastern Canadian-manufactured farm implements because of the huge tariffs placed on cheaper American equipment.

Petitions and meetings held in 1884 involving local Métis leaders such as Gabriel Dumont and Maxime Lepuine failed to get the government to change. Decisive action was needed, the Métis people concluded. As a result, a trio was sent to St. Peter's, Montana, where Métis leader Louis Riel had fled from Manitoba.

The subsequent military confrontations were a turning point in history. The only clear Métis victory in the North-West Rebellion—or North-West

Parks Canada now operates the village as a National Historic Site.
PHOTO COURTESY PARKSCANADA

Resistance as it is known by Métis—came at Duck Lake, the initial outbreak of violence. Engagements at Fish Creek, Cut Knife Hill, and Frenchman Butte were all stand-offs.

The Battle of Batoche was fought over four days. Less than 300 Métis and First Nations People led by Louis Riel and Gabriel Dumont defended Batoche from a series of rifle pits that they had dug along the edge of the bush surrounding the village.

They faced the 800-member North-West Field Force commanded by Major General Frederick Middleton. The turning point in the battle involved Middleton moving north of the church and rectory with about 130 troops, a Gatling gun, and a nine-pound cannon. This action stretched the Métis defensive lines too thin.

Riel and Dumont escaped, but Riel gave himself up later, was put on trial, and eventually was hanged in Regina. Dumont fled to the United States. More than 25 Métis and soldiers were killed in the Battle of Batoche.

Today, visitors to Batoche have the opportunity to converse with knowledgeable interpreters while exploring the site's architectural and archaeological resources.

"Batoche is important to me because it is a vital part of my national history and my local history," said Paulette Gaudet, a local resident who has worked at the site since 1991. "It is economically beneficial to the community because it creates jobs. It's also part of our identity. It's who we are."

Batoche is where visitors can become familiar with Canadian history and Métis culture and heritage. Open from the Victoria Day weekend in May to the Labour Day weekend in September, there is a nominal admission charge.

Batoche is 88 kilometres northeast of Saskatoon. Follow Highway 11 north to Rosthern and then take Highway 312 east to the junction with Highway 225. Batoche is 11 kilometres north of the junction.

FORT BATTLEFORD
National Historic Site

Fort Battleford is a National Historic Site that showcases the role of the North-West Mounted Police establishing law and order in the Canadian west.

The fort, which was established in 1876 and abandoned in 1924, offers visitors a unique glimpse into a pivotal time in the development of the region.

The stockade and bastions have been reconstructed. Four of the original buildings feature period furniture, while the barracks have become an interpretive display.

Kids of all ages can dress up in Mountie costumes and take part in drills, or they can opt to get dirt under their fingernails by participating in an archaeological dig. Visitors are encouraged to identify their finds as they tour Fort Battleford.

"The Province of Saskatchewan is very fortunate to have the Fort Battleford National Historic Site because it is one of the oldest forts in Canada," said Yvonne Michnik, a member of the Friends of Fort Battleford Society.

"We attract many visitors to our province because of the North-West Rebellion of 1885 and the activities that took place in and around our community." Five of the original buildings lend an air of credibility to the site, she said.

"I've enjoyed meeting people from different parts of the world when I volunteer at Fort Battleford," Michnik said. "I'm always very proud to say I'm from Saskatchewan."

Omar Murray, a Parks Canada site interpreter, echoed Michnik's thoughts.

"We ensure that people have a very good understanding of history and the hardships that our ancestors had to endure," Murray said.

"It gives us the opportunity to help people understand that history was made by real people and was not influenced by some 'Hollywood' version of the facts."

Turmoil brewed in the territory only a few short years after Canada become a country. As the buffalo disappeared, the First Nations lifestyle was

Bastions and the stockade at Fort Battleford have been reconstructed.
PHOTO COURTESY PARKSCANADA

Because of the North West Rebellion, the number of North West Mount Police stationed at Fort Battleford grew to 200 from 12.

deteriorated as the NWMP more and more became enforcers of the government's Indian Policy.

Frustrated by the government's response to its concerns regarding the treaties and their livelihood, First Nations, such as the Cree, grew increasingly discontented.

By 1885, violence had erupted, including attacks at Frog Lake and Fort Pitt led by kah-pay-pamhchukwao (Wandering Spirit), war chief of Big Bear's band.

While mistahi-maskwa (Big Bear) might not have condoned the actions of Wandering Spirit and his followers, the government, who viewed these events as a rebellion against its authority, saw Big Bear as an instigator.

As a result of these conflicts, the NWMP force stationed at Fort Battleford grew from 12 men and 16 horses in 1876 to 200 men and 107 horses in 1885.

Fort Battleford now boasted the largest concentration of NWMP in the west.

Fort Battleford then became the focal point for the Canadian Government's military operations during the 1885 rebellion. It was the base of operations during the battles at Cut Knife Hill, Fort Pitt, Frenchman Butte, Steele Narrows, and the search for Big Bear.

Around the same time the fort also sheltered approximately 500 local people who feared an attack from the surrounding First Nations. News of the battle at Duck Lake between the Métis and NWMP made the residents of Battleford uneasy. So they sought protection within the stockade of Fort Battleford.

At the same time pîhtokahânapiwiin (Poundmaker) and his followers were on their way to Battleford to request overdue rations. Expecting to meet with the Indian Agent, Poundmaker was surprised to find the town abandoned.

Through a series of miscommunications, the Indian agent refused to meet with Poundmaker's band. Although Poundmaker tried to prevent it, some of his followers looted the deserted buildings of Battleford.

Later, the militia, led by Colonel Otter, also looted the town on its way to the battle at Cut Knife Hill. Fear, coupled with a succession of violent incidents between townspeople and First Nations

threatened. The new Canadian government wanted to open the west for settlement.

The killing of Nakota (Assiniboine) by wolf-hunters in the Cypress Hills in 1873 confirmed the government's belief that this vast prairie region required administration.

The need for extending law and sovereignty to the west became the motivation for the formation of the North West Mounted Police (NWMP). The force set out for the west in 1874. Battleford was declared capital of the new North-West Territories of Canada in 1876.

That same year, construction began on Battle River Post, later known as Fort Battleford. Situated near the junction of the Battle River and the North Saskatchewan River, the fort was close to large First Nations' populations as well as Government House.

From the moment the NWMP occupied Fort Battleford, one of their main activities was public relations with the surrounding First Nations. The government believed that treaties were required before settlement could commence and that the local First Nations needed to become acquainted with Canadian laws.

The NWMP provided protection for settlers and assistance during the treaty-making process. They were involved with the negotiations and signing of Treaty Six in 1876 and also distributed the annual Treaty payments.

However, the relationship among First Nations, Indian agents, and the NWMP gradually

groups, kept the townspeople crowded inside Fort Battleford for almost a month.

By successfully suppressing the armed conflicts of 1885, the government secured its claims to the west and paved the way for settlement and immigration. Instead of addressing First Nations' grievances, the government tightened regulations governing most aspects of First Nations' culture, including schooling, socialization, livelihood, and customs.

Many First Nations were prosecuted for their involvement in conflict.

Poundmaker went to Fort Battleford to negotiate terms of peace with General Middleton and was arrested. He was sentenced to three years in prison for treason.

The largest mass hanging in Canada, since Confederation, occurred on November 27, 1885, when six Cree and two Assiniboine men were tried for murder and publicly hanged within the walls of the stockade. Many more served time in prison.

These convictions left an impact on the development of the west, serving as examples of the government's response to challenges to its authority. While there was continuing discontent among First Nations, there were no further attempts at armed resistance.

Fort Battleford National Historic Site is located 153 kilometres northwest of Saskatoon in the Town of Battleford, about five kilometres southeast of North Battleford.

Follow the Parks Canada Beaver logo signs from the Yellowhead Highway to the fort, which is open from the Victoria Day long weekend to Labour Day weekend. There is an admission fee.

Visitors can dress in period costumes and participate in drill activities while touring the National Historic Site.
PHOTO COURTESY PARKSCANADA

OLD FLOUR MILL
Esterhazy

The Old Flour Mill in Esterhazy is a pre-First World War building that has machinery from the era in workable condition today.

With grinders and conveying equipment from the turn-of-the-century, the Esterhazy Flour Mill provides a snapshot of the industrial past of Saskatchewan.

The flour mill, originally built between 1905 and 1906, was designated a Municipal Heritage Site in 1996. It's the pride of the east-central Saskatchewan community.

"We think similar structures were built on the prairies, but this is the only complete wood frame flour mill of its type in Saskatchewan and possibly in all of Canada," said Judy Parker, Economic Development Officer for Town of Esterhazy.

"What makes it especially unique is that its integrity has not been compromised by renovations or expansions over the decades. Some of the machines show the patent date of 1879."

After the Town of Esterhazy received title, the property was developed as a heritage property. The Friends of the Esterhazy Flour Mill is a community group committed to preserving, restoring and promoting the flour mill on a provincial and national level.

From June 20, 1907, to 1981, the mill was used to grind wheat flour. Farmers exchanged grain for flour that was stored on site. Western Home Flour was shipped across Canada.

Now, painted a reddish-brown, the flour mill can be easily spotted driving into Esterhazy from the west on Highway 22. The north side of the street is lined with older homes and the south is bordered by a brand new historical park being developed by a town committee.

Overlooking the back side of the park is the Old Flour Mill, which has been transformed, with the help of dozens of gallons of paint, from a weathered-looking, inconspicuous building to a dominant feature.

The flour mill has five-foot-high white lettering on each side. The west side reads: Western Home Flour, while the north side reads: Esterhazy Flour Mill and Western Home Flour.

The building is 65-feet tall and looks like a smaller version of a grain elevator.

From the time the wheat enters the building to be weighed until it leaves as flour, the product travels about 980 feet.

The elevator section of the mill has storage for at least 22,000 bushels of wheat

The metal-drum grinding system made it possible to mill hard Red Spring wheat that at one time was considered low-quality wheat. The hard Red Spring wheat shattered in the stone grinding systems and produced too much very-fine material to make good baking flour. The concept for the system of grinders and sifters came from Hungary and were state-of-the-art when installed. The equipment itself came from Michigan. A similar system is used to this day.

Before the time of protein testing and electric moisture testers, these qualities were determined by the miller chewing the grain, obviously a learned skill.

Local homemakers, in the early years, would test batches of flour by baking bread at home each night. The baking test was important because the wheat delivered by the farmers was of different qualities and had to be blended from the elevator storage bins before it was milled. A poor blend made poor flour.

A steam engine ran the mill until the 1940s, which meant hundreds of cords of wood had to be stockpiled on the east side of the flour mil. A cord of wood is a measurement of wood stacked four-feet high, four-feet wide, and eight-feet long. It took one cord of wood apparently to fire up the steam engine.

The millers weren't always good neighbours.

Sometimes the engine would fire up at 2:00 A.M. With the straight pipe from the engine being the only muffler, everyone in town had a wakeup call, especially the closest neighbours.

"I grew to hate the sound of that engine," remembered Lorretta Common, who lived in a house right next door to the flour mill.

Many that have taken tours through the mill in the past year have commented that they remember when their fathers brought grain to the mill and took home flour and other products from town.

Florence Gray tells the story of her father, Harry Hobart, an early pioneer. "In 1909, he took some wheat into the mill and brought home a load of flour, bran, and shorts, and stored it in a granary," she said, noting it was supposed to be their family's supply for the year.

"A prairie fire came along and burned all the buildings in the farmyard, including the granary and a barn into which the horses had run." Their house was untouched.

Friends and neighbours gave money to the family under the title of "Helping Hands Fund." Mrs. Gray still has the original list of all the donations.

Harvard Zavedosky recalls a school trip made to the mill in 1942 when he was in grade 3. "Fifteen students climbed in the back of a farm truck and drove to Esterhazy on a full day trip," Zavedosky said, a trip of about 11 miles. "The mill part of the Esterhazy tour was the major highlight and very exciting." Zavedosky and these students talk about the trip even today when they get together.

John Jurick, who operated the flour mill for 10 years until 1966, was a very sociable man who liked to tell stories and jokes to all visitors at the flour mill, where he also practised his tuba.

The Old Flour Mill in Esterhazy provides a unique glimpse into Saskatchewan's past. Tour information is available at the Visitors' Centre in the Historical Park. Please contact Ralph May at (306) 745-6455 or Town Office at (306) 745-5405 to arrange tour times.

The Old Flour Mill, at 517 Smith-Dorrien Avenue in Esterhazy, was declared a Municipal Heritage Property in 1996.

FORT WALSH NWMP GARRISON
Fort Walsh

Fort Walsh, which was established in 1875 and became one of the largest and most heavily armed garrisons of the North West Mounted Police, continues to be a source of pride for southwestern Saskatchewan residents.

Fort Walsh now is a National Historic Site operated by Parks Canada.

"This is just a wonderful place where they're bringing history back to life," said Laura Parsonage, who has lived just two miles away from Fort Walsh for the past 55 years.

"I could hear the hammering when they were fixing up the old buildings and saw the trucks driving by with their load of logs for the fort. I'm proud of what they have done."

Jerry Federowich retired in Maple Creek, 55 kilometres north of Fort Walsh, after a 36-year career in the Royal Canadian Mounted Police (RCMP).

"Fort Walsh is important to me because it represents the origins of the force in the west," said the former RCMP sergeant, referring to the fact the North West Mounted Police (NWMP) were the predecessors of the RCMP.

"I've been active in maintaining Fort Walsh as a volunteer because it is part of our Canadian history. People of all ages and even future generations should see Fort Walsh to appreciate what it was like in Saskatchewan in the 1870s."

Federowich was a member of the last troop to graduate from the RCMP training depot on horseback in 1966. As a result, he has a special fondness for the National Historic Site and continues to volunteer to participate in RCMP-related activities at Fort Walsh.

Fort Walsh was reconstructed to allow visitors to experience the facility as a western garrison until 1883 and then as a facility to breed horses for the RCMP and its world-famous Musical Ride from 1942 to 1968.

Visitors can take a guided tour of the fort's buildings, the Fort Walsh town site, two cemeteries, and a reconstructed whiskey trading post. They can also take self-guided trails on their own.

Established in 1875, Fort Walsh would quickly become the most important, largest, and most heavily armed fort the NWMP garrisoned during their early years in the west.

The Mounties, in their early days at Fort Walsh, performed a wide range of duties. They chased whiskey traders and horse thieves, and counselled desperate First Nations peoples dispirited by the disappearance of the buffalo.

In addition, they supervised the thousands of Lakota who had streamed into the western territories of Canada during the Great Sioux War of 1876–1877 in the United States.

The story of Fort Walsh, like that of western Canada, is fascinating. Its pages in history are punctuated with larger-than-life characters, including James Walsh, for whom the fort was named, and Lakota Leader Tantanka Iyotanka, better known as Sitting Bull, who became famous after his clash with the U.S. Seventh Calvary at the Battle of the Little Big Horn.

Fort Walsh National Historic Site of Canada has been commemorated because the fort served from 1878 to 1882 as the headquarters of the NWMP.

The fort played a key role in defending and imposing Canadian law from 1875 to 1883 in the North-West Territory and in implementing Canada's Indian policy.

All groups planning to visit Fort Walsh are urged to register in advance. The site is open daily 9:30 A.M. to 5:30 P.M. from the Victoria Day long weekend to Labour Day. However, tours can be arranged after the Labour Day weekend by calling the Parks Canada office at (306) 662-2645.

There is a nominal admission charge.

Individuals of all ages enjoy the hands-on activities encountered at Fort Walsh.

The guided tour begins with a visit to Farwell's Trading Post and provides visitors with an opportunity to explore the re-furnished 1873 buildings and learn about life in an American whiskey trading post. The story of the Cypress Hills Massacre and the events leading up to that tragic day—June 1, 1873—are outlined during the visit to the Trading Post.

Tours of the historic site of Fort Walsh are lead by a knowledgeable guide dressed in period costume. Students are actively involved in several learning activities, which present the site's historic significance in a fun and entertaining fashion.

Students experience a simulated, recruitment training as a North-West Mounted Policeman and are assigned various tasks, which emphasize cooperative learning and an appreciation for Canada's past.

Fort Walsh National Historic Site, adjacent to the Cypress Hills Interprovincial Park, is located 55 kilometres southwest of Maple Creek, Saskatchewan.

Getting there is sometimes difficult because weather conditions can make roads treacherous.

If you are planning to travel on the "Gap Road" between Cypress Hills Interprovincial Park (Centre Block) and Fort Walsh, or the "Graburn Gap Road" between Elkwater and Fort Walsh, it is recommended that you phone in advance.

To ensure roads are in good condition and passable call Fort Walsh at (306) 662-3590, Elkwater at (403) 893-3833, or Centre Block (306) 662-4411.

MUSEUM OF WHEAT
Hepburn

A restored Saskatchewan Wheat Pool elevator in Hepburn is the first grain elevator in Canada designated a heritage site and provides a unique window into the agricultural history of the province.

The elevator closed for business in 1991 but was reincarnated as the Hepburn Museum of Wheat in 1994 to coincide with the village's 75th homecoming celebrations.

Built by C. H. Nelson in 1928 at a cost of $16,423.80, the elevator is located at the western end of Main Street in the Village of Hepburn, about 50 kilometres north of Saskatoon.

The property now is owned by the village and run by the Hepburn Museum of Wheat. The purpose of the museum is to explain how a grain elevator worked and its role within the Canadian grain handling system.

"While there were many elevators in Saskatchewan and many were built relatively alike, the uniqueness of this building is that it is the first elevator to be turned into a museum and remain on its original site within the province," says Victor Peters, president of the Hepburn Museum of Wheat Board of Directors.

"The elevator is a true example of what distinguished the economy and culture of our province. This building was at the heart of a determined effort by local farmers and businessmen to retain what was a vital service for the larger community."

The Hepburn elevator, he said, also served the needs of farmers for a number of years from the nearby communities of Waldheim, Hepburn, and Mennon.

"During that time, a record handle of 20,743 metric tonnes or roughly 792,000 bushels went through the Hepburn elevator in one crop year," Peters said.

"When the people in the village realized we could no longer save the elevator as a business entity, we decided to turn it into a museum."

The main elevator building, known as Saskatchewan Wheat Pool No 901, remains intact today with most of the original equipment visible for visitors to see. This includes the scale that weighed first the grain wagons and then the grain trucks, as well as the actual elevator that raised the grain into storage bins. Only a few pipes were removed for safety reasons. The adjacent annex was renovated for use as museum office and display area

The Canadian Grain Commission reports there were 3,047 country elevators in Saskatchewan during the peak crop year of 1932–1933. The elevators were located no more than a day's travel by horse and wagon to allow farmers to haul their grain to the nearest railline where the elevators were built. That's one reason many Saskatchewan communities are located about 10 to 15 kilometres apart on railline.

During the 1980s, the agricultural economy shifted, and grain companies began closing elevators when railways began to abandon raillines. Many producers had to haul grain further and further from their farms to elevators because facilities, like Hepburn's, had succumbed to the economic tides of change.

By 2004, the number of licensed primary elevators in Saskatchewan, including high throughput elevators, had dwindled to just 200, Canadian Grain Commission statistics indicate.

The Hepburn elevator is an average in size. Built from 2 by 4 and 2 by 6 British Columbia planks, the elevator is 32 feet by 33 feet and towers 78.5 feet above the driveway that measures 55 feet by 17 feet.

"They called me Mr. Saskatchewan Wheat Pool. I was there to serve the public," recalled Albert Peters, the Hepburn elevator manager from 1948 to 1982.

"They weren't all satisfied with me but most were. It really made my day when former customers came to me and said they wished I were still there. This nearly brought me to tears. You couldn't wish for a better compliment."

The grain elevator provided a substantial tax base for the community as well as providing service to farmers in the area, he said.

Phyllis Siemens, who grew up in Hepburn, returned to teach there and now lives in retirement in the community. "It's encouraging to still have the Hepburn elevator as part of our community," she said.

"Now, as the Museum of Wheat it is an educational asset. Visitors, children, adults, and tourists all may learn from seeing the working of an elevator from the displays of printed material, artifacts, and machinery. It's a valuable link to our past."

For Cornie Willms, the museum still helps her get her bearings. "When we are driving near Hepburn we always know where the village is because we can see the elevator from a distance," she said. "This is something many communities miss—no identifying landmark."

Emil Amendt is proud the village bought the elevator and converted it into a museum. "People from other farming communities come here and ask: How did you manage to save your elevator? They ask if it is used for some business related to farming," said Amendt, who farms southeast of Hepburn.

"Well this is our heritage building. It is one of a very few such structures still remaining on the prairies. One wonders how many more elevators will disappear from our landscape."

Memories of the Hepburn elevator for C. J. Voth touch on the practical side of farming. "I came to the elevator to learn to how farm better. I would listen to other farmers who just happened to be there discuss some issues with their agent," said Voth, who turned 95 in 2004 and has farmed in the area all his life.

"We all had our input into the discussion and came away able to make more informed choices for ourselves. Oh, we did not always agree. Sometimes, the talk turned into quite serious business, but we walked away friends even if we agreed to disagree."

The Hepburn Museum of Wheat, designated a Municipal Heritage site in 1996, provides a window into the rich agricultural past of Saskatchewan and the farmers who built the province.

To get to Hepburn, take Highway 16 north of Saskatoon about five kilometres to the junction with Highway 11, then continue north on Highway 11 to the junction with Highway 12. Travel 36 kilometres on Highway 12 to the Hepburn access road.

SEAGER WHEELER FARM
Rosthern

The farm near Rosthern where Seager Wheeler developed hardier strains of wheat that have been planted by producers on three continents for decades is a National Historic Site open each summer to the public.

All buildings have been maintained as though Wheeler were still pioneering his dry-land farming techniques at the site.

A visitor centre, located at the centre of the Seager Wheeler Farm, includes a restaurant and a gift shop. There are also interpretive displays and a video sharing the life of the man known as the Wheat Wizard.

"This farm is important because it honors the life work of Seager Wheeler who was an innovator and leader in prairie agriculture." said Doug Klaassen, a member of the not-for-profit society that maintains the site and coordinates tours.

Born in the United Kingdom in 1868, Seager Wheeler immigrated to Saskatchewan in 1885. He eventually settled in Rosthern, where he built Maple Grove Farm. Wheeler taught himself the mechanics of dry-land farming and began an agriculture research career. His success made the Canadian prairies a popular place to live and work, and increased the sale of Canadian wheat around the world.

"The farm is important to honor Dr. Seager Wheeler and his accomplishments," said Ewald Epp, who has retired in Rosthern. "We can still use the past techniques he invented in our present day farming practices."

In 1904, Wheeler began selectively breeding spring wheat, developing strains such as Red Bobs, Kitchener, and a superior strain of Marquis. His 10B Marquis was adopted by the Canadian Seed Growers Association as the foundation for all registered Marquis.

Between 1911 and 1918, Wheeler's hard spring wheat varieties won him an unprecedented five international wheat-growing championships, a record that still stands.

Scientists, universities, and farmers throughout North America and the United Kingdom requested the seeds from his wheat varieties.

Wheeler's work also included the development of horticultural varieties such as the Saskatchewan Crabapple and the Seager Wheeler Rose.

Wheeler became remarkably successful in scientific agricultural experimentation, a field that had previously been dominated by universities and governments. In 1910, he became a member of the Canadian Seed Growers Association. The following year he sent a sample of his crop to the New York Land Show and won first prize—$1,000 in gold coins—for the best hard Spring wheat in North America.

Wheeler wrote numerous articles for the *Grain Growers Guide,* leading to his book *Book on Profitable Grain Growing: A Study of Dry-Land Farming,* published in 1919.

Wheeler's fame grew. People began calling him the Wheat Wizard of Rosthern and the Wheat King as he travelled across Saskatchewan delivering lectures to farmers. He was the subject of many articles in a variety of journals in Canada, the United Kingdom, and the United States.

Wheeler received an honourary degree from Queen's University in 1920 and was made a Member of the Order of the British Empire in 1943.

Although best known for his progressive farming techniques, Wheeler was also renowned as a part-time inventor of farm implements, particularly seed-cleaning equipment. He retired to Victoria, British Columbia, in 1947 and died at the age of 93 in 1961.

"The Seager Wheeler farm is important to our community and the province because he was a true pioneer in wheat breeding by developing varieties suitable to our Saskatchewan climate," said Shan Kerber, a retired x-ray technician who volunteers each summer to maintain the gardens at Maple Grove Farm. "It is important to preserve the work that Seager Wheeler did because he is an example for future generations."

The Seager Wheeler Farm, open from the long weekend in May to the end of August, is seven kilometres east of Rosthern, just off of Highway 312. Rosthern is located at the intersection of Highways 11 and 312, about 60 km northeast of Saskatoon, and 70 km southwest of Prince Albert.

For his contribution in the development of the Canadian west, Seager Wheeler was designated a Person of National Historic Significance in 1976. Seager Wheeler's Maple Grove Farm was commemorated in 1994.

GOODWIN HOUSE
Saskatchewan Landing

The fieldstone home Frank Goodwin took three years to construct from 1897 to 1900 after he retired from the North West Mounted Police (NWMP) now is the visitor centre and administration office for the Saskatchewan Landing Provincial Park.

"The house is very important to me because it represents an influential link that my family has to the history of Saskatchewan," said Audrey Goodwin, great-great-granddaughter of Frank Goodwin and now the naturalist at the Saskatchewan Landing Provincial Park.

"It grounds me and offers me a connection to my ancestors. I am very proud that my family has had an impact on the development of our province."

At just 18 years of age, Frank Goodwin left his home in England in 1878 to enlist in the NWMP. His decision had a profound effect on the settlement and development of the Saskatchewan Landing area, about 50 kilometres north of Swift Current, where he was posted.

During the North-West Rebellion of 1885, Goodwin was among the police that escorted the stage and mail coach north from Swift Current to Battleford. The biggest problems occurred when crossing the South Saskatchewan River in the spring and the autumn. For a month during these seasons, it would become impossible to cross the river because of ice conditions. Thus, it was not uncommon for as many as 50 outfits to be stranded at the river, waiting to cross either by ferry or on the ice.

Goodwin saw a business opportunity that involved a career and lifestyle change. He married Mary Rutherford, who had moved to Swift Current to operate the Canadian Pacific Railway Station Dining Room. At the time of their marriage, Mary was one of only six white women living in Swift Current.

He then resigned his commission in the NWMP and began construction of the house in 1897, first by gathering stones for the house's frame from the surrounding rugged hills and the hauling the material by team and stone boat to the site. Each stone was cut and squared by chisels and hammers.

A Métis man helping Goodwin built a kiln and gathered limestone from the surrounding area. As a stabilizer for the lime and sand, hair from horses, antelope, and deer was gathered from various First Nations' camps along the river. Most of the lumber was obtained in Swift Current and Moose Jaw, but some was hauled from as far away as Vancouver.

Meanwhile, Goodwin built a tiny two-room cottage near the construction site where he and his hired help would live in during construction of his home.

The house was designed like a hotel with four rooms and a large hall constituting both the upstairs and the main floor. A summer kitchen was located at the back. The basement was divided into two sections.

One half contained cupboards, shelves, and a wood-burning stove. This side was used for serving meals.

The other half was divided into three rooms: one bricked up for milk and meat, one for a huge coal furnace, and one for a storage and vegetable room.

The house was surrounded by two closed-in and one open veranda. On the top of the house was an iron railing eight feet by eight feet and three-feet high. On the birthday of a family member, a flag would fly from this point.

In 1900, the Goodwin family, now numbering eight, moved into their new home and brought along 150 head of cattle, chickens, and pigs. Their chores consisted of putting up hay, milking cows, churning butter, butchering animals, and cutting wood for fuel. Only a short time after the Goodwins moved in, people began to trek into the country north of Swift Current to homestead.

Thus, the Goodwin stone house became a hotel offering room and board. A large barn was built to accommodate as many as 35 horses at one time. The children often gave up their rooms, sleeping on cots in the veranda during the summer and in the basement in the winter.

Soon, a small store was added to the Goodwins' house, supplying such staples as flour, sugar, spices, tobacco, and candy.

The stone house became a haven for weary travellers going to and from Swift Current for supplies. Roads were not always in good condition so progress was slow. A man could travel about 30 miles a day with horses but only 10 to 20 miles with oxen.

For just $1, a traveller was given a bed, a supper, a breakfast, and shelter for his horse.

With the settlers came the need for broken horses. That created another business opportunity. So the Goodwin boys began taming wild horses and steers to pull the ploughs for settlers.

Even with the heavy workload, the Goodwin family had time to entertain friends and neighbours in their stone house.

Dances would begin at 8:00 P.M. and last all night long. No one would go home until morning for fear of becoming lost or frozen.

The Goodwin children eventually grew up, married, and moved away to make their own homes, except Frank Goodwin Jr., who operated the ferry at Saskatchewan Landing for 20 years until 1953. Frank Goodwin Sr. died in 1934 and his wife Mary Goodwin in 1945.

In 1928, Art and Besse Smith of Swift Current bought the old stone house at Saskatchewan Landing and carried on the business for 30 years, adding a market garden.

A provincial park was created at the historic crossing of the South Saskatchewan River in 1967. It is located at the south end of Lake Diefenbaker that was formed by the creation of the Gardiner and Qu'Appelle dams.

The Goodwin stone house now is the entry point into the Saskatchewan Landing Provincial Park that covers 5,500 hectares, or 13,590 acres.

"There are not many symbols of our heritage left in southwest Saskatchewan. The Goodwin House is definitely representative of the frontier heritage that opened up the west," Audrey Goodwin said. "I would actually like to see more historical recreation at the Goodwin House."

The Goodwin House Visitor Centre is located in the Saskatchewan Landing Provincial Park along Highway 4 about 50 kilometres north of Swift Current.

FORESTRY FARM HOUSE
Saskatoon

Rich in history and a destination spot for tourists, winter at the Forestry Farm House "'tis the season of art serene."
PHOTO COURTESY SAHS

The Superintendent's Residence at the Forestry Farm in Saskatoon, built in 1913, has become a tea house and interpretive centre for the intense work conducted at the former federal facility for almost half a century.

"This award-winning, beautifully restored heritage house is the perfect location for a quiet lunch amid the tranquility of the park," said Bernie Cruikshank, president of the Friends of the Forestry Farm House (FFFH), created in 1996 to preserve and protect the site.

Before the volunteer group was established, the house had faced possible demolition. The group invested more than 5,000 hours of volunteer labour and $143,060 into the restoration of the residence after successfully lobbying the city for a long-term lease.

Cruikshank was so committed to saving the Forestry Farm that she took a leave of absence from her professional job as an operating room nurse to become the project manager for the project. "The restoration project was very intense and yet incredibly satisfying," she recalled. "Looking around the restored house makes the blood, sweat, and tears worth it."

Sitting on the veranda, enjoying home-made lemonade Cruikshank and other long-term members of the group recognize that they have given something back to the community.

"We hope our positive outcome will make a difference in the struggle with the heritage retention and self-sustainability of buildings throughout the City of Saskatoon and the province of Saskatchewan," she said.

The restoration project and adaptive reuse of the Superintendent's Residence was recognized with two awards. Cruikshank won the YWCA Woman of Distinction Award for Heritage in 2001 and also the Municipal Heritage Advisory Committee (MHAC) for Volunteer Public Service in 2000.

The Forestry Farm was originally established in 1913 at Sutherland, a small town now part of

Saskatoon, as a forest nursery station by the Forestry Branch of the Federal Department of the Interior.

During the half-century that it fulfilled its original function, the station played a key role in an important federal government initiative—tree planting on the prairies. Only two such forestry nursery stations were established, the first at Indian Head in 1903.

The two stations became closely associated with the work conducted under the Prairie Farm Rehabilitation Act of 1935.

The Forestry Farm today consists of 144 acres and comprises the core of the original 320-acre station. Several pre-First World War structures, including the superintendent's residence, the former bunkhouse, the packing house, and the pump house, survive.

In 1965, a decision was made in Ottawa to consolidate all of the nursery activities at Indian Head. Title to the remaining 144 acres was transferred to the City of Saskatoon the following year. Few changes were made to the station until 1972, when animals from a local animal park were moved to the site, and the Forestry Farm Park and Zoo was established.

By the early 1990s, financial problems with the park and zoo operation resulted in the City being forced to consider options ranging from demolition to renovation, which resulted in the creation of the volunteer, nonprofit group that still operates the facility today. Major renovations to the interior and exterior of the farm house building were completed from 1998 to 2002.

William Stevenson homesteaded the land in 1886. It changed hands four times before W. C. Sutherland, then Speaker of the Saskatchewan Legislature as well as namesake of Sutherland Village, sold the property to the federal government in 1912 for $14,000.

The Superintendent's Residence at the Sutherland Forest Nursery Station is not a typical prairie farm house in scale or construction.

Constructed of red brick and capped with a complex hipped roof, pierced by a hipped dormer, the residence measures 40 by 40 feet and is an impressive two-and-a-half storey structure. The residence was designed to serve as an impressive focal

point to the lush grounds planned to surround it and continues to serve that function today.

Among the original purposes of the Forestry Farm was to promote the beautification of the prairies, to propagate and distribute seedlings, and to research horticulture.

W. Les Kerr, who became the second superintendent at the farm in 1942, was awarded the Stevenson Memorial Award for horticulture.

His plant-breeding interests and the research conducted under his supervision led to the creation of the Sutherland Caragana, Sutherland Larch, Fangstadt Willow, Golden Elder, Goldenlocks Elder, Pink Spires Crab, Plume Caragana, and the Sutherland Rosybloom Crab.

Kerr was also well known for his gentle touch with animals, which he allowed to live within the forestry farm area, beginning with a porcupine in 1942. The animal population grew to include rabbits, pheasants, deer, raccoons, coyotes, and bear. He retired in 1966, when the Sutherland Forest Nursery Station closed, and a portion of the land was sold to the City of Saskatoon.

Kerr and his wife Blanche were childless but were hosts to Peter and Douglas Wilde under the Children's Overseas Reception Board (CORB) program. The boys were English evacuees from Grantham in Lincolnshire because of the Second World War and returned home in 1945.

Friends of the Forestry Farm House tried to retain as much of the original design during renovations. "The four square layout was kept intact with the kitchen, parlour and dining room changed minimally. The interior porch walls were removed to open up the two porch areas for function sake," explained Cruikshank. "The pantry became the wheelchair-accessible washrooms."

The veranda was originally screened in but during the 1920s was glassed over and the south window became French doors. The French doors were intact but little remained of the original porch interior.

"A brick wall was uncovered and now stands as a focal point in the room and salvaged materials replicated what would have been there during the 1920s," she said. "The cream and green colouring inside the porch was chosen when it was revealed under numerous layers of wood. This colour scheme is also used outside on the new steps and wheelchair access that were harmonized with the house."

The main staircase was returned to its original dark wood. Complementing the staircase is the hallway with original pantry fir wainscotting. The maple floors and windows were rejuvenated.

Sliding doors from the inner office to the parlour were discovered within the wall as were all the original doors under a skin coat of mahogany paneling. All doors were restored, and the original hardware was placed back on them.

The main floor walls of the Superintendent's Residence are triple brick and the second floor reverts to double brick. The basement is first-grade concrete that has lasted more than 90 years.

The superintendent's residence at the Saskatoon Forestry Farm, located 1903 Forest Drive, was declared a Municipal Heritage Property in 1989 and was declared a National Historic Site in 1990.

IMHOFF MUSEUM
St. Walburg

The farm site and studio of Count Berthold Von Imhoff, the province's most prolific painter, have become a museum and tourist attraction near the northwestern Saskatchewan community of St. Walburg.

A bronze statue of a man on horseback at the south entrance to St. Walburg pays tribute to Imhoff, whose legacy includes almost 500 paintings and murals on dozens of church ceilings from the Canadian prairies to Pennsylvania.

The artist's youngest son Carl and his wife Gladyss celebrated their 70th wedding anniversary at the farm and studio in 2003. Their son Bert and his wife Phyliss live in the Imhoff's original home.

From 1914 until his death in 1939 at the age of 71, Imhoff painted hundreds of religious works for nothing but his own spiritual and artistic satisfaction.

"He never painted a picture to sell it," says Bert, Berthold's grandson and the administrator of the Imhoff Museum in St. Walburg. "He just painted to paint."

Imhoff earned his money by being commissioned to work for a specific church. "He'd start by painting miniatures of what he thought would work best for that particular church—he called them his samples," Bert said, referring to one of the miniatures and its full-size companion hanging in the studio that's now a museum. "Then he'd take the miniatures to the church to show them."

Once agreement was reached with a church, Imhoff returned to his studio and reproduced on large canvas the religious scenes selected from among the miniatures. When the paintings were completed, he trimmed the canvases and glued the canvases into their appropriate positions on the walls and ceilings of the church.

Saskatchewan examples of Imhoff's commissioned works can be seen in churches at St. Walburg, Muenster, St. Benedict, Bruno, Denzil, Reward, St. Leo, Humboldt, Paradise Hill, and North Battleford.

Count Berthold Von Imhoff completed almost 500 paintings and murals on church ceilings from the Canadian Prairies to Pennsylvania.
PHOTO COURTESY THE IMHOFF MUSEUM

About 200 of Imhoff's paintings can be seen at the St. Walburg museum, attached to his former home.

Imhoff, who was classically trained in Germany, developed a style similar to Renaissance artists like Raphael. This classical style gives visitors to the rural museum a jarring sensation of being propelled from a Saskatchewan wheat field into a European art gallery such as the Louvre in Paris.

Since Imhoff was prolific and chose never to sell any of his efforts, there is no shortage of his works. Approximately 200 paintings can be viewed at the St. Walburg museum, and an additional 250 works can be now be seen at the Imhoff Art Gallery in Lloydminster, Saskatchewan.

Bert says when the Imhoff family decided to re-open the St. Walburg Museum in 1993, they went to the area where the paintings are stored and simply retrieved enough of them to cover the walls. "What we unrolled is what we hung. There's more."

Thousands of people from around the world have visited the museum over the years and many have asked to purchase a painting. None are for sale.

"Every fall, when the [hunting] season came around, he'd spend two or three weeks hunting big game," recalled Carl Imhoff, Berthold's son and Bert's father in a 2003 interview. "He loved hunting, fishing, and horseback riding."

The outdoor lifestyle is what drew Imhoff to Saskatchewan from his first transplanted home in Pennsylvania. He had fallen in love with the area during a 1914 hunting trip.

Franklin Buchta, an immigrant from Czechoslovakia, built Imhoff's 15 by 30 foot studio in 1920. Five years later, Imhoff's sons enlarged the studio by adding a 20 by 40 north-to-south wing to make a T-shaped building.

"The addition was constructed specifically to meet the needs of the artist, who always mixed his own colours and painted by the light provided by his north-facing windows," explained Phyllis Imhoff, Bert's wife.

"We were told he believed the north light was the true light because there was never direct sunshine, and it remained consistent throughout most of the day."

Because he only painted in daylight hours, his time working on canvas was considerably shorter during winter months. In the evenings though, he would complete other tasks not requiring natural light—stretching and preparing canvases, framing, or cleaning brushes—for these, Imhoff worked from beneath the glow of lights powered by a 32-volt battery-operated system.

Imhoff received the Knighthood of St. Gregory the Great in 1937 from Pope Pius XI. A large celebration, attended by church dignitaries and many of Imhoff's friends from the surrounding area, was held at the studio.

The Imhoff Museum, declared a Municipal Heritage Site in 1993, is open on weekends from the Victoria Day long weekend in May until the Labour Day long weekend in September.

Look for the sign several kilometres south of St. Walburg on Highway 26, or the one just west of town on Highway 3. There is a small admission fee.

CPR Station
Theodore

The Canadian Pacific Railway Station, built in 1902 to link the Village of Theodore with other communities in western Canada, now is a museum that provides a window into the era of steam locomotives.

The station, moved from its original location along the railway into the community in 1975, is the last of a group of five that were built from the same CPR Type 9 Station design in Saskatchewan.

"My most pleasant memory of the Theodore CPR Station was the buzz of activity that was always present," recalled long-time resident Bruce Frederickson. "Trains rolled into the station several times a day, exchanging freight, mail, and passengers, as well as loading and unloading cream cans. The railroad station was the lifeblood of the community as every product, commodity, and service passed through here on a daily basis."

Frederickson remembers Postmaster Richard Mercer loading the canvas sacks of mail onto his two-wheel mailcart and then heading back to the Post Office to start sorting.

"As young children we stood for long periods of time, peering over the counter at the clicking and clacking of the telegraph, not believing how anyone could understand what it was saying," he said. "Nothing can compare in today's world to the sounds of the steam locomotive pulling away from the station with the billows of smoke pouring out of its stack, and the shrill whistle."

Frederickson's most terrifying memories are of a train wreck in 1956 when he was just nine years old. "I will never forget the crash when the trains collided," he said.

"It was like the loudest clap of thunder you have ever heard. I rushed down town, followed by my dog, thinking that maybe an elevator had exploded or fell over. I remember a large pile of grain scattered along the wreck, laden with groceries and meat products, and the immediate area looked like a war zone."

The station in Theodore is the last of a group of five built from the same CPR Type 5 Station design in Saskatchewan.
<small>Photo courtesy Saskatchewan Heritage Foundation</small>

Things literally went off the rails at the station in 1956 when a steam locomotive crashed into the building.
Photo courtesy Saskatchewan Heritage Foundation

No one was injured when two cars of a freight train ploughed through the wall of the station. The force of the impact moved the building six feet off its foundation.

Thelma Gillis, a former Theodore resident, remembers the long hours her father, Postmaster Richard Mercer, had to wait for the train to arrive at the station. "He didn't know when the trains would get through, especially in the winter when there was three to four feet of snow, and the temperature was 35 and 40 below," she said. "In those days, there were a lot of letters and parcels delivered on the train."

The mail had to be sorted even if the train was three hours late, Gillis said. "Some night's dad wouldn't come home until after midnight," she said. "On Christmas Eve we had to wait for dad to come home from sorting mail before we could open any Christmas presents."

Gordon Peterson, whose family operated a garage and International Harvester farm-implement dealership not far from the original train station, had fond business and personal memories of the station.

"There were several trains a day and we could order parts from Yorkton, which was 25 miles east, and receive the order the same day," Peterson said. "The train would stop even if there were only one parcel to deliver."

The Theodore baseball team would often take the morning train to Springside, the next town down the rail line, to play a game and be back in the evening in time for chores, he said. A round-trip ticket cost 20 cents per person.

The CPR Station #6579, located at mile 50.9 of the Wynyard subdivision, was built in 1902 at a cost of $4,000. It was designed by a B. R. Pratt, a CPR architect. The station was sold in 1974 to the Village of Theodore for $100 and moved to its current location the following year.

The original cedar shingles have been replaced with new ones, and there are plans to repaint the exterior and restore the original windows.

The station house, which held its 100th anniversary celebrations in October 2002, had also been a senior's drop in centre since 1975, before it was made into a museum in 2000.

The wood-frame building measures 75 feet by 26 feet and has the pagoda-style roofline, a trademark of the CPR stations of that particular era. The upper level has four rooms, which served as the living quarters for the station agent and his family.

The Type 9 Pratt design is unique in Saskatchewan. Only five such designs were built. The floors are hardwood throughout, and all the original walls are still finished with lath and plaster. The wooden doors are all original, including the freight-shed doors.

The original hardwood staircase still remains intact, with its precision crafted millwork still excelling even by today's standards. The station platform has been rebuilt with new lumber, and the original signal arms have been reinstalled, complete with an original CPR lantern.

A new station agent's workbench has been built, and it contains an original CPR telegraph system. The front of the building has a telegraph line with mostly all original components—poles, wire, insulators, and so on.

"Since this building is a one of its kind in Saskatchewan, the people of Theodore and area are extremely proud to show it off," Frederickson said. "The community has contributed thousands of hours of volunteer labour and a great deal of money towards its restoration."

The Canadian Pacific Railway station is located at 6 Christopher Street North in the Village of Theodore, about 40 kilometres northwest of the City of Yorkton on Highway 16. The CPR station was designated a Municipal Heritage Site in 2000.

DOUKHOBOUR HERITAGE VILLAGE
Veregin

The National Doukhobour Heritage Village in Veregin provides a tangible link between the 7,500 people who fled Russia more than 100 years ago because of religious persecution and their descendents.

"This is a very important place for us because this is where the Doukhobors came to Canada," said Alex Sherstabitoff, chair of the society that maintains and operates the village. "This is where it all began. It is very important for all Doukhobours."

Visitors can stroll around the village and see how the Doukhbours lived and worked.

"My dad got me involved in the idea of having a village more than 30 years ago," he said. "He was the driving force behind the group set up to recognize our past for future generations. That's why I carry on with my work today."

The site offers visitors a unique glimpse in the cultural and political past of the religious group who rejected most of the Orthodox Church rites and beliefs, especially the worshiping of icons. The Doukhobours' roots can be traced to the 18th century.

A Russian Orthodox priest coined the phrase that described the group as Doukhoborets, which is translated to mean "spirit wrestlers."

"This phrase was shortened to be Doukhobours, which we are proud to call ourselves today," said Sherstabitoff, who has farmed near the village his entire life. "We are spirit wrestlers because we wrestle with and for the Spirit of God."

The Doukhobours became pacifists and took a decisive stand against the military and all forms of violence. On June 29, 1895, the Doukhobours burned all of the arms they possessed.

Russian retribution was harsh and swift. Key members of the faith were tortured and exiled, including Peter V. Veregin, for whom the community northeast of Yorkton is named.

Doukhobour leaders at the time realized they had to leave Russia to find a place where they could live without sacrificing their principles, which had

been expanded to include abstaining from eating
meat and consuming alcohol and tobacco.

Leo Tolstoy, who years later would publish
one of the most prolific novels in Russian history, *War and Peace,* was among those who came to
the aid of the Doukhobours, providing money
for their exodus. The group also received assistance from the Society of Friends, commonly
called Quakers.

Negotiations with the British and Canadian
governments resulted in the opportunity for the
7,500 Doukhobours to leave Russia and settle in
Saskatchewan, then known as the North-West
Territory, where they established their communal
lifestyle in 1899.

Peter V. Veregin was released from his 16-year
exile within Russia and was reunited with the
Doukhobours in Canada in 1902.

Their slogan of "Toil and Peaceful Life" was
short-lived. Because many would not take the final
oath of allegiance, the final step required in secur-
ing property under the Homestead Act, most of
their land was released for public sale.

As a result, after only five years in the northeastern corner of Saskatchewan, the majority of the
Doukhobour settlers uprooted themselves and
moved to British Columbia, where land ownership
requirements did not demand swearing an oath.

The National Doukhobour Heritage Village
was officially opened on June 29th, 1980, the day
that the Doukobours celebrate annually as Peter's
Day. It is the day that commemorates the burning
of the arms and which led to the Doukhobour emigration from Russia.

There are about a dozen buildings in the village,
but the focal point is a white prayer home with a
two-storey, wrap-around veranda.

This building is one of the most architecturally
prominent structures in Saskatchewan and features
hand-cut, metal fretwork arches that required an
exceptional design talent to imagine and technical
ability to realize.

Built between 1917 and 1918 to replace a structure destroyed by fire, the building served as a
prayer home and residence for both Peter V.
Veregin and his son Peter P. Veregin.

A smaller, brick prayer home is opposite the
larger building and is reminiscent of the
Doukhobour prayer villages that sprang up in the
first years of the 20th century.

Within the smaller prayer home is a museum
dedicated to Tolstoy, in appreciation of his efforts
in helping the Doukhobours move from Russia to
Canada. It contains a miniature statue and some
photographs donated by the Soviet Ministry of
Culture in 1978. A life-size bronze statue of
Tolstoy, created by Yuri Chernoff, is within the
village grounds.

Sherstabitoff said 1987 was an historic year for
his community. "In 1987, we were honoured to
host Queen Elizabeth and Prince Philip and I had
the honour of thanking the Royal Family personally for accepting us into Canada," he said.

That same year, sculptor Yuri Chernoff visited
the village along with the then-minister of culture
of the Soviet Union, Yory Melentov. Also part of
the group were Eli Tolstoy, the great-great-grand-
son of Leo Tolstoy and the great-great-granddaughter of Queen Victoria, who was the British
monarch who granted the Doukhobour's their land
in Canada.

In addition, on the walls of the museum are
copies of pages from *War and Peace* in Tolstoy's
own handwriting. The narrative is in Russian,
including edits.

Other buildings at the National Doukhobour
Village include a bakery, bathhouse, and blacksmith

shop. There are literally thousands of artifacts lovingly preserved by the Doukhobour descendants for public viewing. The village is open from mid-May to mid-September each year.

The National Doukhobour Heritage Village, named a Provincial Heritage Site in 1982, is located south of the railway line in Veregin, about 75 kilometres northeast of Yorkton.

The National Doukhobour Heritage Village opened in 1980.

TOWN HALL / OPERA HOUSE
Wolseley

Slater Tubman has vivid memories from his childhood growing up one block from the Wolseley Town Hall and Opera House and then working in the community 100 kilometres east of Regina for 35 years.

The building was constructed in 1906 and more than $700,000 in renovations were completed in the early 1990s to ensure the facility could continue to be used for years to come as a community centre.

"This building has always been part of my life because I grew up just one block away," Tubman said. "We moved to Wolseley in 1945 when I was in grade 2."

Memories as a young boy, teenager, and parent are linked to the Town Hall Building for Tubman. "My dad's uncle was the town clerk, so we'd often drop by to see him after school and visit with others in the building," he said.

Tubman, whose father was the funeral director, thinks the name of the building was changed to make it more glamorous.

"I'm not sure who started the rumour about this being the Wolseley Town Hall and Opera House, as far as I know, it's not true." he said.

"I know other communities did have buildings that were named that way and might have even had an opera performed there many, many years ago, but I haven't been able to find anyone or any evidence to prove that we did have an opera performed in this building."

Seven Provincial Heritage Properties are recognized by the Saskatchewan Heritage Foundation in the town hall/opera house category, including Wolseley.

All of the buildings were constructed during the optimistic, economic-boom era of the first few years after Saskatchewan became a new province within the confederation of Canada.

The town hall/opera house in Arcola has been adapted for use as a restaurant, while the buildings in Battleford, Craik, and Melville continue to function as municipal offices. The Prince Albert Town hall / Opera House became an arts centre, while the Qu'Appelle facility has three functions: town hall, library, and hairdresser.

Manitoba architect J. H. G. Russell was contracted to build the Wolseley Town Hall. The community issued $20,000 in debentures to pay for construction and buy some firefighting equipment. A firehall was at the north end of the building.

The north, east, and south walls of the building are Wolseley brick. However, with so much construction taking place in 1906, the Wolseley brickyard couldn't produce bricks fast enough to keep up with demand. So similar bricks were imported from Portage la Prairie, Manitoba, to complete the building. The brick match wasn't exact. As a result, there's a two-tone effect on the building.

The main floor and basement held Wolseley's town offices, council chambers, library, meeting room, kitchen, and even jail cells, while the auditorium was on the second floor. The firehall was relocated in 1989.

A wide range of social and political events have taken place at the Wolseley Town Hall/Opera House over the years."

"We had the school plays and high school graduation exercises there for years as well as the dances," Tubman said.

"Other groups held functions too. The community's New Year's Eve dances were there. I also remember then Premier Tommy Douglas spoke at our 1956 high school graduation exercises held in the hall. Future Conservative Leader John Diefenbaker attended the funeral as a pallbearer for Ernest Perley, a long-time member of Parliament, which was held in the building, there being no other facility of adequate size for that event."

Movies were shown on Thursday and Saturday nights in the hall, that could hold more than 300 people. "Kids got in for just a dime," he said.

"In those days, we'd see the newsreels, Westerns, and serials each week. I remember being so excited when we learned that Wolseley would be getting its first movie filmed in Cinemascope. I can't remember what the name of the movie was!"

Remembrance Day celebrations have always been held in the town hall, and the cenotaph for the community is adjacent to the building.

On a cold winter's night, Tubman and other young boys in the community would often spend time in the furnace room in the basement of the town hall listening to the caretaker tell them stories of his Second World War service.

A bell at the town hall used to ring at noon hour to tell businesses to close and go home for lunch. Today, a siren sounds, instead, he said.

The Wolseley Town Hall / Opera House located at 510 Varennes Street in Wolseley, was designated a Provincial Heritage Property on November 22, 1991.

Built in 1906, the Wolseley town hall/opera house was renovated in the 1990s to ensure it could be used as a community centre for years to come.
PHOTO COURTESY SASKATCHEWAN HERITAGE FOUNDATION

GONE BUT NOT FORGOTTEN

"Old Government House wasn't merely an old building but was one of Saskatchewan's and Canada's treasures."

–Julian Sadlowski, Mayor of the City of North Battleford

The fragile nature of built heritage continues to be driven home by its biggest enemies: fire, neglect, weather, and redevelopment. Each year, our province loses significant heritage buildings.

Saskatchewan is a mere grain in terms of the footprints in the sands of time. The province has never had an architectural heritage to rival the timeless monuments of the Egyptian pyramids and Greek temples of the Mediterranean or the Gothic cathedrals and Medieval castles of Europe.

Yet the importance of built heritage cannot be overstated in promoting or defining the culture of a society, even one as young as Saskatchewan's at just a century. So losing a building that had a significant profile in the province or a role in the economy or culture of a community has an impact on the entire province, not just a particular community.

Gone but not forgotten each year are buildings visited by thousands and often known by many, many more. Two buildings recognized in this chapter—Joyners' store in Moose Jaw and the original government building for the province in North Battleford—are symbols of a lost heritage consumed by fire in the recent past.

Joyners, constructed between 1892 and 1896, had still been operating the oldest cash cable system in North America when fire destroyed the property on New Year's Day in 2004.

The first permanent residence of the Lieutenant-Governor of the North West Territories was consumed in less than three hours in 2003. The building, among only a handful remaining in the province from the 1870 era, was the seat of government for an area covering two-thirds the landmass of Canada, including not only what is now Western Canada, but the three territories and northern Ontario and Quebec as well.

GOVERNMENT HOUSE
Battleford

Once the seat of government for almost two-thirds of Canada, the 127-year-old structure was leveled by a fire in 2003.
PHOTO COURTESY SAHS

Flames took only three hours in 2003 to consume the first permanent residence of the lieutenant governor of the North-West Territories, a building that had taken more than two years to build, ending in 1877.

The Town of Battleford had purchased the building, known locally as Old Government House, and land for $1. There were plans to have the deed transfer completed in the spring, but the legal papers were completed ten days after the blaze.

"Old Government House wasn't merely an old building but was one of Saskatchewan's and Canada's treasures," maintained Julian Sadlowski, a founding member of the Battle River Settlement Foundation Inc. It was one of less than ten buildings in the province that dated from the 1870s.

"In reality, Old Government House was the most significant underdeveloped historical structure in western Canada and perhaps Canada," said Sadlowski, now the town's mayor.

"The North-West Territories at the time, 1876, represented two-thirds of the landmass of Canada. The decisions made in the old capital here would have impacted people living on huge tracts of land throughout western Canada, the territories, northern Ontario and Quebec."

Sadlowski said the flames that consumed Old Government House represent a tragic missed opportunity for the community. "We watched the fire reduce the historic building to a heap of rubble and we lost a tremendous amount of history," he said.

Plans to build Territorial House on top of the Eagle Hills escarpment overlooking the North Saskatchewan and Battle Rivers began almost immediately after the 1876 decision was made to move the capital to Battleford from Swan River, Manitoba.

Contractors John Sutherland and Joseph Wood of the Public Works Department of Winnipeg supervised the construction job done by Jack Oliver's construction crew. With only the stars to guide them, a convoy of 70 men with a long string of Red River Carts drawn by oxen set out from Manitoba for the proposed capital.

Oliver brought a portable saw and shingle mill, steam engine, and boiler. However, he still had to travel west of Edmonton for the big logs that were rafted down the North Saskatchewan River and hauled to the site where he had set up his portable sawmill. Smaller timber came from the neighbouring Eagle Hills.

The two-storey building was constructed of hewn logs put up "Red River style," with the joints plastered with lime and mortar on both sides.

The Territorial Building was an impressive structure, with a foundation of masonary, a stone cellar and a roof of sawn shingles. The outside of the building was strapped, clapboarded, and painted.

The interior walls were lathed and plastered. The ceilings of large rooms had ornamental centrepieces finished, boasting marble mantel pieces, with pointed and grained oak and bird's-eye maple featured in mouldings, floors, and stairways. The staircases were finished with turned ballisters, newels, and handrails of butternut, stained and varnished to imitate walnut. It contained a reception room, drawing room, parlour, office, and eight bedrooms.

The building served as a residence for Lt.-Gov. David Laird and a meeting place for the territorial council.

Battleford was the capital of the North-West Territories from 1876 until it was moved to Regina in 1882. Three government sessions were held there, in 1878, 1879, and 1881.

In 1883, the building became home to what was called an Indian Industrial School under the auspices of the Anglican Church. In 1885, during the North-West Rebellion, it was fortified and called Fort Otter. The school was temporarily moved to a private home.

In 1889, the east wing was added to accommodate more students. With the establishment of schools on reservations, the school closed in 1914, and the building was empty for two years.

Then, from 1916 to 1931, it was used as an academy for Seventh Day Adventists but was sold to the Oblates of Mary Immaculate. St. Thomas College was located in the building until 1950, then it became the seminary of St. Charles Scholasticate.

The building evolved in style from a two-storeyed structure with gabled roof to a three-storey structure with a Mansard roof. Two major annexes were also added.

Government House, located on Government Ridge in Battleford, had been declared a National Historic Site in 1976 and was named a Provincial Heritage Property on March 27, 1984.

JOYNER'S BUILDING
Moose Jaw

A fire on New Year's Day in 2004 destroyed seven businesses in Moose Jaw's historic downtown, including Joyner's, a retail store that was still operating the oldest cash-cable system in North America.

Joyner's, the oldest commercial building in the city, had been constructed between 1892 and 1896, after a fire raced through downtown Moose Jaw in 1891.

The brick-and-stone building appeared, from the outside, to be three individual buildings, but had a connecting corridor throughout. The original owner had leased the building to M. J. McLeod until 1912, when the building was purchased by the Joyner family, who operated a department store in the building until 1994.

The Lampson electric cash-cable system was installed in the building in 1915. As part of a long-term lease with Ted Joyner, the building was operated as a business with a tourism focus on the cable system from 1994 until the tragic fire in 2004. The

system was 1,000 feet in length and carried cash from the point of sale to the bookkeeper's area and back. It apparently was one of only six ever installed in Canada.

Mayor Al Schwinghamer said the loss was a major blow to a city that prided itself on the development of its heritage sites.

Moose Jaw's entire fire department battled the blaze nonstop for 50 hours in temperatures hovering around –20ºC.

"I've been with the department for 28 years and this is one of the worst fires I've ever seen," said Fire Chief Garth Palmer. "It's a huge loss to the city. They've done some extensive renovations in these buildings. It's just a catastrophic loss to the city." In addition to Joyner's, the adjacent Chow building was also consumed. Businesses in a third property that were destroyed included Suzie's Pie and Coffee, Treats R Us, Spencer and Hawthorne Gifts, Promised Land Books, Paws For Thoughts, and Past Times Old Time Photography.

The cause of the fire was determined to be an electrical short.

"I'm kind of sick to my stomach watching the smoke going out," Grant Chow told a local newspaper reporter at the scene. "My building is toast."

Chow said his family had owned the property since the 1940s. "We took it over from my grandmother and it was just mothballed, and we turned it into a viable business," Chow said.

Schwinghamer said the fire destroyed some of the city's main heritage attractions. "What's going to arise out of the ashes, we certainly have no idea. We do know that's a tremendous blow, not just to those people, but to the community as a whole," the mayor said. "As a community, we did lose some cherished structures."

The fire had threatened to spread into the nearby Tunnels of Moose Jaw, a major tourist attraction that offers guided tours of underground tunnels where it is claimed that infamous Chicago gangster Al Capone did some of his bootlegging business. Firefighters, however, were able to keep the blaze from spreading into the tunnel attractions.

Several sites were created on the World Wide Web immediately after the New Year's Day fire began. On the websites, photographs of the blaze were posted along with thoughts from current and former residents of Moose Jaw.

"As an Australian resident, it is really nice to be able to keep up to date with what is going on in my home town," wrote Nicolette Martuo from Sydney, Australia. "I am absolutely saddened by the photos of the New Year's fire. Next time I come home for a visit Main Street just won't be the same."

Joan Miller of Calgary shared dozens of photographs she had taken the previous summer of the cash-cable system in the former Joyner's department store.

Tim Rasch, a former Moose Jaw resident who now lives in California, said he was in disbelief.

"These structures have been burned into the memories of anyone who has spent any amount of time in the city," Rasch said.

Joyner's, which had been located at 28 Main Street North in Moose Jaw, was declared a Municipal Heritage Property on July 12, 1999.

INDEX

ADAPTIVE REUSE

top: Land Titles Building,
Moose Jaw
Photo courtesy SAHS
left: Lane Hall, Wilcox
Photo courtesy Athol
Murray College
Right: Land Titles
Building, Regina
Photo courtesy Saskatchewan
Heritage Foundation

COMMERCE

top: Weyburn Security Bank, Weyburn
left: Saskatchewan Wheat Pool Head Office, Regina
right: Canada Life Assurance Building, Regina

top: Northern Crown Building, Regina
PHOTO COURTESY SASKATCHEWAN HERITAGE FOUNDATION

left: Canada Building, Saskatoon
PHOTO COURTESY SASKATCHEWAN HERITAGE FOUNDATION

bottom: Brick Plant, Claybank
PHOTO COURTESY SASKATCHEWAN HERITAGE FOUNDATION

EDUCATION

top: Thorvaldson Building,
Saskatoon
PHOTO COURTESY UNIVERSITY OF
SASKATCHEWAN
left: College Building,
Saskatoon
PHOTO COURTESY SASKATCHEWAN
HERITAGE FOUNDATION
right: College Mathieu,
Gravelbourg
PHOTO COURTESY COLLEGE
MATHIEU

ENTERTAINMENT

top: Danceland, Manitou Beach
left: The Lyric, Swift Current
right: Assiniboia Club, Regina

top and right: interior,
Capitol Theatre, Moose Jaw
Photos courtesy SAHS
left: Capitol Theatre,
Moose Jaw
Photo courtesy Moose Jaw
Cultural Centre

FAITH

top: *Bishop's Residence,
Ecclesiastical Buildings,
Gravelbourg*
PHOTO COURTESY COLLEGE
MATHIEU

left: *Cathedral,
Ecclesiastical Buildings,
Gravelbourg*
PHOTO COURTESY SASKATCHEWAN
HERITAGE FOUNDATION

right: *St. Mary's Anglican
Church, Whitewood*
PHOTO COURTESY JANET
BLACKSTOCK

faith   285

top: Salvation Army,
Estevan
<small>PHOTO COURTESY SASKATCHEWAN</small>
<small>HERITAGE FOUNDATION</small>
left and right: St. John's
Anglican Cathedral,
Saskatoon
<small>PHOTOS COURTESY SASKATCHEWAN</small>
<small>HERITAGE FOUNDATION</small>

BLESSED ARE THEY THAT MOURN

TO PERPETUATE THE MEMORIES OF THOSE SONS OF THE MARITIME
PROVINCES WHOSE LIVES HAVE BEEN GIVEN IN THE SERVICE OF THIS FORCE

FOR THE TRUMPET SHALL SOUND

TO PERPETUATE THE MEMORIES OF THOSE SONS OF THE MARITIME
PROVINCES WHOSE LIVES HAVE BEEN GIVEN IN THE SERVICE OF THIS FORCE

*top: Third Avenue United
Church, Saskatoon*
*bottom: Holy Rosary
Cathedral, Regina*

SaskPower Building, Regina
Photo courtesy of SaskPower
Corporation

GOVERNMENT

*top: Albert Memorial
Bridge, Regina*
Photo courtesy SAHS
*left: Water Tower,
Humboldt*
Photo courtesy Saskatchewan
Heritage Foundation
*right: Public Library,
Moose Jaw*
Photo courtesy Saskatchewan
Heritage Foundation

top: Court House, Weyburn
PHOTO COURTESY SASKATCHEWAN
HERITAGE FOUNDATION
*bottom: Land Registry
Office, Battleford*
PHOTO COURTESY SASKATCHEWAN
HERITAGE FOUNDATION

HOMES

*Stebner/Alexander
Residence, Saskatoon*
Photo courtesy Annette
Stebner

homes 297

HOTELS

The Bessborough Hotel, Saskatoon
PHOTOS COURTESY DELTA
BESSBOROUGH HOTEL

*top and left: Hotel
Saskatchewan, Regina*
Photos courtesy Hotel
Saskatchewan Radisson Plaza
*right: Brunswick Hotel,
Moose Jaw*
Photo courtesy Saskatchewan
Heritage Foundation

OUR RURAL ROOTS

top: *Schmitz Barn,*
Moose Jaw
Photo courtesy SAHS

left: *Convent of the Sacred*
Heart, Willow Bunch
Photo courtesy Saskatchewan
Heritage Foundation

right: *University of*
Saskatchewan Barn,
Saskatoon
Photo courtesy Saskatchewan
Heritage Foundation

PIONEERING SPIRIT

*top: Town Hall/Opera
House, Wolseley*
PHOTO COURTESY SASKATCHEWAN
HERITAGE FOUNDATION
*left: Doukhobour Heritage
Village, Veregin*
PHOTO COURTESY SASKATCHEWAN
HERITAGE FOUNDATION
*right: CPR Station,
Theodore*
PHOTO COURTESY SASKATCHEWAN
HERITAGE FOUNDATION
*bottom: Forestry Farm
House, Saskatoon*
PHOTO COURTESY SAHS

GONE,
BUT NOT FORGOTTEN

top: Joyner's Building,
Moose Jaw
<small>Photo courtesy Saskatchewan</small>
<small>Heritage Foundation</small>
bottom: Government
House, Battleford
<small>Photo courtesy SAHS</small>